Tied To The Mast

Graeme C Berneville-Claye

Published in 2018 by Amazon Publishing.

TIED TO THE MAST

(which roughly translates as 'no going back')

'On such a full sea are we now afloat
And we must take the current when it serves
Or lose our Venture'

Brutus,   Act 4   Scene 3
Julius Caesar

'And In The Beginning'

I may, sometimes, have suggested that it was my mother who sent me to sea but, in reality, that was not so. She may well have been relieved to see that, at last, her sole offspring was gainfully employed. She may even have felt a weight of responsibility lifted from her shoulders but, by pressure or by suggestion, she did not influence my decision to choose a career in the British Merchant Navy. She did make the necessary enquiries and paid the £30 indenture fee and, as I remember it, not reluctantly, but it was my own, if slightly guided decision. She missed me when I first sailed away, I know - as did my maternal Grandmother. But , I feel, it was a bit like missing a sore thumb rather than missing a child of her womb. I don't mean this or say this unkindly. I merely point out that through a dysfunctional parentage where my father influenced my upbringing by not one jot, I became something of a self inflicted focal point and something of a self inflicted burden to my mother and because of this, as the sole breadwinner, she left much of the aforesaid upbringing to my grandmother. More about my father later maybe, but a little about my grandmother now. She was the great influence in my early life but perhaps not in the way she had intended. Signing the 'pledge' at the age of nine and being introduced to the 'little white ribbon' during a visit to the Great Yorkshire Show at Huddersfield in 1949 having the opposite effect on me throughout my career! It would be some years however before Bacchus enrolled me as a follower, convincing me that I had been hoodwinked and allowing me to break the 'pledge' and abandon the 'white ribbon', feeling no qualms, but I digress. My grandmother, was herself a good Christian but, in trying to instil the same beliefs in me, she tried too hard and managed to achieve the exact opposite effect. For neither of the above do I blame her. I was loved, had a good upbringing and a reasonably unadventurous childhood. I don't think that I was in anyway rebellious but I was naughty at times, like a good wine, but there I go again.

It had been my intention to finish 'A' Levels at Technical College and then to take a university degree in Forestry. How I went from 'tree' to 'sea' I find a little difficult to explain after all these years. My 'A' level results were anything but brilliant but in my defence, I did sit them six months ahead of schedule. I vaguely remember a brochure or career film stressing the advantages and possible, adventures to be enjoyed in a career at sea, and this, coupled with the discovery of beer, snooker and girls, convinced me of the way forward. Beer, snooker and girls, not necessarily in that order. A yearning for far away places and dusky maidens was upon me. Grandma, good Christian as she was, in virtually her last words to me prior to my departure urged me 'not to bring a dark lady home'. Again, and unwittingly, she fed fuel to my investigative aspirations. In the few weeks before my departure I assembled my cadet's uniforms and the necessary accoutrements as advised by something called the Merchant Navy Establishment, who claimed to know about such things. I learnt later, that a boiler suit and a pair of shorts would have sufficed along with 'civvies' for the occasional run ashore. I use the word 'occasional' but I could have equally used the word 'infrequent', as my personal 'run ashore' was at the whim of my seniors who frequently objected to this and in doing so, regularly banned my shore leave. But that came later so back to the beginnings of this story. However, let us not get this wrong, I liked my uniforms and now realise that this must have been something of a throwback to my father who, apparently, tried on a few different ones during his lifetime.   I felt taller, broader, more alive.   All of this until I stepped onboard my first ship and had all the inward pretensions of grandeur that I felt, instantly and mercilessly removed, extracted, or crushed by the Officer of the Watch who just happened to be an Australian.   I have admired Australians ever since.   Like Yorkshire folk, they say it as it is, but even more so and, with a lot more colour.   His dry sense of humour, caustic admonitions and colourful tales would be with me for many months during my first voyage.   The initiation was about to begin!

On a grey February day my mother accompanied me, took me, delivered me, take your pick, to the bottom of the gangway of my first ship.   Those who know Liverpool docks or remember them during the early 50's will know what I mean by a grey day.   Those who know Liverpool docks on a wet and grey February day will understand that particular wet greyness.   A quick farewell and then a struggle up the steep gangway with my new 'kit'.

I have memories of faces, Oriental and European watching me climb that steep gangway from one well known, if not fully appreciated, way of life to another, read about, but otherwise completely unknown way of life. Apart from a few words from pre-sea instructors, the nautical jargon was virtually a new language to me and to be greeted by a uniformed officer telling me to 'bugger off' while I still had the chance was a bit unsettling and unexpected to say the least. I had been on a ferry to and from France and I wonder if this influenced my career choice, but this was my first 'real' ship and where 'welcome onboard' was replaced by 'bugger off' followed by ribald remarks about my obviously too pristine uniform cap, I found discouraging. Too late though, the taxi had gone and I was abandoned to my fate! The Australian officer who I later understood to be the 2nd Officer and Navigating Officer introduced me to the 3rd Officer, a jovial Londoner, who escorted me, still struggling with my kit in the unusual surroundings, to the Captain's cabin. Serious initiation was about to begin! Devices intended to keep seawater out of the accommodation became obstacles, steep and narrow steel stairways became obstacles, narrow corridors became obstacles. My introduction to the Captain was both brief and abrupt. 'Come in, keep your cabin clean, now get out' was, I learned, something of a speech from this short, square Yorkshireman. Some weeks later when he instructed me in the ways of the world, the evil of drink, loose women, houses of ill repute and some horrible diseases that would result in the loss of my 'willy' was, for him, a marathon speech! On the odd time when I was not totally correct in my attitude or attention to duty, his admonishments were short, sharp and colourful. The 'Old Man' was a bit of a tartar but for the first few weeks I did not see much of him. At meal times, in the saloon, I was seated as far away from him as was physically possible in the space provided. Entering or leaving port, I was stationed either forward with the Chief Officer or aft with the 2nd Officer - I preferred the latter arrangement. For one, you could not be seen from the Bridge and for two, the Chief Officer was another bloody Yorkshire tartar!

But I race ahead. I must return to that

aforementioned grey, wet Liverpool day and the Gladstone Dock. For my first full day onboard, I was allowed to roam freely around the vessel to 'familiarise myself with the layout' of my first ship. After a long and early interview with the Chief Officer, I was instructed to 'look and learn and to be aware of my surroundings'. I think that my first impression was that anywhere outside the accommodation block was bloody dangerous. The open decks were hazardous with cargo being loaded at the five hatches, so I peered carefully and briefly into the cavernous holds while keeping a watchful eye open for the swinging nets full of cargo. Boxes and boxes of what and for where? The Deck Officers gave me directions to the 'sharp end' or the 'blunt end' and even the 'monkey island'. At the time I thought they were joking. The Engineers made vague reference to such things as 'steam on the Old Man's organ' or the 'golden rivet' and talked of things such as the 'pit' or the 'shaft tunnel'. The Hong Kong Chinese crew were friendly but distant. The Liverpool wharfies were unintelligible. Much later on in my career during subsequent visits to Liverpool, I managed to break their code. The noises and smells were strange and to this day, some sixty years on, unforgettable. I learned that the cargo was being loaded for South Africa, Kenya. Aden and for some unpronounceable place names in the Persian Gulf.

Apart from the Liverpool wharfies and their ribald, barely intelligible remarks, I met Tally Clerks, Foremen, Chandlers and Provedores. I heard talk of Agents, Shipping Clerks, Shipping Masters, Pilots and Port Captains. Some, I knew what they did in connection with the ship but others, I would learn about later. I had been issued with something called a Discharge Book, an ID Card showing my photograph and fingerprints, and had several needles stuck in me so that bites by foreign insects or, the, unlikely, ingestion of unclean water would not give me some horrible disease or infection. When being inflicted with and instructed about the latter, I nurtured some doubts about my chosen career. I learned new words such as 'dunnage', this from tripping over a pile of this seemingly haphazardly scattered timber around the deck, much to the amusement of those Officers, crew and wharfies in the immediate vicinity. Hatch beams, hatch boards, hatch tarpaulins and wedges would soon become as familiar to me and so much part of my new life as bread and butter.   The intricacies of mast rigging and the complexities of derricks, I would learn in time but in these early days, I viewed them with some misgiving.   I was told that the 'Boatswains Manual' would help me.   This was just one of the many books that I had been advised to purchase before joining, again on the advice of the aforementioned Merchant Navy Establishment. All this was on my first day onboard ship.   It was all strange but interesting and the day passed quickly.   I don't remember disgracing myself at table on that day but I do remember wondering about the food, but eating the lot.   It was English food with a hint of Chinese. By the time I had completed my 'sea-time' I had developed a taste for the latter.   This ship was a tramp ship, but even so, there was a strict formality in the saloon to be followed by all, especially by first trip 'snotties'.

But now the light was fading and I was facing my first night onboard ship.   I had found the 'officer's mess room'.   The ship was quiet apart from the background hum of the generators. The wharfies had gone for the day and the drizzle and wetness made the deck lights something of a picture but a gloomy one. I made my way to the empty mess room and started twiddling with the dials on the PYE radio managing to receive a few squeaks and hums but not much more. A voice behind me offered assistance and introduced himself as 'Sparks'. Seeing my confusion and realising that I was 'a first tripper' he advised me that 'sparks' was the Radio Officer. He was a tall, gangling Irishman who became a good friend over the next couple of years. He was also quite a character. Anyway, to move the story along, he offered to take me ashore and introduce me to the delights of Liverpool by night. I accepted and after changing into 'civvies' we proceeded ashore through wharf detritus and the seemingly permanent drizzle. The darker side of my education was about to begin! We descended the dark, wet steps into the Anchor Bar, The Chain Locker or some such name but I do remember it being under the Liver Building. It was a dimly lit, noisy pub but since this was my first ever, I found it fascinating. A lovely lady joined us at our table and 'Sparks' bought her a drink. After that there was a long discussion about something that would cost me over one months wages. We finished our drinks and left.   Me, reluctantly, because I thought she was a lovely lady.   Of course I soon realised that this was,'education without consummation' so to speak and without the great expense.   She was nice though.   We then made our way to Lime Street and entered another pub and therein followed a similar procedure.   By now I knew what was going on but this time, I didn't   much like the lady and anyway, the price was silly.   After that we made our way back to the ship and I ran headlong into my first storm.   I was immediately summoned to the Chief Officer's office and given a 'first class bollocking'.   Apparently for a 'first tripper' at the tender age of sixteen years, to go ashore without first asking permission was a heinous crime and my shore leave was stopped until further notice.   There followed a long lecture on the burden of responsibility on the shoulders of the Captain and Officers for those, and in particular me, in training onboard ship.   I retired shaking a bit and dreamt of the lady in the pub under the Liver Building.   This was my first 'bollocking' and my first 'shore leave ban'.   There were to be a few more   over the next four years.

The following morning I was 'put on the shake' at 0630 hours. Something of a shock to the system at first but this was to be the daily routine for much of my four years sea-time apart from the last few months when I stood watch on the Bridge with the Officer of the Watch or OOW. I was to report to the Chief Officer at 0700 hours on the Bridge when at sea or in his office when the ship was in port. There I would receive my orders for the day. It also coincided with the Chief Officer being served with a plate of hot, buttered toast which sent my hunger pangs into overdrive. He never once offered me a slice. Here I must add, that I was not starved and enjoyed a hearty breakfast at 0800 hours each day. But to continue, on this particular morning I was very much in the 'doghouse'. Maybe not a nautical term but one that amply described my situation. I was told to work as directed by the Boatswain for the day, and so started my instruction on washing down, chipping, scraping, sanding and eventually, some months later, actually applying paint. Which reminds me of a story told by one of my tutors at Nautical College some years later. It was about an advert in the window of an East End shop. 'Painters required, seamen should not apply'. Throughout my training and later as an Officer, I understood why! Chuck it on and spread it around comes to mind!

After my first day of work onboard ship, I spent the evening mastering the PYE radio in the mess room, managing to keep the admonishments down to the minimum. I was ticked off by the Chief Officer for having the volume on the radio turned up too high. His dayroom was next to the mess room and I soon learnt that the bulkheads were not very thick. Another lesson! After that I managed to further subdue my enthusiasm by standing on deck looking across the dock at an ancient Soviet freighter. Dimly lit and rusty, the only bit of colour to be seen was the 'hammer and sickle' on the funnel. The darkness and the drizzle didn't add anything to the depressing picture. I was told that the old tub was a coal burner and that, at that time, there weren't many like that left in the world. I was thankful! Thanking my lucky stars. At least my ship was a good one, bright and clean. My senior officers may well have been a pair of Yorkshire tartars but the alternative across the dock was much less appealing!

One other incident served to teach me that being cheeky to my seniors was not an acceptable approach. One evening I was asked by the 2nd and 3rd Officers to make a pot of tea. When I jocularly refused I was given a rapid and rude lesson on how first trip snotties should behave to their seniors. Another lesson that I would never forget. Well, except for the odd occasion.

And so the days and nights in Liverpool passed by until, at last, sailing day arrived. Cargo work was finished and the hatches closed and battened down for the sea passage. I watched as the crew lowered the derricks and the amazing jumble of steel cables were coiled and secured for sea. Assisted by tugs the ship left the dock and proceeded to sea via a narrow cut and one sea lock. I was positioned forward of the bridge on the ship's side holding onto a length of rope with a lump of timber on the other end. 'Move that fender forward' I was yelled at from the bridge. Assuming that the way the vessel was moving was forward, I moved my 'fender' in that direction. My assumption was incorrect and I was roundly abused from the bridge wing. Apparently we were being manoeuvred astern through the first cut.   Another lesson learnt.   Some laughed, some sniggered, some turned away and I went bright red with indignation.   How was I to know. 'Bugger it'.   See, already I was adjusting to onboard jargon.   My piece of rope and bit of timber was used successfully in the sea lock as the ship manoeuvred head first into the murky, choppy waters of the Mersey.

The sounds, the smells, the movement of my first ship moving out to sea for my very first time, I will never forget.   The ship's whistle, the tug's horns, all were to become very familiar sounds. Out of Liverpool and into the Irish Sea, as I recall, was not an unpleasant experience.   Away from the damp dreariness of Liverpool into the fresh air and moderate sea was something of a relief.   The adventure had begun.

The Irish Sea, I had seen on maps of the British Isles.   The Western Approaches had an adventurous ring to it.   We were buzzed by a Coastal Command Shackleton   in the Western Approaches which I found very exciting as it roared seemingly below mast height past us.

However, the Bay of Biscay was renowned for bad weather and my shipmates had filled my mind with tales of colossal seas and dangerous swells. Most of the black and white sea movies of my youth featured this stretch of water and usually showed ships being tossed around in vicious seas. Probably exaggerated I thought then. Later in my career I would reflect on that thought but now, for my first passage, the sea was calm and the sun shone. Life was good!

We had regular meals, breakfast 0800 hours, lunch 1200 hours and dinner 1800 hours. At 2130 hours there were sandwiches in the pantry refrigerator, one for each of us. In between there were no pickings. I tried once to get something from the galley but had to beat a hasty retreat followed by an irate Chinese cook. He threatened me with a meat cleaver and that was quite enough for me! On the odd occasion, one of the deck officers or engineers would let me have their sandwich but these feasts were few and far between. The meat paste sandwiches were, mainly, a subject of daily derision and scorn but there never seemed to be any leftovers! The occasional Spam sandwich was wolfed down with relish by all and the very rare luxury of a beef sandwich was much celebrated. In the Officer's Mess these sandwiches were washed down with canned beer from cans which reminded me of Brasso tins. I hasten to add that, much to my chagrin, I was not allowed to drink onboard. It was only when the Chief Engineer's wife joined us for a voyage that I tasted the stuff, when she would hide a can for me in a fire-hose box. Even this stopped when she was caught in the act. When I was allowed ashore I usually managed to end up in a pub, bar or similar establishment, depending on which country we were in. This was also frowned upon but, what the heck. On wages of £5 a month, I couldn't get far. However, back to food, a subject close to any cadet or apprentice's heart, I wasn't starving, I did put on a little weight and I did grow - but not much. The food onboard my ship was 'Chinglish'. Sometimes very tasty, sometimes bland and sometimes, ney alltimes, with the vegetables boiled to a mush. On Chinese Festivals we ate Chinese food and I, for one, eagerly looked forward to these occasions. However, the hard working Hong Kong Chinese crew didn't celebrate enough Festivals in my opinion. I have to say at this point that, on the odd occasion, Cookie would allow me to have a taste of something   -   after several days at sea he had forgiven me for my earlier poaching incident -   and now and again, one of the Chinese able seamen would let me have a bowl of something. I keep saying 'something' because I never knew what it was but, it was always tasty.   God bless Cookie and Wong Kwai whichever or whatever God they believed in.   I managed to get the odd meal ashore but as some of them were either spectacularly tasty or sickeningly bloody awful, I will talk of these as they crop up throughout my career at sea.   Later in said career, I experienced food cooked by British cooks, by Mainland Chinese, by filipino and by one Mongolian.   The latter cooked a mean steak but his speciality, 'chicken arseholes', was somewhat less palatable, but more about George later.   Apart from one Mainland Chinese cook, the British were by far the worst but it was to be a few years before I suffered under their efforts.   I hasten to add that when they were good they were, generally, some of the best, but when bad, they were spectacularly bloody awful!   But back to voyage number one.

My education proceeded apace.   For six

days thou shalt work and on the seventh day thou shalt enjoy relaxation apart from those days when the Chief Officer would have something for you to do.   This appeared to be quite often.   I was allowed one afternoon a week for study.   I had a yearly set of levels to achieve which would culminate in a yearly written examination.   My tutor, guide, was the 3rd Officer, possibly because he was the youngest and therefore the most up-to-date amongst the officers or, more likely, because he was the one who drew the short straw.   As you can see, I was becoming a little cynical.   I had to start learning the 'Rules of the Road', the nautical equivalent of the 'Highway Code'.   I understood their importance but, learning them parrot fashion was a pain in the posterior.   More enjoyable was learning the Morse Code and how to use the Aldis Lamp.   I learned how to send AA AA AA, What Ship, Where from, Where to,   but I forget for the moment, how we used to finish the contact.   AR I think. When called up to the Bridge to make my first live contact with another ship, I was terrified. To the Norwegian Officer who replied to my stumbling efforts, I apologise.   He replied in English, or so I was told by the 3rd Officer who read the signal and told me what to say in reply.   I was a trembling wreck.   Over the years I became more confident and 'spoke' to many Norwegian ships. Where were all the British ships? Considering that Britain had fifty percent of the world's fleet at that time, I found this most strange. Blue Funnel and Blue Star were amongst the British companies who did reply to my signals. Shaw Savill and Union Castle also chatted to me. The ships who replied were going to, and coming from,   exotic places, some of which I had never heard of.   My knowledge of these place names was growing, my prowess with the 'lamp' was taking time, my reading of the lamp was, to say the least, stuttering.   When I started to enjoy it, my signalling and reading of signals improved apace. I mastered Semaphore for my examinations 'on the way up'   until this method of communications was withdrawn much to my relief.   However, I should add, that Semaphore was the only non mechanical/electrical way of communicating ship to ship so, I wonder!   As I said earlier, I was allowed one afternoon a week for study. Principles of Navigation,   Chartwork, Seamanship, Basic (and I do mean basic) Engineering and Meteorology amongst other subjects.   Fortunately my mathematics at school had somewhat blossomed with the introduction of Geometry, Trigonometry and Spherical Trigonometry, the basics of navigation. It would be many months before I would be allowed to hold a Sextant, or even the bridge binoculars or even peer into the radar screen. When I look back to those early days, the sextant was a sextant, the binoculars were nothing special but the radar was primitive. The sextant and the binoculars were in daily use but the radar could only be turned on with the Captain's permission. No wonder there were so many 'radar assisted collisions' in those days. Or , could they have been 'radar unassisted collisions' in our case. Fortunately, during my time on the ship, we had only one minor bump and that was in the Suez Canal at anchor. My Chief Officer jumped up and down and the British officer on the other ship did the same thing but, hey, blame it on the Egyptian pilots. Later on in my career I blamed the aforesaid for just about anything. But back to the studies. I had my own parallel rules, dividers and a spherical slide rule, Nories Nautical Tables and several books on terrestrial or stellar navigation. Tide Tables, Nautical Almanacs and Pilot Books belonged to the ship and I was allowed to use, look at them, only with the permission of the OOW. It would be a few weeks hence before I would be challenged to calculate the Noon position of the ship but this is a tale for a little later. The 3rd Officer, the jovial Londoner was patient in my schooling, the Australian 2nd Officer was patient but caustic in my training, the Radio Officer was humorous in my training, the Chief Engineer, realising my negative engineering abilities, was supportive in my studies but the Chief Officer was a sarcastic Yorkshire tartar! My training/schooling proceeded but slowly.

Having completed my first crossing of 'the Bay', we were now off Cape Finisterre, the seas were calm and the temperature was rising rapidly. We were now instructed to change into 'whites'. White shirt, white shorts, long white socks and white moleskin shoes. I started to appreciate the costly outlay made by my mother, who was now hundreds of miles away astern. To picture the uniform just watch 'The Cruel Sea' or any other fifties sea movie. Shorts were affectionately called 'Empire builders'. Bloody ridiculous in appearance but the sea breezes did reach places where, in a different attire, sea breezes may not have reached.   This was the dress uniform worn at mealtimes and during the evening hours.   The work uniform was a blue long sleeved shirt and blue shorts.   Much closer fitting than the 'whites'. We had Blue Uniform, Whites, Battledress and working uniforms - plus overalls, wetsuits and Wellington boots.   Things that are now provided by the company were in those days provided by, in my case anyway, 'mother'.   Along with the sun and the uniform change, spirits seemed to lift onboard.   The gloom of February in the UK and in particular, Liverpool, was now far behind us. 'Smoko' could be enjoyed sitting out on deck. We had loaded several huge MOD tank transporters for Aden and these were ideal for sitting on or reclining against, clutching a cup of tea or coffee.   Of course, one thing that had not featured in my view of a life of adventure at sea was the fact that I had to do my own 'dhobi' - my own laundry, but I soon learnt how to wash, scrub and do the ironing!   To this day, some sixty years on, I still reckon that I can iron a shirt better than my wife -   and pack a suitcase. However, let us move quickly on!

By this time I knew all the Deck Officers of

course, but new Engineers seemed to keep popping up from the 'pit'.   Actually there were only six Engineers plus one Electrician but in   their different guises, from fresh white uniform through the spectrum to oil and grease stained boiler suits, there seemed to be many more.   They were a jovial, hard working bunch, who spent a lot of time talking, loudly about 'effing' Doxfords,   bloody Doxfords and many other colourful expletives regarding   our   main   propelling   machinery. Boilers, generators and a multitude of other engine room 'bits' received regular, explicit and critical assessment   in   the   Duty   Mess,   the   Officer's Messroom, the Saloon or sitting out on deck in the sunshine.   To my first trip ears it appeared that the 'elastic band' was about to break and that, this happy band would then descend into the 'pit' and, armed with sledgehammers would beat the 'ess aitch one tee' out of the bloody thing.   They were a good bunch and I enjoyed being in their company but, they managed to get me into trouble more than once!   Now, Lecky, I was never sure about him.   He made too many references to the golden rivet for my liking.

The Hongkong Chinese crew consisted of

one Boatswain, a very elderly, wrinkled person. The Kassab, or Storekeeper, was a small rotund fellow who reluctantly dished out my work tools in the morning and who muttered Cantonese curses, I supposed, under his breath when I returned them in the evening. At least I assumed the mutterings to be curses, they most certainly weren't compliments. Two Quartermasters and six Able Seamen completed the deck crew. One Leading Hand and four Ratings made up the Engineroom compliment. A Chief Steward, two Cooks and two Stewards made up the Catering Department. Cookie prepared food for the 'Gweilos' and the 2nd Cook fed the Chinese. One thing about the catering puzzled me but I never did find out why the Chinese crew enjoyed fresh vegetables while we 'Gweilos' were generally fed canned mixed vegetables. It wasn't just this crew, I was to experience this phenomenon later in my career but by then I was in a position to do something about it. Staying with catering, the Provision Store was a large area, part dry stores, a couple of large refrigerators and a walk in freezer compartment. To get into this area one had first to unlock a hefty steel door and, secondly, one had to get through the padlocked wire mesh cage which surrounded all the goodies.   I never did manage to penetrate Fort Knox, at least, not without company.   As I mentioned earlier, we weren't badly fed, it was just that I always seemed to be hungry.   Hardly a growth spurt because I only managed to gain an extra half inch and even this was disputed by those who needed to check my height for record or medical reasons. So, my perma-hunger must have been due to the sea air.

Onwards and upwards or, in this case, southwards.   I was given my orders for the day but this was to be a special day.   The ship was due to dock at Las Palmas mid morning to take on bunkers.   I was given the job of assisting the AB's to get the mooring ropes up on deck and uncovering the wire ropes ready for berthing.   I remember being very excited about the prospect of arriving at this exotic foreign port,   my first foreign port, but in this I appeared to be the only one.   The pilot boarded, the ship berthed, the huge bunker line was attached to the ship and the bunkering operation started.   The smell of fuel oil in the hot Las Palmas sunshine was one of those smells that would stay with me for life. I was to smell that smell many times and in many exotic places but it would always be the bunker berth at Las Palmas that would come to mind, closely followed by the Shell bunker berth on the island of Pulau Bukum off Singapore. Beyond the bunker berth I   could see the palm lined waterfront of Las Palmas but this was out of bounds, at least to me. However, to make amends, Las Palmas came to us by way of the 'bumboat'. 'Bumboat' by name but in fact, in this case, it was a rickety stall on the wharf piled high with exotic goods, in my eyes, or crap in the eyes of others.   I don't recall purchasing any of the aforementioned 'crap' but others did.   There seemed to be a constant, if somewhat surreptitious, line of ship's officers of the junior kind, carrying unmarked boxes from underneath the stall to the ship.   It was Sparks who enlightened me and told me about the cheap booze racket.   Strictly frowned upon by Company and Senior Officers,   indulged in by everyone else.   But to progress, our stay in Las Palmas was a short one and with bunkering completed, the ship turned southwards again, now heading for Cape Town.   The Tropics and the Equator lay ahead!

My mind was adjusting to the discipline and the way of life and my body was adjusting to the Tropical heat. The dangers of sunburn, of sunstroke, and of heatstroke were much talked about and I was introduced to the joys of salt tablets. I had already had a personal hygiene lecture from the Chief Officer regarding such things as 'dhobi itch' or 'prickly heat'. However, the lecture from the Captain on what the 3rd Officer referred to as 'galloping knob rot' was imminent. One fair tropical morning I was summoned to the Chartroom by the Captain. He normally had a loud voice but on this occasion it was even louder. No doubt about it, this was definitely not one of his favourite chores. As I remember, he started off by running through the terms of the Articles of Agreement which every seaman must sign on joining a ship, easy stuff. From there he went on to the Indentures that I had signed when joining the company and particularly the bit about 'drinking establishments and houses of ill repute'. After that he launched into a tirade against 'booze, birds and brothels' followed by a lurid description of gonorrhoea and syphilis, or the aforementioned 'galloping knob rot' as my shipmates called them. I seem to remember him closing this meeting with 'remember what I have said and now bugger off'. He went below to his cabin and I walked out into the Wheelhouse, where I found the Third Officer doubled up clutching his stomach with suppressed laughter. My introduction to the wicked ways of the world was much quoted in the Officers mess room that evening. The bastards took the micky out of me unmercifully.

Life at sea was really a matter of strict routine especially for the Bridge and Engineroom watch keepers. To us day workers, it was a little less so, but there were weekly scheduled happenings that could not be avoided, much as we would have liked to. These were inspections, fire drills and lifeboat drills. Inspection was a twice weekly happening at 1100hrs on Tuesdays and Fridays. Our accommodation was subject to inspection on both days but on Fridays, it included the dry stores and the cold store. The Captain, the Chief Officer and the Chief Steward would do the rounds, peering and poking into the corners of our cabins. They always seemed to concentrate on my cabin and volunteered such comments as, *wash that, iron this* or *clean that. Put that straight, tidy that up* and occasionally, *disgusting,* when they managed to find my meagre food stash. After that I would be ordered to follow them and they would inspect every cabin, locker, public room, shower and toilets, pantries and the galley. I remember one inspection shortly after leaving Hong Kong. We got to the crew washroom and found a live chicken tied to every tap and there were about twelve washbasins. It caused a bit of a rumpus but the crew enjoyed fresh chicken for a while. Another time in the dry stores, the Chief Officer spotted weevils in the rice causing some dismay. I couldn't see the harm in a few small black things sharing the rice but my opinion was not generally shared. Until it could be replaced, it had to be carefully sieved. Between Las Palmas and Capetown on my first trip much anger was shown when the inspection trio found lines with multiple fish hooks attached, in the crew quarters. These were, I was told, for casting over the stern to catch seabirds. I thought we were in for a mutiny when the said trio found a live albatross in a sack in the galley. Both wings had been broken to subdue it or fit it in the sack and this caused outrage amongst us Gweilos and outrage amongst the Chinese when it was humanely dispatched and tossed overboard.

There were mutterings in the Officer's Messroom that evening with occasional misquotes from 'The Ancient Mariner'. The inspection team usually managed to find something to grumble about but the albatross, the weevils and the chickens stand out in my memory. It was some years on when I came across the white gloves technique during cabin inspections but more about that later.

As I remember, the following days passed rapidly as the ship pushed southwards towards Capetown. The days were a set routine on this passage, work, eat, sleep, with just one exception - the 'crossing the line ceremony'. Later on in my career at sea, this ceremony was a much more lavish and traditional production but not on this ship. At about midday I was ambushed by a group of Engineers who proceeded to plaster me with some vile gunge which smelt like a mixture of galley slops and engine room waste. The 3rd Officer then washed me down with a high pressure fire-hose. It was more of a battering than a wash down but it did remove most of the muck. I showered and showered but the smell stayed with me for days! The unjust part of all this was that I had to clean the mess off the deck. Later I was issued with a certificate signed by Neptune giving me the freedom to roam the Seven Seas. Now I really was part of the team, or so I thought!

Our scheduled stop at Capetown was to be a short one. I think it was just to discharge some bags of mail and quite a few cases of Scotch Whisky. I have visited Capetown several times since this initial visit, but the city with its magnificent backdrop of Table Mountain, has never failed to impress. Here, we were due to receive our first mail from home and everybody onboard eagerly awaited the arrival of the ship's agent. Later, when it was distributed by the Chief Steward, I seem to remember getting two letters. One from mother and the other from grandma. I really can't remember the content of either letter. Just receiving them was enough. I also observed the reverse effect on those few who didn't receive any mail. The 2nd Officer just shrugged it off with 'well no bugger writes to me anyway' but one of the younger Engineers was distraught. We would all experience this emotion at one time or another.

The passage to Mombasa, after the ship had cleared the swells off the coast of South Africa was remarkable for only one thing - my first navigational calculation. The fact that this put the ship's noon position as being 'halfway up bloody Mount Kilimanjaro' caused the Chief Officer to sniff expressively and the other deck officers to enjoy a good laugh. Since I did not personally plot the position on the chart, to this day I believe it to have been Aussie bloody humour. No getting away with it though; the story stuck!

We sailed onwards, up to the Horn of Africa and round Cape Guardafui into the Bay of Aden. By now I was coping with the heat, but from now on, the rays of the sun brought to mind the flame of a blowtorch. Aden came as something of a shock - the heat, the number of ships working at anchor and the mass of people along the waterfront. When the ship was safely anchored amid the other ships and the bustling boats, barges and tugs, the first arrival was the 'bumboat' but a real one this time. Along with the same sort of junk offered in Las Palmas were Japanese cameras, binoculars and tea-sets. Definitely a much upgraded type of 'bumboat'. The next arrival would have been the agent with the mail or the port authorities with papers covering entrance formalities. The next one was the 'liberty boat' with a timetable to and from the town quay. This was to be my first 'run ashore' after Liverpool and I received a long talk on how to act ashore in Aden. I seem to remember going ashore with Sparks, one Engineer and the Lecky. Sparky admitted that he too had had a lecture on what to do and what not to do with first trip snotties when accompanying such on a foray ashore. I also know that he ignored these instructions. But before going ashore there was a ritual to perform. Those members of the ship's company requiring a 'sub' or advance of pay, had to queue up before the 'Old Man'. There he sat in splendour before a table with cash and cash book in front of him. On one side he had a box containing 'French Letters' and on the other side, a box containing 'Dreadnoughts'. I received and signed for my cash advance but when I peered into the two boxes I was dismissed with the usual 'bugger off'. I was told later by one of those in the know, that the condoms were of MOD industrial standard that would withstand the bite of a Cobra. Somewhat reassuring I thought, not wishing to have my 'willy' bitten by a bloody snake. The 'Dreadnoughts' were more interesting to a snottie like me - consisting of a small tube with a long spout and a piece of pink cloth in a vacuum pack along with instructions. Apparently, after sex, one had to insert the long spout up the penis and squeeze the contents of the tube into said penis. After this, one was supposed to moisten the pink cloth and wash around the contact areas. Having only experienced a couple of 'hand jobs' administered by two local girls back home, I found all this both intriguing and a bit disturbing, but I was learning. The allowance was, one pack containing three 'johnnies' and one 'dreadnought'. This did not apply to 'snotties'. On reflection I found this quite a conundrum. Was my 'willy' to be sacrificed in the line of experience or was I to remain celibate?

Back to the tale. Now in civvies and eager to get ashore, we climbed down the very steep gangway to the small launch that was to ferry us to the town quay. Then through the arched portals and out into the main waterfront street of Aden. I remember the shock of meeting so many people in so many different guises and speaking so many strange languages.   The locals seemed to be dressed in varying mixtures of Arab and European attires.   Then there were seamen from the ships at anchor.   Matelots from the warship also at anchor and quite a number of British soldiers and air-force personnel.   Already we had been called 'draft dodgers' by   National Service sailors on the RN ship, much to the indignation of my companions. The 'grey funnel line' was not popular with my lot. Sparks, because he was from the Republic of Ireland and the others, because as members of the Merchant Navy, they were exempt from call-up and did not like the accusations.   We walked along the waterfront peering into shops and narrow alleyways.   The shops seemed to sell just about anything from just about anywhere.   The narrow alleyways were jammed with people.   We turned into one alleyway which opened up into the bazaar.   The goods, the food, were piled high   - the smells.   Some good, some?   There were many things that I had never seen before and things that, had you put them on my plate, I would have been instantly sick.   Back to the relatively fresh air of the waterfront we made our way to the Rock Hotel.   It was in the bar of the Rock Hotel that I tasted my first beer since leaving Liverpool and it tasted wonderful.   Apart from being told to 'be careful' by the RAF Police, nothing of much note happened after that and eventually we returned to the ship.

Now we headed for the Persian Gulf where the remaining and bulk of the cargo was to be discharged.   The port rotation for the Gulf was Muscat, Dubai, Bahrain, Mena-al-Ahmadi, Abadan, Khoramshahr and Basra.   The first three were anchorage ports where we discharged into lighters.   I think it was Muscat where we anchored off and viewed a lot of sand, a fortress and a huge rocky headland with the names of ships painted high up on the rock face.   There did not appear to be much else but as shore leave was not allowed, it didn't matter.   No shore leave in either Dubai or Bahrain.   I do recall being given the job of cargo watchman in one of the holds and discovering some of the Arabs drinking HP Sauce. I left them to it.   We did go alongside the oil jetty in Mena-al-Ahmadi   and again I was given the job of cargo watchman.   At one point, all the Arabs in the hatch headed for the hatch ladders and, wondering what was happening, I followed them.   Halfway up the ladder I could hear the sounds of a military band and when I put my head out of the hatch there was a truly magnificent sight. HMS Ark Royal was approaching her berth with personnel in whites lining the flight deck and a Marine Band playing. I remember my chest swelling with pride. The fact that they were allowed ashore while we had to put up with a sort of club house on the jetty caused a few mutterings though. Mutterings without cause really, because I was told that there wasn't much to go ashore for. The 'Ark Royal' launched a few sailing dinghies and some of their crew enjoyed themselves that way.

One thing, or should I say several things, stand out in my memory of the Persian Gulf and that was the 'thunder boxes'. Because the Arab wharfies lived onboard during cargo operations they had to have somewhere to relieve themselves. These timber constructed boxes hung over the ships side rails or bulwarks secured by ropes. Inside they had a plank with hole cut in it so that the crap went straight into the water below. Primitive but effective. It was my job to chop the ropes and let these constructions fall overboard at the end of their use. It was a mucky job!

Unfortunately some of the aforesaid wharfies used to crap down the anchor hawse pipe so that when the anchor was lifted, the chain was covered in Arab crap.   Another   hose job that I was nominated for!   My love of the Middle East waned rapidly.   It was at anchor in the Shat-al-Arab that I first came across the term 'flashy for dashy' where a canoe type craft would approach the ship with a man paddling and a female sitting forward.   Those crew members on deck would offer a can of beer, a plastic bottle or a packet of cigarettes and the female would lift her top revealing her breasts.   Say no more but we all looked!

Really, the only bright spot of my visit to the Persian Gulf was meeting a young, attractive Iraqi girl in Basra.   She invited me to go with her to the swimming pool at Basra airport.   As I recall we had a very pleasant day together but when I tried to get her back to the ship, things went badly wrong.   The guard at the gate said something to her and she ran off, he then said something to me and ripped up my ID card.   I said rude words to him and was arrested.   The ship's agent arranged my release and gave me a bollocking, I returned to the ship and the Chief Officer gave me a bollocking, I went before the Captain and was given another bollocking and then had my shore leave stopped indefinitely. It was becoming a habit!

I do recall another incident while at anchor in the Shat-al-Arab when the ship started dragging anchor. By the time we got to stations and the engine was made ready the ship was drifting sideways quite rapidly down the waterway past other anchored ships. It wasn't funny at the time although we laughed about it later. However, later in my career and when I was in charge, this happened twice and I remembered the Shat-al-Arab. We learn by others and our own mistakes and I didn't find it atall funny on the second and third occasions.

From the Persian Gulf we backtracked to Aden where the ship loaded bulk salt for Ube, Japan. Looking back, times must have been hard because bulk salt was not the ideal cargo for a ship designed to carry general cargo. I realise now that any cargo is better than nothing. Empty ships do not make money, but the corrosive properties of salt in bulk did nothing for the steelwork in the holds. The cargo was loaded from lighters and this operation took several days giving us plenty of time to explore Aden. Exploring Aden meant the waterfront and maybe the bazaar but we were advised to go no further afield. Actually, we spent most of our time ashore at the Rock Hotel because of unrest amongst the local population. The RAF Police told us to be careful and the Royal Navy SP's made sure that we returned to our ship before curfew. Exciting times!

From Aden we moved on across the Indian Ocean to Pulau Bukum, a Shell bunker island just off Singapore. This via the Malacca Strait. The smell of wood smoke in the middle of nowhere - little wooden fishing boats in the middle of nowhere. I saw my first waterspouts on this passage, in fact, a whole line of them. When the strait narrowed on the approaches to Singapore the traffic volume increased and I had my first lesson in ship spotting. In those days, ships of the major companies had distinctive outlines and I soon became familiar with the shapes and colours of Blue Funnel and Glen Lines. The shape, colour and intricate paintwork of Ben Line. There were many, many more at this time. There were the immaculate Scandinavian ships of The East Asiatic Company, Wilhelmson and the Swedish company with the Royal Crest on the funnel. Then there were the host of rust buckets. I became relatively efficient at identifying a company by outline or funnel shape when a ship appeared over the horizon. It doesn't happen these days. Apart from the distinctive hull colour of the Maersk Line. Now you have to get close enough to read the company name on the hull - definitely not the same. Since that time I have always enjoyed passages through the Malacca and Singapore Straits though, having to take pirate precautions in my last few years at sea, somewhat tempered the enjoyment.

But back to life onboard. lifeboat drill was a once a week interruption to the routine, but not one to be looked forward to by the majority. I experienced this reluctance to take the drill seriously throughout my career. Later, as a senior officer, I tried to instil some amount of enthusiasm into the proceedings but with little success. When the alarm was sounded on the ship's whistle and alarm bells, we were expected to don lifejackets and proceed immediately to our 'boat stations'. If the weather was clement, one of the four lifeboats would be lowered to embarkation deck then re-hoisted and stowed, this after answering the roll call. If the ship was in port and the Port Captain or authorities gave their permission, both offshore lifeboats would be lowered to the water with full complement onboard. Those lucky enough to be on the boat with the engine would then go for a short trip round the harbour. Those on the boat propelled by oars would struggle and splash and curse in Anglo Saxon and Chinese in a short but ragged circle. On occasion the engine on the other boat would fail and then they would have to take to the oars to get back, much to the amusement of those who remained onboard. Only once were we asked to try to sail a lifeboat and we failed miserably. We agreed that the sail provided was really only meant to catch rainwater during a prolonged emergency. Raising the boats afterwards was quite easy when the air hoists worked. When they failed, it was a long, tedious and sweaty procedure. Lifeboats were meant for launching, not for recovery, was one reason given for it being so difficult. At times we would have to put the lifeboat embarkation rope ladder over the side to get important people back onboard after hoist failures. The cooks and the senior officers or engineers would be the first up the ladder whilst the rest of us would sit there until the hoist was fixed. These ladders with their heavy wooden rungs and long wooden spreaders were easy to throw out but very heavy to retrieve. These drills were usually held at 1600hrs and it was not unusual for them to overrun the 'dinner gong'. Hence the reason for the cooks either being excused from attending the drill or being first up the ladder. We were not allowed to remove our lifejackets and in the tropics we would perspire profusely to put it politely. When the engineer in charge of the lifeboat engines was called upon to fix one of the latter, it would not be long before, amid muttered curses, the lifejacket would be chucked into the bilges. I have one or two amusing tales about lifeboat drills but these are from drills of later years. I must add that one good thing about being in China was that it was forbidden to launch lifeboats. Come to think of it, even launching the painting dinghy to paint the ship's sides was banned. During my cadetship there was no occasion when we had to launch a lifeboat for an emergency situation and having observed the ritual, I am to this day, greatly relieved.

Part of my duties was to look after the lifeboat equipment and to regularly change the water in the tanks. There didn't seem to be much water to me and the scoop for rationing the water out between occupants looked very small. It is every sailors aim to keep his feet dry and the size of these water tanks convinced me that this was a good idea. The short mast had to be stepped every two months and the red canvas sail along with all the halyards and ropes had to be spread out on deck. The lifeboat pyrotechnics had to be checked to make sure that the container was still watertight and that the various flares and rockets were still in date. Sometimes the oars had to be oiled also the rudder and tiller had to be checked. The lifeboat davits and wires and the lifting equipment were looked after by the Kassab. Under supervision, I was allowed to grease the wires on the drums, but I was not thought to be ready to maintain the lifting/lowering gears. I quite enjoyed my time in the lifeboats and could occasionally get away with a bit of sunbathing when the Chief Officer was taking his afternoon nap. If I was caught it would be by the 2nd Officer peering down on me from the wing of the Bridge and issuing forth some Australian expletive. I learned some good sayings from his impressive repertoire. Sometimes I would join him on the Bridge and would enjoy some of his tales about Australia and the South Pacific. Now he really could weave a story! I have to add at this point that my visits to the Bridge in the early months of my career were very limited. Fetch something, carry something or polish the brasswork being the main reasons to be up there. The Old Man slept every afternoon and the Chief Officer being a watch keeper usually took a short afternoon nap and it was at these times that I managed to see some of the magic that was to come. Much later I would be allowed to take a watch with either the 2nd or 3rd Officers. The Chief Officer obviously didn't want to share his toast.

Fire and Emergency Drill was yet another regular occurrence. This one greeted with somewhat more enthusiasm than Boat Drill. Here was an opportunity to spray water everywhere, to get wet and enjoy ourselves in the sunshine. I hasten to add that this was not the purpose of the drill. The drill was not so enjoyable in the colder climes however. The alarm would sound and senior officers would direct us to the area of the fire or emergency. At the scene of the assumed fire, two members of the team would done fire suits while back up rigged fire hoses and the engineers started the emergency fire pump. Starting the latter always seemed to be a bit hit and miss and sometimes the resulting 'jet' of water would have been better supplemented by the team pee'ing on the fire. In these cases a rather larger and more efficient pump would be started down in the engine room which would result in the hose team hanging onto the hose as if to an athletic Anaconda, and in managing to hold on to the aforesaid, also managing to hose down all in the vicinity. Senior officers would vainly attempt to stop things being reduced into something of a farce and after about thirty minutes of running around, success would be declared and a wet, bedraggled bunch would put all the gear away until next time. Emergency Drill was a much more sober proceeding as we were exercised in casualty recovery and the general principles of first aid. Even then, humour did manage to creep into some exercises as the poor 'volunteer' would be bandaged, bound up, mummified and then strapped into the stretcher and finally bounced, without dignity in the general direction of the ship's hospital or dispensary. All we juniors suffered this indignity at one time or another. All part of my training I was told by way of explaining why I was favourite to be tied up, tied down and bounced around.

From Singapore up through the South China Sea and a bit of the Pacific Ocean towards Japan. To the Bungo Suido entrance to the Inland Sea of Japan and the passage to the tiny port of Ube, which I found very interesting. We anchored off Ube and tugs brought lighters out to the ship into which we were to discharge the salt. Things became even more interesting when the discharge gang boarded and it turned out to be an all female operation. Most of them were a bit wizened but out of the hundreds who boarded, there were a few nice ones. When they stripped off topless and started to shovel the salt into bags even the

Engineers took a sudden interest in cargo operations. Early on in the discharge operation I received a lecture from the Chief Officer which condensed meant 'look don't touch'. Nobody told the 3rd Engineer and he turned up the heat on one of the ladies. Me; they just took the mickey out of me and made me blush a lot. When they climbed out of the hatches and washed down on deck, they would surround me and say things in Japanese. They didn't have much to waggle but what they did have, they waggled and scared the living daylights out of me, much to the amusement of ships personnel and the ladies. It was here that I first heard the term 'cherry boy' mentioned. When the Japanese foreman translated this term for the ladies, I suffered a severe groping.

However, this was not to be the only embarrassing experience for me during our stay at Ube. Via the Agent, one of the local schools asked for two officers to sit in on an English lesson and to speak to the pupils. I was volunteered as one and the 3rd Engineer volunteered to be the other. We were driven to the school and firstly had to meet the Head and join him for a cup of green tea. I, for one, had never tasted the stuff before but immediately marked it down as my least favourite tipple. After that we were taken to the classroom and introduced to the teacher and the students. We sat and listened to the lesson for a while and then the teacher wanted us to show the class whereabouts in England we lived. My companion was a Scot and didn't like this and from here on things started to go downhill. First of all I looked around for a map of the British Isles but was informed that I must draw a map on the board and then point out my home town. My companion then drew a line through my map separating Scotland from England and launched into a short, brutal and totally biased history of conflict between the two. They were confused and I was confused. The Scottish 'wanker' had high-jacked the school visit. I had a reasonable knowledge of the history of the British Isles and its internal conflicts but most of those being aired before the Japanese students, I had never heard of. To cut things short, our visit was cut short. The Agent reported back to the ship and I received a severe lecture on diplomacy and how I should be careful what I said in such circumstances. As I recall it, I hadn't said much atall. I didn't get the bloody chance. As for the 3rd Engineer, the bugger, got away with it completely!

From Ube we moved on a short distance to the bustling port of Moji. Because of the strong current flowing from the Inland Sea out to the Sea of Japan the ship had to moor at buoys forward and aft using one anchor cable forward. I seem to remember it taking hours to hang off and unshackle the anchor but eventually the mooring operation was completed. It was here that I first met 'Moji Mary' bumboat lady extraordinaire. This permanently happy, rotund lady could get one anything one wanted, including girls. Instead of buying things from the boat, 'Moji Mary' and her female assistants set up shop on deck. Japanese binoculars, Japanese cameras, all manner of electrical goods and the usual 'crap'. In a rush of enthusiasm, I bought a Japanese tea-set for my mother which she kept for many years but never used. Not only could you buy the goods but Mary could also arrange to have them sent back home. The humour of Mary and the glamorous assistants promised a very happy stay in Moji!

As I recall it, shore leave on that first evening in Moji was an early evening affair. I was to venture ashore with Sparks, but for some reason he was taking his time getting ready. I was eager to 'get going' and couldn't understand why my Irish friend was 'farting around' getting ready. When we eventually got ashore it was to be lead to a small Japanese bar which seemed to have been completely taken over by off-duty Deck Officers and Engineer Officers from my ship. When I look back I can see that it was a setup right from the start. Like a 'lamb to the slaughter' except my experience that night was a bloody sight better than slaughter! Having gone through the ritual cleaning of hands with hot towels and then the necessary ordering of drinks, we settled down to enjoy ourselves. The Japanese hostesses, and there were quite a few of them, settled down amongst us. Some of the lads were drinking warm Saki, others were enjoying more familiar spirits, I was allowed to drink beer. It was a jovial evening, the music was good, the girls were lovely and my companions were intent on enjoying themselves. The light snacks were different. The paper games and tricks that the girls showed us were amusing and I kept on getting the feeling that I was being coralled by the ladies. It was lovely! There was much chatter or banter in

English or pidgin English and I soon realised that a lot of the banter was at my expense but hey, I was relaxed, I had a beer in my hand and a girl at my side! My initiation ceremony was underway! I was collared, captured, selected and about to be seduced and, if you are still out there Mitchiko (or Matchiko) , may I thank you again. The evening continued, food, music, drink (although regarding the latter, mine seemed to be severely limited) until the Mama-San (who was hanging onto Sparks) decided it was time to shut up shop and that we should all move on elsewhere. Elsewhere turned out to be a Japanese hotel with a central area for drinks and snacks and a lot of small rooms with sort of paper walls. Like a lamb to the slaughter I was led away by Mitchiko to a large bathroom where I was stripped, dunked in a sunken bath and parboiled, hauled out and lathered, washed down and then boiled in the sunken bath again. I then watched and did my bit as Mitchiko did the same bathing routine to herself. After that we had a mutual drying and touching session before I was led off to our paper walled room. There on a floor level mattress, I lost my cherry and it was wonderful! It didn't end there. I was then taken back to the communal area wearing a Kimono where all my shipmates and their partners waited holding drinks. This time I was allowed a Saki and the party really began. Never mind the 'crossing the line ceremony' now I really was one of the team! After a few drinks everybody drifted off to their own rooms again but, in the morning, they made sure I made it back to the ship in time to report for duty. During the day whilst dwelling happily on the nights events I realised how my comrades knew when to gather in the communal area. Those bloody paper walls!

Here having related the experience of my first real 'climax' of the voyage I suffered a few moments of writers block but, to continue. The few days that I enjoyed in Moji came to an abrupt end when I stuck a marline spike in my leg while being taught how to wire splice by the Kassab. It wasn't a deep wound, in fact I went ashore that evening, but by the morning my leg looked as if I was suffering from elephantitis. I was taken from the ship to hospital where I spent an unhappy three weeks. I wrote to my Mother complaining, she wrote to the company complaining, they got in touch with the agent complaining who then got in touch with the hospital complaining who then confronted me and delivered a bollocking in broken English! I was in a three bed ward with a hole in the corner to be used as a 'loo'. The only other occupant, an American suffering from syphilis, soon warned me that being on the second floor, one had to move quickly to get away from the rising fumes. Since I was reduced to crawling, rapid movement was difficult but I soon perfected the art. Apart from Mitchiko, I was visited by the British Consul, and when a visit from the latter coincided with a visit from the former, I was in trouble again. He decided that there were far better things to occupy my mind and lent me the 'Works of Shakespeare'. Not a great deal more to be said about my stay in hospital apart from the fact that it was an American doctor from a nearby military establishment who 'saved' my leg for which I am eternally grateful. From hospital, I was removed to a Japanese hotel. Unfortunately, not the one where I lost my cherry but a 'real' Japanese hotel. Here I experienced the bath routine once more but this time with a kimono clad maid doing the honours. I remember getting to like the experience because she was very meticulous in her work. From hotel in Moji, to hotel in Tokyo, but here, the very personal touches were missing. The 'sleeper' train from Moji to Tokyo was another new experience and I shared a sleeper cabin with an American Army officer and his wife. It was more like three in a bed and they were not keen on the idea. I recall being ordered to put my face to the wall and keep it there.

I went from Tokyo by air to Vancouver via the small island of Chemya in the Aleutian Islands and then Anchorage, Alaska. I had a short stay ashore in Vancouver before rejoining my ship and, while waiting for the ship to arrive, I remember visiting the Seamans Mission and looking at the long list of names of 'displaced persons' on the notice board. I felt a bit lonely but what must they be feeling - wherever they were. Even today when I think of it, I feel a wave of sadness. However - back onboard and back to work. The ship was loading bulk grain in Vancouver for ports in China, and after only a few short days in Canada, the ship headed back across the Pacific, this time with me onboard. The first port of call was Darien in north China. It was a large city which had been at various times Chinese, Russian,

Japanese and again Chinese over the years.   In those days it looked grim and was grim.   We were allowed ashore but really to only one place - the International Seamen's Club and there was a 2200 hrs curfew.   Papers were checked going ashore and returning.   If you got into trouble, and we did, you were arrested and would appear before a military 'court'.   One officer would do the questioning and translating while the others looked on.   We soon learnt that if you made a wrong answer there would be reaction before your answer had been translated and passed to the court.   Most of them spoke English.   You would be asked about your parents, your home, your schooling and if you pleaded poverty they would mostly be lenient.   No shore leave was the usual form of punishment.   It was a familiar kind of punishment but being applied by the shore authorities gave it an extra degree of achievement and anyway, being banned from visiting nothing really meant nothing. The club was grim,   the town was grim.

After discharging the cargo of grain the ship was chartered to carry cargoes up and down the China coast.   Most of the time these cargoes appeared to be made up of scrap metal, steel plates and 'pig iron' ingots.   This was our contribution to Chairman Mao's red revolution or his current five year plan.   We did one trip to North Vietnam to the port of Haiphong which was interesting to say the least.   It was the very first time that I was shot at and I can picture the incident today after many, many years as if it happened last week.

Going ashore in North Vietnam was even more tedious than in China.   Apart from having to produce your papers and   having to empty your pockets, any cash you had was counted and recorded.   When you returned to the ship the same procedures were followed and if there was any difference in the cash tally, you had to show them what you had spent the money on.   Apart from fresh fruit or a sugar cane drink produced on the street by putting the cane through a mangle, there wasn't much to spend our money on anyway. It was returning from one trip ashore that the 'shooting' incident happened.   The 3rd Engineer, who was a large, jovial Geordie, was asked what he had spent his money on, and after pointing at the banana he was eating, he then stuffed it in the guard's face.   By this time I was legging it!   I think there were four of us, each suddenly blessed with Olympic athleticism.   Concrete dust started erupting close by as we rounded the corner of a wharf shed and   we took the gangway in a couple of bounds.   Of course, the guards knew the culprit, knew the group and knew the ship.   The 3rd Engineer was carted off to the local lock up for a few days and the rest of us had our shore leave stopped.   Amusing afterwards but   certainly a bit hairy at the time.   Losing my life because of someone else's banana was not part of the career dream.

Prior to this incident I had been 'chosen' to show a group of East German officers around our ship.   They all spoke very good English especially the Political Officer.   They were a little critical about some of our Bridge navigation instruments,   very interested in our worldwide pilot books and viewed with humour our bulkhead mounted chart showing the silhouettes of Soviet naval vessels.   After their tour I was allowed to give each of them a beer in our Officer's Mess. After this they borrowed a couple of films from our library and returned to their own ship.   Our officers were invited across for a return visit but it was me that was 'sent'.   There I had a very pleasant evening sitting with their Captain and Political Officer, drinking German beer, eating a delicious stew and watching one of our films. If this was being brainwashed, I enjoyed it. Prior to this I had a short tour of their ship and I could see what they meant about our lack of Bridge instruments - they appeared to have everything and everything duplicated. There was one short break in the film when a large cupboard was opened revealing a very large radio which spoke to the German crew for about ten minutes. I was told to keep drinking and keep quiet. It sounded a bit like Hitler speaking to the masses to me but I did not pass on this observation. All over, cupboard doors closed, film resumed and formalities over. I met the Political Officer some years later in Shanghai and we had a good laugh at our first meeting and my 'observation'.

From Haiphong we went to Whampoa in southern China after a short call at Hong Kong for bunkers. The bunkering took place at anchor and there was no shore leave but there was a very nice bumboat. It didn't last long though - the hoards of lovely ladies who swarmed onboard were soon rounded up by the Captain, the

Captain's wife who had joined us somewhere along the way and the Chief Officer. One was found in my cabin by the Captain's wife, which resulted in another lecture. Unfair really, because I had been out on deck enjoying the fun, totally unaware of the intruder. Anyway, the girls were sent back the way they came and the bumboat departed. The rails were lined with waving Brits and Chinese much to the Captain's wife's disgust and annoyance.

Whampoa I remember as being totally different to the industrialised or militarised ports further north. It was a lot warmer too. Cargo operations took place at anchor and forays ashore were via sampan. Shortly after we anchored two small coal burners tied up alongside and cargo work began. These relics belched black smoke from their funnels in varying amounts but enough to quickly start turning our white paintwork to a dirty shade of grey. Ventilation was shut down to try and stop both fumes and coal dust from getting into the accommodation. All this made the forays ashore that much more pleasant. They made a grim pair these old tubs and they were manned by even grimmer looking crews. Once ashore the formalities were the same as other ports in The Peoples Chinese Republic and the only place that we were allowed to go to was the International Seamen's club. However, an open sided bamboo hut serving cool beer was a lot better than the bleak concrete buildings of the frozen north. I think we all managed to stay out of trouble here. However, it couldn't last and northwards we went again. When I say it couldn't last I meant staying out of trouble and enjoying the sunny south. The pattern was mainly Shanghai, Tsingtao, Tientsin, Chinwangtao and Darien and back again. We braved the Formosa Strait between the then island of Formosa, now Taiwan and mainland China being buzzed by American aircraft and spoken to by American naval vessels. I think we were stopped and boarded once but my memory may well be playing tricks. It did happen later on in my career, off Cuba. We used to listen to the top one hundred records from a radio station in Taiwan or was it Korea. Anyway a very sexy voiced lady would talk to us between records. When in port in China the radio station was jammed as were most of the BBC Overseas programmes including our own Merchant Navy programme!

Apart from being famous for the beer it produces, of which we took good advantage when ashore, Tsingtao was also a major naval port and I was told that one amongst our senior officers was taking note of what was to be readily observed. I recall seeing many submarines but not much else. Perhaps one needed a trained eye. It was all very intriguing anyway, to think that we may have had a spy amongst us. Not much else to say about the place. It was industrial, militarised and I can't remember it ever being warm when we were there. I experienced one sticky moment when I was sent ashore to read the draft before departure where I was momentarily detained for doing something suspicious. If they were going to detain me for reading the draft, what would they do to our 007 whoever he was.

From Chinwangtao some of us were taken by bus for a day trip to the first gate of the Great Wall of China. It was an enjoyable outing and we were freely allowed to take photographs although our cameras were confiscated on the journey out and back and only returned to us on reaching the ship. The one thing that I remember most was the lack of facilities and thus I claim to be one of the very few foreigners to have 'peed' on the Great Wall of China.   Fortunately for me, I wasn't caught   -   I hate to think what the consequences might have been!

Shanghai was a great bustling port and a very large city even in those days.   I imagine that now it is a city of light with modern buildings, much traffic and many shops.   Back then the Bund was quiet traffic wise apart from military vehicles and cargo wagons, the side streets were dimly lit and there was an air of darkness about the place. There were bicycles everywhere and mass movements of people.   The International Seamen's Club was a very large building which must have been quite spectacular in the days before communism switched the lights off.   It had at one time been home to the longest bar in the world.   The magnificent polished wooden bar was still there but I believe it had lost first spot to a bar in Australia.   To enter the building you had to climb wide curving steps and pass through huge pillars into a large domed entrance hall with a statue of Chairman Mao in the centre.   Off to the left and through very large and splendid wooden doors was the club bar and this wonderfully ornate structure stretching away into the distance. I think I may be exaggerating a bit but it really was a fine bar. However, the choice of drinks was severely limited. Beer at something like 30 pence a bottle or vodka at about 15 pence a bottle. On the opposite side of the entrance hall was a shop where visitors could buy some souvenirs, some food and an amazing amount of communist literature in an equally amazing number of languages. The latter being gratis to any gullible sod who wished to partake. Pictures of happy workers singing patriotic songs while holding either a sheaf of wheat or a hammer in one hand and a huge red flag in the other. I do remember looking at a transistor radio that required something about the size of a car battery to power it. Anything purchased in the shop and that included drink and food was then delivered to the ship. Where for example a bottle of beer would cost 30 pence in the bar, by choosing to have it delivered to the ship it would cost 15 pence. Some took advantage of this - I was still not allowed.

It was during one of our *visits* to the 'Club'

that the riot started. It involved several ship's crews with the main protagonists being two British ships and one Scandinavian ship. I hasten to add that it was not an inter-ship brawl. In my mind I remember it as being the result of the officials over-reaction to an admittedly raucous inter-ship party wherein much of the banter was against our Chinese hosts. When said officials started arresting us in groups of about half a dozen at a time, things got a little more violent. As I recall the 'border police' were quite zealous in their task of cutting us down to size but then there were quite a number of Brits and Vikings charged up with vodka or beer and armed with the bottles that had contained the latter. Part of the evenings entertainment had been endeavouring to slide bottles of vodka along the highly polished bar, points being scored for how far said bottle would go before it fell off and shattered on the mosaic floor. We were all arrested! The following morning most were returned to their ships - eight were not and I was one of the eight. I still believe that we were selected at random from the crowd and not because of any outstanding action during the riot. Anyway, that was it. We each appeared before a tribunal which followed a similar pattern to the previous ones but this time, no amount of pleading poverty or suppression of human rights did any good. We were to be made an example of to others showing what would happen to them should they choose to step out of line.

The following three months were not the brightest in my career. The solitary cell was actually only slightly smaller than my cabin onboard ship. Admittedly, the facilities were certainly not as good and the food was bloody awful. When my ship was in Shanghai which was every two or three weeks I was allowed food packages but no visitors. Once a day our group was exercised in a small yard but no talking was allowed. If you tried to talk, the guards would threaten you with and sometimes did jab you with the butt of their rifle. It was only during these exercise periods in my stay that anything threatening happened. The rest of the time I saw hardly anybody. We could shout to each other and this was mostly tolerated but only for short periods and I got the impression that it depended on who was on duty or who was in charge. The amount of literature that I was given to read was mountainous and even then they had to produce some Soviet literature to fill in.   Needless to say, when I was unexpectedly released and delivered back to   my ship I was overjoyed first, and much relieved second.   I expected a severe telling off on my return to the ship but nothing was said. Actually, I was a bit of a hit for a few days amongst the junior deck and engineering officers. But that didn't last long and it was soon back to being a 'snotty' again.

At the moment I can only remember one other incident which caused the Chinese authorities some concern and provided us with a few moments   of humour.   I hasten to add that I was in no way involved in this incident.   We were in Dairen and amongst the shore revellers was our Electrician, a bloke in his mid forties.   Anyway he broke the curfew and did not return to the ship at or after the set time.   We onboard were alerted because of the great agitation amongst the guards at the gangway.   They even searched the ship just in case he had slipped onboard unnoticed.   We found out the following morning that he had been arrested sleeping in a tree along the tree lined boulevard where the Club was situated.   His excuse, apparently, was that he felt tired and climbed the tree to get away from pedestrians. He was locked up for twenty-four hours, had his shore leave stopped and was subjected to a minor brain washing.   See I was not the only one.   We enjoyed a good laugh at his expense.

During one visit to Tientsin we were warned of an approaching Typhoon and since it was apparently too late to put to sea, we had to take action to face a battering in port.   Ropes and wire ropes were being strung out from every available bollard.   Even the 'insurance wire' was taken out of storage and put into use.   I particularly remember this bit of wire because it was a bugger to manhandle.   This was to be my very first experience of a Typhoon direct hit and I wasn't sure exactly what to expect. The precautions being taken by us and other nearby vessels were a sure indication that it was not expected to be a pleasant experience.   This turned out to be true. It was not a pleasant experience, but the adrenalin burst kept us, certainly me, active, alert and out on deck.   I stood on deck in the torrential rain and watched the insurance wire carve its way through a solid steel bulwark like a knife through butter.   When it eventually held, it then pulled the wharf bollard off its mountings. The ship shuddered and crashed throughout the night until at first light, the main fury of the storm had passed. Later on in my career I mused on why most of these nasty happenings seemed to happen during the hours of darkness, but I digress. We had suffered quite a bit of superficial damage, some main structural damage and some side plate damage - but we had survived. Others were not quite so lucky. At least one of the local ships had her plates sprung and was listing heavily. There appeared to be a lot of damage ashore but for us it was all hands on deck to look to our own ship. The storm passed, calm returned and then it took a long time re-stowing all the extra mooring wires and ropes that we had put out. I was told that our hull plates were buckled but not sprung and would have to wait for dry-docking for repair. I later viewed the damage internally in one of the empty holds and it looked rather like a step in the plating in a fore and aft line at the level of the wharf where the ship had been repeatedly bashed against the unforgiving concrete of the wharf.

Our contribution towards Chairman Mao's five year plan and his dream of a perfect socialist state was complete and at last the charter came to an end and from Darien we headed southwards towards the South Pacific island of Nauru where we were scheduled to load phosphate for Northern Europe. This was to be my first visit to a Pacific island and I looked forward to it eagerly. Nauru, at that time, had the deepest moorings in the world and tying up to them proved to be quite a challenge. I seem to recall many hours on deck hanging off anchors and attaching the anchor chains to buoys with huge shackles. I must add that when I say 'hanging off anchors' I mean separating them from the anchor chain and not me personally hanging off the anchor by my fingertips gazing into the deep blue beneath me. Oh no! Once moored, a great cantilever arm was positioned over one of the open hatches and a steady stream of what appeared to be mainly dust to me, cascaded into the hold below. To keep the trim of the vessel right this arm was moved from hatch to hatch and slowly everything turned grey. It was very hot but all the ventilation systems had to be shut down to try to stop the dust getting into the accommodation. I say try, because it seemed to get everywhere. Even the vegetation on the island was covered with the stuff and the nearby buildings were caked with it. Because of the depth of the moorings a close watch had to be kept on the weather, and in particular, the sea conditions. I forget what the sea condition was that would mean letting go from the mooring buoys and proceeding to sea, but we had to do it once, returning only when things calmed down and conditions allowed after about six days at sea just drifting and waiting. When at the buoys we were allowed ashore but only briefly so I did not get a chance to seek out dusky maidens. The run ashore was quite interesting though. We boarded what looked like a miniature tank landing craft which headed out to sea then turned and raced for a little man made harbour beyond what appeared to be a line of impenetrable surf. Very impressive. On the way back we all got a good wetting as the craft burst out through the surf. Great fun! Never mind the dusky maidens, the time was spent surrounded by dusty Chinese labourers which was definitely not the same thing! During one lunch break I went swimming off the end of the gangway. The water was warm and very clear and it was a very good way of clearing the phosphate out of the nasal passages. I remember that I could see the whole of the ships underwater form. The rudder and the propeller. When one of the engineers shouted 'shark' and I caught sight of a dark form in the water close-by, it proved to me that it was possible to climb up a ships vertical side using only rivets for hand-grips. Well maybe not - but I was out of the water with astonishing speed and agility. The dark form turned out to be a pair of rays gliding gracefully past but it was enough for me and I did not venture into the sea at Nauru again. From Nauru we sailed eastwards towards the Panama Canal and from there onwards to Northern Europe.

The voyage back to *Europe* was long and uneventful apart from the night passage through the Panama Canal. At anchor at the Pacific end of the canal the amount of sea life and bird life, I recall, as being amazing. Actually transiting the canal at night had a magical effect because there are lights along much of the canal highlighting the green and density of the jungle. In the narrower parts of the canal the sounds of the jungle at night conjured up pictures of exotic birds and animals and slithering things. I had recently read an article in the Readers Digest about a bloke who woke up in his sleeping bag with a snake curled up with him somewhere out there in the jungles of Panama and I immediately resolved to stick with the ship whatever happened. The 'mules', the engines which tow the ships through the locks was another amazing sight. It was very hot and very humid! I enjoyed my first passage through the canal but later in my career it became something of a hot and tiring chore. When, later on, the ships I served on became too big to transit the Panama Canal, I was quietly relieved. If only the same could have happened with the Suez Canal. I'm sure there are not many ship-owners who would agree with this sentiment but I think the majority of the worlds seafarers would most definitely be on my side.

It was on this passage from Panama to Europe that I was introduced to the word 'LEFO' and to the magical name of Portishead Radio. Not really magical but it was from this place that great messages of portent were received usually regarding our next destination and or cargo. LEFO was the abbreviation for Lands End For Orders which virtually meant that nobody knew where the hell we were going to next. Our future, our very destiny lay somewhere between the London office, Portishead Radio station, LEFO and the ship. I experienced this phenomenon a few times during my cadetship but afterwards when I joined ships on regular trade routes, the liners, this was a thing of the past and an occasional source of mirth - but not so funny when it applies to the ship you are serving on. Anyway, we had two discharge ports in Europe and nothing after that so LEFO applied. Sparks became the centre of attention and when he left the radio shack for a cup of tea, a meal, or for more basic functions he would be set upon. When the shack buzzed with dots and dashes, rumours would start. If Sparks left the shack and went to the Old Man's cabin, interest would reach fever pitch and rumours would start. Amazing really that grown men, many of whom had been at sea for many years, would turn into mumbling wrecks at the sound of a few dots and dashes. I was young, first voyage, and amongst the worst effected. We had been away for well over a year by then and some amongst us thought of home. It wasn't going to be much in consolation in that we would be able to see the UK coastline in the distance as we passed through the Dover Strait. The Western Approaches still had an exciting ring to it and being 'buzzed' again by Coastal Command patrol aircraft just added to the excitement. The line of fishing boats marking the change of water depth from the deep Atlantic Ocean to the shallower European Shelf was another indication that we were approaching home waters. The schedule for the voyage had the ship discharging her cargo at Rotterdam and Copenhagen and then, when eventually our LEFO orders did come through causing joy to some but disappointment to the majority, the orders were to proceed to Safi in Morocco to load phosphate for China. This induced me to spend my money in the bars of Katendrecht in Rotterdam and the bars in the Nyhavn in Copenhagen. The fact that we then put into London to load sheets of steel caught us all on the hop. I was granted four days leave but had to borrow some money to get home. Fortunately at that time our rail fares were subsidized by Forces Passes. I arrived home at some disgusting hour in the early morning and had to throw stones at my Mothers bedroom window to gain entry. After two years and five months away, this was most definitely not the triumphal return that I had long envisaged.

Back onboard and onwards,, the only two things that I remember about Safi was watching a naked French girl walking along the beach adjacent to the ship.   I was not alone in this observation.   We did not know for sure that she was French as all this was viewed from the wing of the bridge and that was as close as we got but she was certainly very sexy, so we decided that she must be French.   The other happening was when I stopped to buy food from a street seller with an oil can full of red hot coals.   Whatever it was. it tasted delicious when it went down, but it didn't stay down for very long.   From those mild adventures we sailed again for China fully laden with steel plates in the bottoms and topped up with phosphate, this time via the Suez Canal. Now correct me if I'm wrong but having loaded phosphate in Nauru which is but a spit from China a few months earlier for Europe, now to be loading phosphate again in Morocco which is but a spit from Europe for China seemed very strange to me. Keep the ship fully loaded and world trade ticking over I agree, but I still don't get it.

Now, after forty years at sea I can still recall some points of that passage through the Canal to the Red Sea.   I did not really enjoy it then and after multiple transits I actually hated it.   I have to admit though that I found this first passage through the Canal interesting.   My duty for the whole of this passage was to try and stop boarders and to make sure that those who were permitted onboard did not manage to acquire that which was not theirs.   Apart from being approached to buy some much thumbed dirty black and white photographs and model camels and other trash, there was not much to cheer about on that first passage.   The bumboat did not match the attraction of those in Japan and Hong Kong.   The gilli-gilli man, I think that was what he was called, was amusing when watched in a group but his conjuring and pick pocketing skills were not so enjoyable when he caught one alone. The boatmen spent most of their time begging for food or wandering around in places where they should not have been.   I spent a lot of time chasing them out of the accommodation.   They are a persistent lot, the Egyptian canal employees.   I do remember seeing the remains of vessels, sunk during the Suez conflict to block the canal and then salvaged, cut up and dumped on the side of the canal. And still, I remember, how relieved I felt when the mooring boats were lowered to the water, the pilot departed at Suez and we moved out into the relative peace and quiet of the Gulf of Suez. That evening the Chief Officer was particularly grumpy but I could understand why.

We stopped off at Aden to bunker but apart from a crewmember dropping a heavy shackle onto a persistent wooden bumboat causing a rapid ingress of water and an even faster retreat to the safety of the shallow water, it was a quiet stay. As usual, the harbour was full of mainly British merchant ships loading, discharging or bunkering. There were also naval vessels and ships of the Royal Fleet Auxiliary. On our jaunt to the Rock Hotel, we were again called 'draft dodgers' as our liberty boat passed a naval vessel. Aden was even more of a problem at this time and the increase in the presence of the military onshore was very obvious. It was an unhappy place then, but bunkering there a few years later when Aden was part of the Yemen Republic, it was an even more unhappy place.

Sport at sea in these early days was very hit and miss. On our occasional visits to Europe, the Mission to Seamen would sometimes arrange inter-ship soccer matches and very occasionally, inter-ship cricket matches. On the China coast we would meet up with ships from various parts of the Soviet Union who were always game for a game. Fortunately, there were very few Soviet ships on the coast at that time due to some tiff between these communist giants. I say, fortunately, because their teams generally managed to slaughter us. As it was the defeated ships privilege to play host to the winners our limited stocks of goodies suffered somewhat. Occasionally our Russian adversaries would take pity on us and invite us back to their ships, usually when they wanted to see one of our films. We would always add some of our Western grog to the proceedings as a gesture and this seemed to be appreciated but they knew how to throw a party. I have to add that one of the added attractions was that there were females onboard these Soviet ships and most of them were gorgeous. They were very friendly but it was strictly, look don't touch.

I fell in lust many times but it was never to see them again.   Any good from the game healthwise was soon lost with the intake of some strange Eastern European alcoholic drinks.   Someone did suggest at one such party, that our hosts were pouring surgical spirit.   After that we were a little more selective.   The food that they laid on for us was always very good.   As a team we were a ragged lot, whereas the opposition were usually properly kitted out in full ship's strip.   The games were usually good fun if a little brutal.   We could barely put together a team but they had much larger and fitter crews, larger, not only in number, but in size as well!   Because of this they got to provide the referee   -   need I say more.   The after game analysis would have made a good recording.   'That bloody Cossack was aiming for me not the ball'   or 'Ivan the bastard could touch both goalposts without moving a muscle' or 'I'm sure they had more than eleven men in their team' or   'What did they put in *their* half time drink'. Of all the countries that I have visited, New Zealand was by far the best for ship involved sporting activities.   I will say it again   -   it wasn't a bad place for parties either!

Onboard ship during the long sea passages there was nothing to encourage us to keep fit. Much later on, the ships would have games rooms and gymnasiums, but in these early days, work as exercise would have to suffice. That and elbow bending! One thing we did have onboard that first ship was a swimming pool. At least that was what it was called. Really it was just a plunge pool. There were two reasons why we saw very little of this though. One - it was awkward to erect and two - the Chief Officer had a thing about salt water on his steel deck. It had to be a long spell at anchor in the tropics for our pleas to be answered - and even then reluctantly. And that was about it in the early years of my career - our employers did not invest much in our health. Things would eventually change for the better but it would take a few years.

Medical health was another thing. On my first ship, the person in charge of the dispensary was the Chief Officer, and if that wasn't enough to put you off, then viewing the contents of the dispensary surely would. I have to say that the contents of this dispensary would not look a great deal different from the one on my last ship apart from an update in pills and potions.   The devices for extracting teeth or removing limbs were the same and   brought to mind instruments of extreme torture.   Lockers marked poison added to the feeling of repulsion like a 'do not enter' sign. Pictures of buttocks indicating the correct area to insert a needle.   Metal needles looking like something designed for spraying the garden and not for inserting into the posterior.   Disposable needles came in sometime later.   All these things did nothing to improve the ambience of the place. The fact that they had chosen one of the gloomiest rooms on the ship did not help either.   This was most definitely not a place to visit unless when absolutely necessary.   I visited this 'chamber of horrors' on a regular basis during Emergency Drills to fetch and carry the stretcher, a wood and canvas construction that had all the trappings of a straight jacket with its straps and loops, ties and tassels.   Apart from the odd plaster I had no other reasons to visit the place during my time onboard.

By now I was well into my third year at sea. The Captain had changed, the Chief Officer had changed and so had many of the Engineers.   The new Old Man was a very large gentleman from East Anglia and his attitude to life was completely opposite to that of his predecessor. I don't think I ever heard him raise his voice in all the months that we sailed together and there were one or two moments when I wouldn't have blamed him. This man took great interest in my training and I must thank him for making my passage from sea to college to gaining my Second Mates Certificate a much smoother passage than it might have been. I had already had two of the annual examinations with varying results. I achieved 90% in my first years exams helped by having the necessary text books with me whereas I only achieved 56% in the following year without said text books. The company showed a degree of unhappiness with this trend. Anyway, with the change of command came a change in routine. Now I was able to keep a Bridge watch with either the 2nd Officer or the 3rd Officer. Now I was able to handle a sextant regularly, use binoculars, even peer into the radar. My calculations were looked at and corrected where necessary. I was given a study schedule and regularly questioned on the Rules of the Road. I was allowed on the Bridge arriving and departing from some ports. I even did the occasional engine room watch but this only confirmed to me that I had chosen the right department. It did make me appreciate what the lads down below had to put up with. I still had days working on deck but even these tasks were now educationally orientated. The complexity of rigging derricks and mast rigging were made clear. Wire and rope splicing were a regular task. Even painting was treated as more of a science than a slap it on technique.

However - back to the tale. The voyage continued onwards through the Malacca Strait, the Singapore Strait and once again to bunker at Hong Kong. This time, shore leave was granted and I forayed ashore with Sparks. We took the Wanchai ferry across to Hong Kong island and enjoyed a couple of hours wandering around and window shopping. Back across by ferry and we managed to wander into a military area where we were picked up and transported back to the ship by the army. We were given a beer in some bar on the camp so this was counted as a successful if minor adventure. I was not to see Hong Kong again for many years and by then the place was virtually unrecognisable. We thought it was a bustling place then, but it was a mere backwater to what it was to become.

From there onwards to our discharge port of Dairen. It hadn't changed atall in the few months that we had been away. The usual arrival formalities had to be gone through. All crew members were studied one by one by blank faced frontier police. Everything was done by at least three policemen. Once again all cameras and binoculars were confiscated, locked away and the locker sealed. I felt that they peered at my papers for that little bit longer than other crew members but that might just have been me. One would look at the ID Card and the crew pass and when satisfied would write on a list in front of him. Another would then take the crew pass and write on a list in front of him. Yet another would take the ID Card and write on a list in front of him. Then all three would stare at the crew member in front of them and then with a gesture of the hand the crew member would be dismissed. I must add here, that our Hong Kong Chinese crew members were not allowed ashore atall in the Peoples Republic of China. While this was going on, two groups of policemen would be searching all the

89

cabins, lockers and public rooms escorted by a senior officer. All other members of the crew were confined to one room while this was going on and it could last up to four hours. Dairen was our port of entry but this routine was followed at every port on the China coast!

Dairen was a huge rail junction and the massive trains and equally massive wagons were on the move twenty-four hours a day. I can still hear their whistles blowing throughout the night. The whole of the port and railway area was floodlit at night with an orange glow, apart from the high wire of the perimeter and the guard stations which were brilliantly lit. The icy wind, the blowing snow, the eerie glow, the mournful whistles, the hiss of steam and the smell of coal dust all made for a fairly grim picture and one that I hold in my memory today. It wasn't much better during daylight hours when we had the additional entertainment of music being blasted out from the seemingly hundreds of loudspeakers dotted around the port area. From ship to gate or vice versa could be something of a obstacle course at times and on more than one occasion, we had near misses when crossing the railway lines. On one particular occasion when returning from the Club, the 3rd Engineer while scrambling between two huge bulk wagons had his clothing caught between the buffers when the train started to move. Fortunately for him it was a bit of a stuttering start and the buffers separated and released him. When we picked him up, he was as white as a sheet and shaking but unharmed and by then, completely sober.   He later joked about   the waste of money that incident had cost him. However, after that, we were much more wary during our forays ashore.   I can recall only one other incident during this call when the Electrician was arrested and charged with   breaking curfew and spying.   The fact was he had fallen asleep in a snow drift and being found by the frontier police probably saved his life.   He was locked up for the remainder of our stay in Dairen.

On the odd occasion we would be invited to attend a Chinese opera or a Chinese circus.   The operas were a bit long for us, sometimes lasting up to four hours but they were very colourful and very noisy.   The circus had its moments but I for one found the dancing bear routine distressing.   The acrobats and jugglers were very good.   However, the bonus for these events was a meal ashore and if you liked Chinese food, as I did, they were excellent. It was more like a banquet and thoroughly enjoyed and appreciated by all. The rice wine I could easily leave alone, as to me, it tasted something like I imagine sweaty socks would taste. During the meals there would be speeches and much clapping. Nobody bothered translating but we didn't mind. At least we got bussed from the gangway and back to the gangway thus avoiding any close encounters with shunting trains. Again, on occasion we would be treated to a film show at 'our' Club. These were always propaganda films and were usually greeted with rich and ribald remarks. One immensely amusing evening a giant Scandinavian threw his bottle of vodka at the screen when the propaganda got a bit over the top for him. This caused something of a rumpus. Most of the other filmgoers tried to interfere with the guards as they struggled to remove the perpetrator of this heinous offence. Bearing in mind earlier experiences, I stayed exactly where I was. The club officials saw this and I was one of the few who didn't get locked up that night. I even seem to think I got a free beer for not getting involved.

Once again we found ourselves or at least the ship, on charter to the Chinese and employed carrying 'stuff' up and down the coast. Most of us were now well used to the routine but I could have wished for other places on this planet on which to pass those few months.

We experienced two major incidents during this sojourn on the China coast, neither of them in any way humorous at the time. Somewhere along the line, a new Third Officer had joined the ship. He was in his mid twenties and appeared to most of us to be a bit lacking in the sense of humour department which we all thought to be a vital component for survival on that China charter. He was rather stiff and staid but got on with the job and was very keen when it came to my periods of instruction. However, mingling with the rest of the officers when off duty was certainly not his thing. One morning, when the ship was alongside in Shanghai, there was an awful kerfuffle along the corridor from my cabin. I remember poking my head out of the door to see what was going on and being told, rather sharply, to get inside and stay where I was. On a working day this was a most unusual order. Anyway, I learned later that 3/O had finished his shift on cargo watch and had immediately retired to his cabin. This was not unusual for him. The following morning when he had not reported for the next cargo watch, the Second Officer went to his cabin and found him lying on his bunk with the top sheet covered in blood by his feet. I was told later, that after retiring, he had apparently undressed, lay down on the top of the bunk and had supped most of a bottle of vodka and had then proceeded to shoot at his toes with some sort of gas gun. It fired small ball bearings which had made a terrible mess of his feet. He was carted off to hospital ashore and we never saw him again.

The second incident again took place in Shanghai, but this time it was just a few hours before the ship was due to sail for Europe with a general cargo bound for Rijeka in the then Yugoslavia, Trieste, Venice, Leghorn and finally, Genoa. The electrician had been complaining of toothache for some days and on the final day one side of his face came up like a balloon. He was taken ashore to some medical facility where they removed a tooth and subsequently returned him to the ship. Here he complained of being in even more pain than before the extraction. The ship sailed and headed southwards towards Singapore. After a few hours at sea and feeling no less pain after being dosed up with the ship's pain killers, one of the Engineers gave him a bottle of vodka. This had a remarkable effect in that his jaw swelling subsided and the pain became acceptable. A constant supply of vodka was arranged and 'Lecky' was kept in a more or less alcoholic stupor until we arrived in Singapore. Here he was transported to hospital where they diagnosed a broken jaw. So much for all these tales about alcohol being bad for you! Another member of the crew to be left behind. One good thing about the departure of the Third Officer, as far as I was concerned, was my temporary promotion to Watchkeeper on the 8 to 12 watch until a certificated replacement could be flown out. Unfortunately, it didn't last long as the new 3/O was waiting on the quayside as we docked in Singapore. However, it stood me in good stead, as later I was to be transferred to another ship as Uncertificated Third Officer to finish my cadet seatime. The fact that it was a terrible old tub will be told later.

As I recall, the passage through the Malacca Strait, across the Bay of Bengal and the Indian Ocean to Aden was uneventful. I was told about fierce warriors on the island of Socotra and on the coast of the Arabian mainland to the north and these tales were partially verified by the Pilot book for the region. Aden was its usual hot and busy place, but now there was open conflict between the British forces and the locals, so shore leave was banned. While we were there a large part of Aden away from the waterfront seemed to be on fire. The bumboats still plied their trade but all was definitely not well ashore. After Aden we had the passage up the Red Sea and the Suez Canal transit to look forward to but really, we were all looking forward to getting to Rijeka.

After clearing the Suez Canal, on the transit between Port Said and Rijeka the ship experienced some of the worst weather I had seen so far. In fact, apart from the odd Typhoon or Hurricane that I encountered in later years, the Eastern Mediterranean was perhaps the most violent stretch of water that I was to come across in my years at sea. That and the bit of the

Mediterranean between Algeria and France. Higher seas in the Atlantic, longer swells in the Pacific but for violence, I think the Mediterranean takes the biscuit. It was blowing hard shortly after we left the canal and by the time the ship was off the south coast of Crete, things were very uncomfortable. Fortunately, by this time, everything that could be lashed down was lashed down and everything that should be battened down was battened down. However, one derrick did break loose from its lashings and jumped out of the derrick crutch which the derrick head was supposed to sit in when at sea. It swung violently until, by manoeuvring the ship, the officers on the bridge managed to control its movement long enough for the sailors to get more lashings on it. One of the lifeboats had also started to move in the davits at the same time and this time it was the Third Officer and myself who went out onto the boat deck to re-secure it. He took the bow and I took the stern and our co-ordinated efforts were by visual direction only as the howl of the wind made conversation impossible. We both got very wet! Our speed had been severely reduced and the ship was still rolling, pitching and spiralling in the very rough confused seas. My cabin was a mess -

fellow shipmates at the time would say that it was always thus, but I protest. The old sea adage 'if it falls leave it' comes to mind. I had been told this much earlier on in my cadetship accompanied with 'once its on the deck it won't go much further'. So, I left everything on deck piled in a corner of my cabin and held on to something immovable. The only thing I can say in favour of Mediterranean storms is that they are quick to arise and equally quick to die down. Our voyage to freedom was delayed but by not too much and by the time we had rounded the corner into the Adriatic all was relatively calm again. By the time we reached the anchorage at Rijeka all was 'shipshape and Bristol fashion' once more. One sobering fact was that a British ship, owned by one of the major shipping lines, had foundered off Crete in the storm. I tell many tales of adventures ashore and lessons unlearnt but when it comes to adventures at sea, whatever, make a mental note and hang on to it. I learned this lesson very early on in my career. For those worst hours of the storm we lived on bowls of hot, thick soup or mugs of cocoa and condensed milk - one of the catering lessons I have never forgotten. Much later on in my career I found that offering a Pilot a mug of hot soup in the middle of the night rather than the traditional cup of tea or coffee, especially in the colder climes, was much appreciated.   A mug of soup or stew in the middle of a storm was much appreciated by all onboard.

But back to looking forward to our arrival at Rijeka.   Never mind that it was yet another communist country, anything had to be better.   A better experience than China.   Nobody onboard had been there before so, what little we knew, was gleaned from the appropriate Mediterranean Pilot Book.   The now defunct version of this book not only gave guidance to the mariner regarding navigational points, pilot and port authority instruction, but they also included some history, some trade information, some places of interest and even some politics.   So, we knew before we got there, that Rijeka was a major port, a major shipyard and that it was also   -   and here the ears pricked up -   a major tourist centre for Western Europeans.   This all sounded like a much better type of communism.   When we got there, the ship was anchored some way from the port and, apart from boats carrying Port Authority people, agents to ship and our Captain to shore, no liberty boat was laid on. We had all been cleared to go ashore and had been issued with shore passes but much to our disgust the company had decided against the expense of the liberty boat. We could swim around the ship in the clear waters of the Adriatic and wave longingly, sometimes frantically at the passing tourist boats but that was it. On one occasion a passing West German pleasure cruiser circled us waving and beckoning. This was too much for the Third Engineer and he dived in from the wing of the bridge. He was hauled onboard the cruiser by the German family who then took him on a tour of the area, returning him to the gangway some hours later, a burbling but happy wreck. When he eventually managed to tells us about his trip our appetite for 'liberty' was even more intense. I think it was about three weeks before the ship eventually berthed and, to a man, all those allowed ashore on that first night, were arrested, escorted back to the ship and had further shore leave banned for two days. The police were friendly, smiling, even seemingly understanding but we were told to 'cool it' in future. This really was a different type of communism. Away from the docks, the bars, restaurants and nightclubs in the old part of Rijeka and along the waterfront proved to be a magnet to us and as long as we behaved ourselves we were left alone by the authorities. We were there for several days, several very happy runs ashore and I thank you Rijeka for returning our sanity. Well nearly. One evening ashore in my favourite bar the regular and extremely shapely singer was strutting her stuff when I decided that she needed a rose down her cleavage. Not a good move as I forgot to remove one of the thorns. She shrieked, thumped me and I went backwards off the stage. She was very angry but the crowded bar thought this was hilarious. I was picked up and ceremoniously carted back to the 'ships' table. Later I got close enough to apologise.

From Rijeka, we then moved onwards to Trieste, just a very short way up the Adriatic. This was a very busy port and our berth was about half a mile from the centre of town. Here we were discharging and loading at the same time. The walk ashore was along a wide road with water on one side and high security fencing on the other. On leaving the port area through the guard gate there was a bit of a park on the right hand side surrounded by hedges and to the left, on the harbour side, was a large open air swimming pool. Both have some significance to my tale. As we walked ashore day or night or returned to the ship, night or day, a voice from behind the hedge would offer all kinds of sexual things for 500 lire. Female we thought, but to my knowledge none of our team stayed behind to find out. The swimming pool was all flags, bunting and posters advising us that Bridget Bardot was to appear there one afternoon. I was even allowed shore leave to go and see her but the crowd was so dense I couldn't get near. By now, the ship had adopted the bar 'Vito' as our main shore base, and the ladies of the house were very friendly. When the ships of the United States Mediterranean fleet tied up, stern to, along the road from our ship to the security gate, all hell was let loose upon the town. Until 9pm every evening hordes, of American sailors took over the bars, restaurants and clubs to the disadvantage of the rest of us. However, when they went back to their ships, sometimes reluctantly, the town was ours and the ladies were most generous. I remember one of the girls at the Vito opening a bag the size of a small suitcase and revealing it stuffed with dollars. That night and most others whilst the fleet was in, drinks and food for us were on the house.

Onwards again, this time to Venice, which was again only a very small trip across the Adriatic. To get to the commercial docks of Venice, the ship sailed past some of the wonderful sights of that amazing city. St Marks Square and the Lido are the ones I remember and I still have a black and white photo of the ship with the square behind it. Again we were loading and discharging at the same time and the walk into town was quite a way - but well worth it! We did the tourist thing and enjoyed the sights. One day, after crossing the Rialto Bridge, we came across a group of English girls sitting at tables outside a canal-side bar. When we asked if we could join them we were told in no uncertain terms to 'fuck off'. These were the first English girls we had seen for over two years! We moved on. The only other thing that I remember was that there was, at that time, a brothel just up one of the streets off St Marks Square. I was told of this and even had it pointed out to me but took no advantage of this knowledge. However, in a certain James Bond film where the hero disappears

up this very same alleyway I do wonder   -
surely not though.

From Venice we *moved* on to Palermo in
Sicily to load.   This port, plus Leghorn and
Genoa had been added to our European schedule.
On our arrival there was only one other ship in the
port, other than a ferry or two and this was a
medium sized West German freighter.   As I
recall, all German freighters were of a restricted
size at that time, but I digress. Here, in a
waterfront bar, the two nationalities mixed quite
amicably until the 'liberty men' off an American
warship upset the applecart.   Within minutes of
them entering the bar, the place erupted.   It was
Europe versus the US in a short but sharp bar
brawl.   When the 'shore patrol' accompanied by
an Italian policeman, entered things became even
more confused with the long white battens wielded
by the patrol hitting anybody within reach and the
policeman shooting lumps out of the ceiling.
Fortunately nobody had taken advantage of the
rooms offered upstairs.   It was over very quickly
and the American seamen were marched off by the
'Shore Patrol'.   We received an on the spot
lecture in Italian and were marched off to our

respective ships   -   and that was it.   No fine no
nothing.

'that the mind moves more freely in
The presence of that boundless expanse,
That the sight of it elevates the soul and gives
Rise to thoughts of the infinite and the ideal'

Gustave Flaubert.   Madame Bovary

'Onwards and Upwards'

My elation on being promoted to
Uncertificated Third Officer was only slightly
tempered by the tales I had heard about the ship on
which I was about to serve.   During the long
hours onboard my first ship it was not unusual to
talk about other ships in the fleet and my next one
seemed to crop up in conversation a lot more than
the others.   The story was that she had been sunk
by the Germans during the last war and had been
dug up again by the British when hostilities
ceased.   The general opinion of my shipmates

was that she would have been better left where she was.   Such names as 'the rust bucket' or 'the old tub' or even 'that heap of scrap' or was it 'crap' frequently entered into the conversations which lead me to gather that I was in for a somewhat less comfortable experience than I had experienced on my first ship.   Nobody could agree on when she had been launched but the majority agreed that it was way back.   I had read in my tutorial books about steam winches but. this was mainly to do with tankers but the tales I was told of these cranking, hissing monsters filled me with some trepidation. Tales of steam reciprocating engines and 'oilers' and 'greasers' only mildly worried me. The colourful descriptions of the accommodation brought to mind that un-colourful Soviet coal burner way back in Liverpool when I joined my first ship.   Even this did not entirely put a damper on my enthusiasm for my promotion.   This promotion was said to be for the last three months of my seatime, after which I would proceed to college to study for my Second Mates certificate.

The day I joined 'the old tub' was a very cold and wet day in November in a wind and rain swept dry-dock in South Shields.   The freshly painted hull showed no signs of the aforementioned rust but the accommodation block looked decidedly grey and unwelcoming. The ancient lines reminded me of the silhouettes of old ships on the inside cover of one of my training manuals. I don't recall how I found my way to my cabin but I do remember the shock when I did find it. One single small porthole above a high, narrow bunk above several drawers. I found out later that day that I would have to pull out the lower drawer so that I could climb up to the bunk. One small fixed table and cracked lino on the deck. On my first ship I had the luxury of my own 'facilities' but not here. On this ship we deck officers shared. Right outside my porthole was a steam winch which, fortunately, was silent when I joined. The accommodation was split with Captain, deck officers and sparks forward then a cargo hatch and then cabins for the engineers and catering staff and then right aft above the steering gear for the rest of the crew. All this I would learn later but on joining, my main concern were my quarters. Why I use plural for a 6 foot by 10 foot box I know not. Suffice it to say my personal box was dull and drear.

No cheerful greetings at the head of the gangway on this one. I had to find my own cabin and then find my way to the Captain's quarters to introduce myself. The captain turned out to be a middle aged Welshman accompanied by a very attractive wife. Anyway, I remember him making me sign the Articles of Agreement with suspicious haste probably before I could change my mind. All this came to me afterwards but by then it was too late. It was up to the 2nd Officer to show me around as there was no 3rd Officer to hand over the job to me. Even that was suspicious - what was I letting myself in for? The Bridge turned out to be a three windowed box containing an ancient steering wheel and a brass telegraph and not much else. However, I considered this to be a small but much appreciated mercy as it could have been an open Bridge. Oh yes, she did have a radar set which at first glance could well have been one of the very first. Because of the small wheelhouse the bridge wings were quite spacious and I was quite surprised to find a Vincent motorcycle on the starboard wing. I mentioned this to the 2/O but he wasn't very forthcoming so I let it pass. The rest of the tour only convinced me that all those tales I had heard before were definitely not exaggerations. I stowed my kit, put on a boiler suit and explored further. The four hatches were open so I was able to peer into these battered and rusty caverns. I was able to closely inspect the steam winches with all their levers, valves and taps. I even had a look down the engine room onto this sort of open engine with long legs and arms. I hadn't made much headway studying the Doxford on my first ship which compared to this one was neatly enclosed. What chance would I have with a steam reciprocating engine in my next three months. I decided there and then - very little. I recall meeting various crew members as I wandered around. One was the 3rd Engineer, a German named Willi. He too had just joined so we were able to discuss the shock quite openly. Sparks was another, but he had been on the ship for a long time and appeared to think she was magnificent. As usual, the engineers were a cheerful lot apart from the Chief who had an acidic tongue. This was to be my first experience with a British crew and it came as a bit of a shock. They weren't all bad by any means, but the bad ones were really bad. I got on well during the voyage with the boatswain, I considered the cook to be a crook.   One of the sailors was studying for his 2nd Mates certificate so occasionally we would study together or take a run ashore together.   Later on the team was to be myself, Willi, occasionally the sailor and the Captain's wife, who would foray ashore together.   I say foray because some of the ports we were to visit were very much like that.

I had a couple of days to get used to things onboard as the ship was about to leave the dock and to proceed southwards to London to load a general cargo for West Africa.   She was on charter to a company known onboard as 'Elder Gangster Line'   which was not the real name but it was a top British company.   I must say here, that it took me much less than three months to decide that when I passed my 2nd Mates certificate, the Elder Gangster Line was one company to whom I would most definitely not apply.

I don't remember much about the loading in London Docks apart from watching the rope slings with boxes of all shapes and sizes being lowered into the holds.   I soon learnt that in a particular game of cards there should only be four players and not five and that when the wharfies smoko was over, the box they had been using as a card table would be empty.   Particular care had to be taken when loading cases of whisky, but the cheeky buggers would still get away with it.   Those noisy, steamy and smelly steam winches cranked and clanked and kept me awake when I was off watch.   When in use, they were constantly requiring attention and when not working they had to be drained or if it was very cold, they had to be left 'ticking' over. Was it ticking over or clanking over.   Anyway, cargo watch on that ship was most definitely a boiler suit job.

Now I had done a few days as watch keeper in the Pacific on my first ship and had also the experience of the 8 to 12 watch on the coastal run down from South Shields to London but on departure from the latter my education was to really begin.   My very first passage through the Dover Strait as officer of the watch was as I recall it, somewhat worrying.   The Old Man had left orders to be called if needed and left me to it.   On a cold, dark winter's evening on a darkened bridge with an antique radar with a screen that seemed more like a much decorated blue and white porcelain plate than a true representation of what was going on around me. In a dimmed chartroom seemingly with space only for the chart and me. It may have been rough out there but that bit I don't remember. To my unskilled eye the surrounding waters appeared to be alive with ships all doing their very best to get in my way. I was relieved to get past Dover. I was relieved when I spotted the Varne light and at the end of my watch, I was relieved to get relieved. Never mind - I had followed the course laid down on the chart and I hadn't hit anything - that called for a beer at midnight. The rest of the passage southwards gave me a chance to really familiarise myself with my surroundings. I managed to master the intricacies of the radar though I had one on a cabin cruiser after retirement that was quite a bit bigger and certainly, better. My noon sights eventually came within hailing distance of the 2nd Officer's positions. After clearing Cape Finisterre and the Bay of Biscay I believe that I really stated to enjoy my watch keeping. The Captain and sparks seemed to spend most of those days at sea stripping parts of the Vincent motorcycle with occasional assistance from the Chief Engineer. I was left very much to myself and found that I very much liked it that way.   Off watch, I would do a bit of studying   -   sometimes.   Then again, I used to enjoy a beer with Willi and the Captains wife in the mess room.   And it really was a mess -   a gloomy little room but with the usual PYE radio and a few books for entertainment.

After a short bunkering stop at Dakar, the real shock, I recall, was reaching our first port of discharge which was Freetown, Sierra Leone. Capetown, even Mombasa appeared orderly compared to this place, but later in the voyage other ports of call were even worse.   I had thought that the Liverpool and London dockers were a noisy lot but compared to the West Africans they were positively monastic.   I remember it being hot, colourful and smelly.

One morning somebody had handed in a bunch of car keys they had found on deck.   Now, we were not carrying cars but another British ship tied up ahead of us had cars on deck.   As junior officer I was dispatched to see if they belonged to that ship.   I recall meeting their Captain and Chief Officer, presenting the keys and then being shown around by their boatswain.   He told me to wait in his cabin while he went to the toilet so I walked in and was confronted by a bloody great chimpanzee. I must have made some startled reaction because the boatswain was standing behind me laughing. It is the only time in my career that I have enjoyed a beer with a chimp sitting on my knee knit picking in my hair. They also had a ship's cat and a ship's dog. Quite a menagerie. We had cockroaches! We had cockroaches who revelled in the hot, humid West African climate. We humans wilted. No such thing as air conditioning on that one. If you left your porthole open you were either robbed or you let in some nasty looking wildlife - if you closed your porthole you sweltered and gave the cockroaches a bloody sauna. And this was just the first port.

We discharged the general cargo in Freetown, Takoradi and Lagos and then loaded in Port Harcourt, Abonema, Lome and finally Takoradi. By then we had all had enough. Our cargo for the voyage back to Europe was timber - huge tree trunks floated to the ship, slung with chains and then lifted onboard. The derricks shuddered and the steam winches clanked and protested under the weight of these water blackened, saturated lumber lifts. The holds slowly filled with timber and the hold bilges overflowed with water.

There was nothing to go ashore for, but of course, we did go ashore.   At Abonema up the Bonny river these huge logs were floated out to the ship and loaded at anchor.   To get ashore one had to agree a price with the oarsman of what was literally just a dugout canoe.   When Willi and I were halfway to the landing stage the oarsman demanded double pay and stopped rowing.   Now I don't recall seeing the punch land but Willi in one go knocked him overboard, retrieved the paddle and continued us on our way.   This in a dugout with not even a wobble, takes some doing. We watched each others backs during our very short stay ashore.

Another couple of things that I remember about our trip up the Bonny river.   The first was 'Blue Jack' the river pilot.   He was very short, very black and very happy.   The other was the sight of the Old Man on the wing of the bridge wielding a shotgun and a Lee Enfield 303.   Now I had seen him firing at targets on the voyage south but here he was firing into the dense forest/jungle on the riverbank with gay abandon. Anything that moved - bang! It is the only time that I have ever fired a shotgun and my bruised shoulder hurt for a couple of days. 'Blue Jack' seemed quite amused at this white man's madness, obviously not considering that it could be one of his own on the receiving end. He howled with laughter at every bang and sucked on what looked like a clay pipe. The helmsman rolled his eyes and I prayed for deliverance.

The Old Man and sparks continued to work on the Vincent whilst myself, Willi and the Captain's wife enjoyed the odd trip ashore. It appeared to be a strange set up to me, but everyone seemed to be quite happy with this arrangement. I enjoyed their company, in fact I quite enjoyed the ship, but for me the West Coast of Africa was a definite no no. I recall witnessing a few near major accidents while loading these huge wet logs but fortunately we survived and sailed onwards and as far as I was concerned - upwards. We, the team, did enjoy a run ashore in London before I left the ship, and even here we managed to get into trouble.   This time in the local pub for playing an Anglo/German record too many times but it was a pleasant evening. I signed off in Tilbury and went ashore to study for my 2nd Mates certificate.   Onwards and upwards - yes!

I won't go into the details of my study period and the examination in Hull.   Let it suffice to say that I enjoyed my stay but had already made my mind up to try elsewhere for my First Mates certificate because Hull was too much of a party town. So six months later and armed with a 2nd Mates certificate on which the ink was still wet, the world appeared to be my oyster.   I had already received a letter from China Navigation offering me a position, but the memories of China put me off that one.   I had also heard from the company with whom I had served my time but I did not believe their assurances that there would be no more two year trips.   So now was the time to apply to a company that I thought would take me to the part of the world I wanted to explore.   I was accepted by one of the major liner companies of that time and kitted myself out for my first voyage as Junior Third Officer.   Any previous contact with this company had the ships trading between London and New Zealand or Australia. Therefore, I was dismayed to find that I was being appointed to a ship loading in Cardiff for Newfoundland, Quebec and Montreal. Not only that, but the ship was 35 years old and that was a few years older than the last one. It did have one advantage though, she had not been sunk by the Germans! Actually she turned out to be a fine old vessel apart from the steam winches and the accommodation. My cabin was even smaller than the last one and the bunk was one drawer higher. This, I reasoned was so there was drawer space enough to stow all the extra bits of uniform required by a liner company. I think I had about eighteen inches clearance when lying in the bunk. Oh yes, I did have a small wardrobe but my desk was even smaller.

I was introduced to the Chief Officer and soon realised that I was being indoctrinated into a much different system to my old one. Here 'bull' ruled. He was so terribly far back and all the crap that he spouted seemed incongruous in the old fashioned somewhat dishevelled surroundings. He told me of the long history of the company, he told me about the long history of the ship and he told me what was expected of me.   He also told me that if I wished to see the captain at any time other than on the bridge, I should see the purser to make an appointment. By this time, I was wondering what the hell I'd let myself in for! Such and such a uniform should be worn until such a time when one should change into such and such a uniform except on Sundays when such and such a uniform should be worn.   Gone were the days of blues, whites or boiler suits.   I have to admit, I was not impressed and I had to do the sea watch with this bloke.   However, I had signed the Articles of Agreement, this time in front of the purser, so I was committed.

We sailed from Cardiff for Cornerbrook on the western part of the island of Newfoundland to load newsprint for Sydney, Australia.   Joy at last! I don't remember much about that passage across the North Atlantic except that after the first few watches I was left alone much to my satisfaction. The constant line of bull dried up and I was able to get on with the job.   Apart from getting into trouble for smuggling a girl onboard in Cornerbrook and, later on, enjoying the sights of

Quebec, there is not a lot to say about my time with that company. The voyage from Canada to Sydney via the Panama Canal was uneventful until I had an accident in a fall and managed to damage my right knee. This resulted in my being landed to hospital in Sydney and to my refusing to rejoin the company. The latter gave me a hard time but the Australian seaman's union backed me up so that was that.

My next ship was an entirely different kettle of fish and one that I still have very fond memories of. I had been told to present myself at the Hunter Street office of this particular company to be interviewed by their superintendent. On presenting myself at the front desk I was told, by a very attractive Scottish lady, to go across the road to the pub and to have a beer and wait there. Now to me this was a definite up and up situation. The super eventually turned up and interviewed me over a few beers and we shook hands on the deal. It was the one and only time that I have ever been interviewed in a pub and I thank Australia for the experience. Not only that, a few days later I was again called in to the office and the superintendent took me to one of the towers on

Sydney Harbour bridge to watch my next ship arriving.

This ship was a bulk carrier. Built in Belgium for a British company and bare boat chartered to an Australian company. For some reason the Australian unions refused to man her so volunteers from amongst the delivery crew got the job. Fortunately for me, the Third Officer was not one of the volunteers. The ship ended up with British mates, German engineers, the seemingly inevitable Irish sparks and a Hong Kong Chinese crew and I thought this was bloody marvellous! I was on that ship for a long time and the combination of nationalities, though it varied at times, worked exceedingly well.

The ship was new, she was big and the accommodation was excellent. OK, I still didn't have my own facilities but then I only had to share with the 2nd Officer. The Bridge was a dream compared to my first three ships and the huge, side sliding steel hatch covers were magic. All in all I was well happy to be joining my first bulk carrier even though she was loading bulk grain for China. Being an Australian ship although flying the Red

Duster, she was dry. That meant that the consuming of alcohol onboard was not allowed. The fact that you could not move in the ship's hospital for cases of canned beer much relieved me. The food was again Chinglish but with a little more bias on the Chinese and this was another pro as far as I was concerned.

I remember standing on the raised walkway above the hatch lids peering down into one of the nine cavernous holds and watching the grain being poured from a towering chute and being directed into the four corners of the abyss. I remember walking under the huge hatch lids all along the deck and thinking that a bicycle would help. And not a steam winch in sight. Not a derrick, not a mast apart from a short stubby one on the forecastle deck and the tall radar mast above the monkey island. She had electric mooring winches and one huge anchor windlass up forward. After the hissing, clanking steam winches these were virtually silent and anyway, they were only really used on arrival and departure so did not involve any sleep loss in port. There was one downer I remember. In good ports such as Sydney, cargo operations were smooth and fast so our leisure time in these places was sorely restricted. There were the odd times when we had to go to a lay-by berth or when we arrived in the middle of a strike and we took full advantage of these occasions. I retain fond memories of Kirribilli Dolphins just below the Governors residence in Sydney Harbour. In places that weren't so popular such as Darien it took days to dig the cargo out. However, I had by some stroke of luck, ended up on a ship that I really liked.

It was on this ship that I first became aware of such monumental pubs as the Newcastle, the Captain Cook and Montgomery's Hotel. The first one was a place for all, the second was a place to be a bit more careful but Monty's was a world renowned sailor's pub. I didn't see much of them that first time but during subsequent calls and with another shipping company, I got to know them quite well.

The coastal trip from Sydney northwards, or southwards for that matter, I always found very enjoyable. At one time I could name all the points or distinctive places on the coast until we were too far off land up by Cape Byron. From there we headed up across the Coral Sea towards the passage between the islands of New Britain, New Ireland and Bougainville. Past the small island of Fini and out into the wide Pacific. There is something about the Pacific Ocean that can't be matched by any other. Sea like glass. .Sky merging with the horizon. Those magnificent sunrises and sunsets. Up past the island of Yap and on through the Ryu-Kyu Islands and into the East China Sea and then into the Yellow Sea. All roads seemed to lead to China for me back then but this was a much better ship to suffer on! It had been quite a few months since I had last been in Dairen but I remember thinking that things were getting a bit lax there when I was accosted for cigarettes by a wharfie. It was either getting lax or he was taking advantage of being underneath one of the giant steel hatch covers. The discharge was painfully slow. They had portable suction units but most of it had to be shovelled into huge slings and crane lifted out. I took great pleasure in our lack of derricks. The facilities ashore had not changed, neither had the security, but we still ventured forth. On one subsequent visit I was invited onboard a Polish freighter for a meal and a film. It was one of our films but never mind. They had a few females onboard, wives and crewmembers and some children so when I went over I took a few souvenir Koalas and Boomerangs. I must have overdone the praise of the meal because they sent me back loaded down with food parcels. Actually it is the only time that I have ever eaten tripe and I suffered it then because I thought it a bit rude to complain. Never mind, they were very sociable and very friendly and I had a wonderful evening. Onboard our 'dry' ship things were also quite sociable. Our Anglo/Irish stroke German evenings were very pleasant and we got on very well together. Some of the engineers had been working at Mount Isa before a strike sent them down to Sydney looking for employment. Their tales of Mount Isa kept us going on many a long evening. If anybody tells you that the Germans don't have a sense of humour, don't believe them. Some of the tales had us in stitches. They were a good bunch. The 2nd Officer came from somewhere in the south of England and was reputed to be a remittance man. He was certainly a character. He was very tall, very thin, white bearded and wizened. He took advantage of the 'shop' in Dairen and filled his cabin with vodka much to the old man's concern.   He was also a bugger for relieving me at midnight.   One particular night I actually left the bridge and went down to his cabin to shake him.   I was caught by the Captain and all hell broke loose.   I got a severe bollocking for leaving the bridge and he, the 2nd Officer, got a severe telling off for being late on watch and he had his stock of vodka impounded.   He was always a gentleman and always polite and in this case very apologetic but he didn't change.   I think the only time I heard him curse was when he dropped a bottle of Bundaberg.   Amongst the engineers, big Rolf, the 3rd engineer was my particular pal.   He was a very big lad from Hamburg   -   big enough to get me out of trouble should that ever happen.

I could and probably do wax lyrical about the South Pacific   in parts of this tale but one happening on this ship stands out in my memory, but it certainly wasn't a wax lyrical moment.   It was during a morning watch en-route from China to Sydney.   Nothing around but calm blue sea.   I was gazing into the distance when I saw what appeared to be a reef right ahead of the ship. What appeared at a distance to be broken water! We were still some way off so I had time to check the Admiralty Chart which indicated nothing to be aware of in our position. I called the Captain and altered course to run parallel to the 'reef'.   We got in as close as we dared and found it to be a line of discoloration, miles long but only a few yards wide.   We eventually resumed our course and went through the discoloration.   Our two echo sounders registered nothing - no bottom.   If those machines had been able to register heart beats -   they would have gone into overdrive!

The ship did several voyages between Sydney and Dairen carrying grain but when that season was over, we were transferred to the coal run from Gladstone up to Yawata in Japan.   The cargo took one day to load in Gladstone and nineteen hours to discharge in Yawata hence we didn't get to see much of either place.   Shame really because Moji was right next door to Yawata.

One voyage away from our Australian season, we left China and sailed for Port Elizabeth in South Africa to load coal for -   you guessed it -   China.   It was quite a long passage out, broken only by bunkering at anchor off Singapore, and by the passage through the Sunda Strait between the Indonesian islands of Sumatra and Java. At the Singapore anchorage we were visited by the Coca Cola girls and later, with the pilot onboard ready for departure and the 'Old Man' still entertaining, we very nearly got into trouble with the authorities. The passage through the strait was impressive. The turbulence as the waters of the Indian Ocean met the waters of the Pacific Ocean was quite interesting but not a patch on the turbulence that we were to experience on the return passage through the Lombok Strait.

At Port Elizabeth, we realised we were going to be in port for some time, as the method of loading the coal was a bit primitive and very labour intensive. The cargo was loaded onboard in small grabs. These were landed on the hatch lids and then the grab releases were opened and the contents poured into the abyss. Quite a bit of the stuff actually landed on the hatch lids and this had then to be manually shovelled over the edge into the hold. It was a day and night operation but, even so, it took about ten days to get our quota.

The 'apartheid' policy was in full swing in

South Africa. We received all the warnings about where to go and who and who not to get mixed up with. Large notices in bright red were posted around the ship, warning of severe retributions should we stray. On one occasion, whilst ashore, I fell foul of the system when I met up with our Chinese carpenter and we went into a hotel bar for a beer. The barman refused to serve us until I managed to persuade him that 'chippy' was Japanese. Strange really, but I make no comment. Between us the 2nd Officer and I did the cargo watches - twenty four hours on and twenty four hours off - or at least that was the plan. However, I drew the short straw and copped for the first duty, but when my time was up my relief failed to appear. Four days later, he was spotted weaving along the wharf followed by several natives carrying large jars of some potent local hooch, looking like some great white explorer trekking through the jungle. He even had a silver tipped walking stick but how he managed to hold on to it during his absence was the cause of much conjecture in the mess room. We reckoned that he must have broken every rule in the apartheid book but, if so, he managed to get away with it. His usually smart white suite was crumpled and dirty.   He apologised to me profusely at the head of the gangway but was then grabbed and unceremoniously hustled up before the Captain by the Chief Officer.   I hasten to add that I did not do four full days without relief.   The Chief Officer stepped in and did a cargo watch, now and again.   He was somewhat less than amused.   The booze was confiscated, work continued as usual and I had the sniff of promotion in my nostrils.   But not just yet!

The passage back to China was again a long haul, but this time we went through the Lombok Strait and on this occasion, really experienced turbulence.   I remember taking the wheel from the quartermaster in an effort to control the violent swings and surges of the ship in the tide rips   - but, I hasten to add, without effect   -   the whirlpools spewed us out into the Pacific end of the strait sideways.   The seas on each side of the strait were relatively calm, but the strait itself was a maelstrom of whirling waters.   A good job we were alone for the passage.   Bali was a blurr! From there we went up to Balikpapan on the Indonesian part of the island of Borneo to bunker. I seem to remember that British and Chinese were not allowed ashore but Germans and Australians were. No matter - we were only there for a few hours and those who did get ashore, assured those that didn't that they had missed absolutely nothing. And from there back to China.

Our next voyage was to Vancouver, Canada or rather to Port Moody to load a cargo of sulphur for Japan. Then onwards again from Japan to Laurenco Marques in Mozambique to load soya beans for China. The cargo operation at Laurenco Marques was a long process as the bags were landed on the hatch lids, opened and then poured into the hold. Some of the bags were hoisted onboard in slings but the majority were carried onboard over the shoulders of the wharfies, climbing ramps from wharf to hatch lid. Mozambique was still under Potuguese rule at the time so the bars and hotels had a European feel with an African touch in that all the whores, the strippers and the barmaids were black. The place was full of South African white males calling us, naughty Europeans - very strange. And after that run, back to Australia. The trips to South Africa and Mozambique and Canada were a pleasant deviation but going back to Australia was like going back home. Here I was promoted to 2nd Officer and the ship resumed its season carrying grain from Sydney to China. I thoroughly enjoyed being Navigating Officer and the quiet solitude of the 12-4 watch was a pleasure. Sitting on deck after my watch in the morning enjoying a beer and a club sandwich while watching the sun rise over the Pacific I still count as one of life's great pleasures!

By this time I had been onboard for many months without leave, and the company insisted that I take some time off. When I requested leave in the UK they agreed but said I would have to pay my own way. I went home, had a good leave and then returned to Australia at the company's request. Not only did they pay for my return flight but they refunded my home flight expenses. They were a good outfit to work for and when they got rid of all their sea-going vessels I was very disappointed.

However, when the Australian company decided to get rid of all their seagoing ships, I was transferred to one of the parent companies vessels back in the UK. I joined this old freighter at anchor off Dundee, Scotland and instantly regretted my appointment. However, as a redeeming factor, I was only appointed for the passage from Dundee to the dry-dock in South Shields. I can't remember what had hit her but she had a gaping hole to the steering gear compartment and I do mean a gaping hole. All the steering machinery was open to the elements. The crew who also had been appointed for the short run down the coast, showed their concern by calling in the local union rep who in turn called in higher union authorities. The result was a bonus payment and a choice to sail or not to sail. Two of the crew chose not to risk it and the rest accepted the bonus. We, the officers, received a less than tempting 'fiver'. The weather for the passage was moderate and at the end of each watch the off going OOW had to make sure that any ingress of water was being successfully pumped back to where it belonged.

From this less than tempting appointment I was transferred to another freighter, joining in Singapore. This one was a much more seaworthy prospect without holes. An added bonus was that this vessel had already loaded her cargo in China and was now on passage to West Africa and Cuba. Perhaps I should have remembered my earlier voyage to West Africa and the experiences therein! Given the choice between West Africa and China I think I would have chosen the latter even after my, sometimes, unhappy experiences there. The cargo was a gift cargo from the Chinese to Guinea and Cuba.

Our stay in Conakry was unremarkable. Labour intensive but very slow. The gift cargo joined the huge pile of boxes on the quayside. Half marked with the gift sign of the United States, others from Europe and then our cargo from China. All gently rotting in the hot, humid conditions.

From Conakry we went on to Havana, the capital of Cuba, to discharge the remainder of our 'gift' cargo. The Cuban crisis had happened quite some time before our visit but the United States Navy was much in evidence as we approached the island, and showed a great interest in our cargo, but they let us proceed. Although Fidel Castro had been in power for a few years there was still much evidence of his 'takeover' with many of the old establishments closed and with an abundance of attractive, if humourless, ladies in uniform guarding all the shops. They were definitely not receptive to any forms of address or banter, and since they were armed, we gave them a wide berth. One or two of the old nightclubs and bars were still open, but we had to sell American cigarettes on the black market to be able to afford to visit these places. The sale of said cigarettes was a complicated affair involving Customs Officers, bribing port guards with cigarettes and all this before reaching the point of sale, but it was worth it. American cigarettes were the currency of the day. The girls in the nightclub shows wore magnificent costumes and were very attractive. We were very surprised that these shows still existed under the communist regime but we certainly didn't complain. Again the discharge of our cargo was slow going and we had about two weeks there - again we didn't complain!

We sailed from there to Falmouth where the ship was due to drydock and the only exciting happening on that passage that I recall was when we found a stowaway a couple of days after departure.   He had been hiding in the engine room but gave himself up when the heat became too much for him.   He was either Dutch or Belgian and had somehow been stranded in Cuba. He was cleaned up, given a cabin, then set to, to work his passage back to Europe.   Anyway, the British police carted him off on arrival at Falmouth and we heard no more.   From Falmouth I went home on leave and then went to college in South Shields to study for my 1st Mates Certificate.

The Australian company's   final dastardly and distressing act of selling off their seagoing ships was done while I was on study leave in the UK studying for my 1st Mates Certificate.   They were paying for my time at college in South Shields and they stuck with me until I passed my exams, but then I was high and dry, so to speak, and without employment.   I knew where I wanted to be   -   Australia   -   but being short of funds I took the first ship I could get sailing out of Hull. Not my best career move!   I 'chose' this ship from the 'pool' at Hull.   As I remember 'the rule of the pool',   you were given a choice of three ships and if you failed to choose one of them you were punished.   I can't remember what the punishment consisted of but I made my choice, went back to sea, and later wished that I'd taken whatever they could have threatened me with.

I joined my 'choice' vessel in King George Dock, Hull on New Years Eve and spent a miserable evening looking around the ship.   She was a small bulk carrier but she had started off as a small tanker many years before.   It was back to cramped quarters and shared facilities.   The Captain was a man close to retirement, the Chief Officer was a youngish Irishman pushing for promotion,   I was 2nd Officer and the 3rd Officer was a Nigerian with an attitude.   The engineers and the crew were from all parts of the UK. What I later heard to be called, a scratch crew. Back in those days most men would keep their heads down and enjoy the Festive Season but some, the more desperate, would put their names forward at the 'pools' around Britain and those ships requiring a crew would drag them in from all quarters - no questions asked.   This lot turned out to be quite good as they go but I met up with some real corkers later on.

The vessel sailed in ballast for Dutch Guiana

to Paranam, a small river port a few miles upstream of Paramaribo on the Suriname river. Here, we were to load bauxite for Chaguaramas Bay, Trinidad. Because of draught restrictions we could only take on so much bauxite each voyage but our purpose there was to top up the pile in Trinidad so that other ships could load to capacity for onward destinations. We were advised to shut down all power ventilation, to batten down all portholes and to keep all doors closed. But still the red dust got everywhere. There was nothing ashore to warrant a foray and the nearest populated area was a leper colony on the opposite bank of the river. The latter made us put that extra turn on the screws battening down our cabin portholes! The loading operation was quite efficient so we were not long in port and then after the short run up to Trinidad the discharging operation was super efficient so the turnaround was even shorter. Backwards and forwards we went covered in dust and sweat at each end and frantically trying to clean up in-between. Never mind the tensions onboard and there were a few, the red routine was awful! The day eventually came when it was our turn to fill to capacity at Chaguaramas Bay and to sail out into the open sea and the clean air on our way up to Port Alfred on the Saguenay River, Quebec Canada. I recall the relief onboard when we got away from the dust, sweat and flies. There was nearly harmony onboard - nearly. At least in Port Alfred we could go ashore and stretch our legs - but I don't think there was much else to do there at that time.

From Port Alfred we sailed up the St Lawrence river, then the St. Lawrence seaway and via lakes Ontario, Erie, Huron and Superior to Duluth, Minnesota and Superior, Wisconsin to load a cargo of grain for Hull. It was still early in the season and we were delayed for four days at the Sault Ste Marie lock between Lake Huron and Lake Superior because of ice. The easterly wind had blown a mass of broken ice into the lock approaches and we had to wait for a Canadian icebreaker to do most of the clearing and a Norwegian ice strengthened freighter to do the final clearing before we could pass through the lock. It was an arduous passage from Port Alfred to Duluth in that, apart from the normal watch keeping, and the time at stations passing through the locks on the Welland Canal, all hands had to turn to wash down the cargo holds prior to loading grain. After months of shuffling Bauxite around, the bloody stuff was everywhere, and it took a lot of time, energy and pressure hoses to get rid of the it!

I repeat myself, but the passage from Port Alfred to Duluth was quite long and, in parts, hard going. The deep locks in the Welland Ship Canal were much different to the more sedate Panama operation. We had to rig a small derrick forward so that we could swing a crewman out and land him on the lockside. He would then take the ship's wires to moor at the entrance to each lock. The sounds of steel against concrete or timber, and the sound of taught wires singing, and being cold and wet and hungry are the lingering memories. The transit was not interrupted for meal breaks - it was a case of grab a bite when you could. It was an experience not to be missed but I would be hard pushed to say that it was pleasurable. The following voyage, when things warmed up a bit, it was a bit more to my liking. However the passage through the Thousand Islands and the passage from Lake Erie to Lake Huron via Lake St Clair were wonderful. All in all it was an experience not to be missed.

We enjoyed our stay in the twin ports - there were bars, steak bars and other places of entertainment. During the week, Duluth was jumping, but on Sunday when the place closed down, Superior, just across the bridge, was jumping. A group of us managed to get into trouble in a nightclub where scantily clad maidens cavorted in cages just above nose level. However, we moved on before the lynch mob could catch us!

From the St Lawrence we went through the Strait of Belle Isle between Newfoundland and Labrador, and then passed just to the south of Greenland before going 'north about' through the Pentland Firth into the North Sea and onwards to Denmark. Yes - Denmark. The cargo had originally been loaded for Hull, but due to a dock strike its destination was re-negotiated for ports in Denmark. Shortly after passing through the Strait of Belle Isle we encountered my first iceberg. Perhaps I should have phrased that 'we saw my first iceberg'. Anyway, it was a very large bluey white object in the form of a 'C'. When the Old

Man nearly took the ship into the bay to let his wife have a close look, I was on the verge of asking him to sign over the watch as, though I was enjoying the view, I was not enjoying the proximity. On the Grand Banks we weaved our way through the fishing fleets and out into the North Atlantic. I don't recall it being a bad passage but it was very cold. We pushed hard against the current through the Pentland Firth, across a foggy North Sea onwards through the Skagerrak and the Kattegat towards Copenhagen.

Usual stuff in Copenhagen, myself and the 3rd Engineer went into a bar in the Nyhavn. A Swedish sailor punched the barmaid, so I punched the Swede, the police removed the Swede and the 3rd Engineer went to bed with the barmaid. Not much more to say about that interlude apart from that Copenhagen is a nice place. The ship moved on to Aarhus and then finally on to Esbjerg. In a bar called The Flame Restaurant (I think), our crew got into a bit of a one sided fight with some German fishermen where, in an attempt to even the odds and also to protect my steward, I raised a chair to flatten his opponent. However, the Germen ducked, the steward didn't and the chair broke over the head of the latter.   It stopped the fight - both sides fell about laughing - apart from the steward.   But a pleasant evening was then had by all.

From Esbjerg we sailed back to the Great Lakes to Duluth and Superior to load grain again but this time we managed to get the stuff to Hull. By the time we got back there, I'd had enough, so I signed off and decided to look for pastures green.

I enjoyed a spot of leave and then started looking for another ship.   I approached one of the big liner companies and, after an interview at the head office in London, I was accepted and, within days, appointed to my first passenger ship.   I needed a few days because I had to be kitted out with all the necessary uniforms required for such a service.   I thought that my last liner company required a few changes but the assortment required for service on passenger ships was, to say the least, startling.   Expensive too!   However, fully booted and spurred, I made my way to Southampton to join my first passenger ship.   But what was my first uniform to be - a boiler suit provided by the company.   The ship was in drydock   -   no passengers, no entertainers, nothing really.   At least I had time to find my way around the maze of alleyways, stairwells, lounges and restaurants.   I use the term restaurants loosely as at the officer's dining table,   in one of said restaurants, the service was not up to much.   The 'staff' table always seemed to be at the back of the queue.   But this judgement was to be made over the next twelve months.   In the beginning I found everything interesting and unusual and even exciting. Although there was just a skeleton crew onboard during the time in drydock,   I had time to look at crew lists to see what or who was to come. As Junior Third Officer, one of three,   I was on the bottom rung of the ladder regarding Deck Officers. Going upwards we had one Third Officer, one Second Officer, one First Officer, one Chief Officer, a Staff Captain and then 'God Almighty' - the Captain himself. Then there were five Radio Officers, hosts of Engineer Officers and Electrical Officers, Pursers and Catering Officers and then crew.   In all, just over six hundred souls.   I started to get used to the passenger ship jargon and to know a few new names such as 'Fluff Alley' or female officers quarters.   'Steam Queens' or the ladies who worked in the ships laundry. 'Dads Army' or relief officers. I'm sure there were many more but perhaps they will come to mind later. It was all very bright and very new and I thought this must be what pure luxury was really like - until it came to our accommodation. It was clean, bright and airy but very small and, as was pointed out to me by others, very remote from all the action. Our cabins were on the deck immediately below the Navigating Bridge, approached by a narrow spiral staircase. Which reminds me of another saying. 'Running the bus' or getting a female passenger up to your cabin. However, going back to the whereabouts of our accommodation - should the passengers or the crew revolt it was an easily defensible position. Strange thoughts at this early stage. I stood by that ship for the month that it was in drydock and at the fitting out berth and then transferred to the sister ship for the forthcoming voyage. I boarded against the flow of disembarking passengers and settled my kit into a near identical cabin to the one I had just left. I made myself known to the deck team and was told to go and find my way about. There were some differences between the two ships but having spent one month on the sister ship certainly helped.   This was a Friday and the ship was due to sail on the following Monday. My education, induction was about to begin!

On one day over the weekend, the relieving Captain asked me to go to a hotel in Southampton to bring his car down to the ship.   It was a little green Austin 1100 and after driving it very carefully through the town, I parked it at the forward gangway between the Chief Steward's Mk X Jaguar and the Head Barman's chauffeur driven Bentley.   I did not know who these cars belonged to at the time, but when I found out I suffered some doubts about my choice of department.   I had cause to reflect on this a few times over the next twelve months.

My first duty onboard was to man the Deck Office during the first night   in port, under the supervision of the First Officer.   Actually, he left most of it up to me but with strict instructions to call him if necessary.   It wasn't long before I found it necessary!   I sat there before a bank of telephones both internal and external.   Lines direct to Southampton Fire Brigade.   Lines direct to Southampton police.   Fire plans.   Emergency plans. Banks of lights and switches. Fire Door and Watertight Door indicators. All those and much more. Immediately in front of my position was a bookshelf full of reports of disturbances during previous voyages and I gained an insight into what I had let myself in for by glancing through a few of these books. I don't know what happened to them in the end but I do think they should have been published - some of the incidents were hilarious. Breaking and attempting to enter the ship's shop was a regular occurrence. 'Coitus interruptus' in some amazing places and positions could be found on most pages. Even a brothel - where some enterprising maidens worked their passage so to speak! Riots, near riots, crew insurrection, crew invasion of passenger accommodation. Break ins, bust ups and break ups. Assault, battery. You name it - it would appear in one of the books! Hosts of drink related happenings - some humorous, some painful. Hosts of romance related happenings - some humorous, some disastrous, some long lasting. Nudity or near nudity - skinny dipping in the ship's pool. I was about to add a few more! The following twelve hour shift was to pass rapidly!

Sitting up there in the relative solitude of the Deck Office, the frenzied activity of the day now much reduced and anyway, what activity remained was a few decks below. I looked forward to or at least hoped for a quiet night. Then it started. My first telephone call was from an irate female from Liverpool wanting to know 'where the body was'. She laid into me before I could get a word in edgeways. The First Officer who I rapidly called, was also newly joined, and couldn't answer the question either, so the next one in line, the Chief Officer, was called. After a bit of exploring, enquiring, it was found that the body of her 'father' (I think) had been landed and buried somewhere in New Zealand. The level of abuse went up by several octaves! I started filling in the 'disturbances' book. The next phone call was from an equally irate female, but this time from South Africa. This lady wanted to know why her parents had been refused entry into Great Britain and why they were being held onboard to be returned to South Africa on the next voyage. I was directed to pass this one on to the Purser's office but I had to remain talking to the lady for quite a while until somebody in the know could be found. I never did find out why they had been refused entry but I did meet them and they seemed like a kindly elderly couple. There were many more calls during the night but all were much more mundane. I had to use the ship broadcast system a couple of times and I am sure that my voice must have echoed the terror I felt. *Baggage Masters contact so and so* or *Would the Children's Hostess contact so and so.* Quite simple stuff but terrifying for the novice. Anyway - I survived my first night onboard. During that first night I spoke on the internal phone to, or broadcast for, many crewmembers. Over the next couple of days I was introduced to or bumped into a host of male and female officers and crew putting a face to some of those I had contacted by phone or tannoy. It was just a blurr but I would get to know them all over the following twelve months.

Twenty-four hours prior to departure from Southampton all members of the ships company were required to attend the Board of Trade boat drill. Here, inspectors from the Board of Trade would randomly ask crew members what they were assigned to do in the case of an emergency.

We had to stand at lifeboat stations for quite some time as these inspectors moved amongst us. Over six hundred men and women wearing uncomfortable lifejackets and wishing that they were somewhere else. I can't remember whether or not it was cold or damp for my very first BOT inspection but I do remember that after checking all the names off on my boat muster list, I had a hell of a job keeping some sort of order. Trying to keep orderly lines and prevent crewmembers leaning on the ship's side rails or lighting cigarettes or sitting on the lifejacket boxes was some task and Senior Officers yelling and shouting didn't appear to help. When the inspector arrived at my boat we were in a reasonable semblance of order but his first victim to question was a newly joined steward and, I fear, this lad did not know which way was up! I was called upon to check my 'checklist' and to instruct the crew member on his assigned duties and to reprimand him for not reading up on his duties before the drill. Fortunately, the next crewmember questioned was an old hand and was able to reel off his duties 'word perfect'. Again randomly, some of the offside lifeboats had to be lowered to embarkation level thus prolonging the agony. Anyway, eventually the BOT inspectors were satisfied and the end of the drill was announced. Then six hundred and odd life jacketed crewmembers tried to get back to their quarters. The stairwells and alleyways were chock-a-block and I reflected on what it might be like if fourteen hundred passengers were also involved and it wasn't a drill.

The weekend rushed by and then came Monday and the time for the 'Boat Train' and passenger embarkation. Admittedly, as a Deck Officer, I had little or nothing to do with this but I kept peering over the side to see what was going on. The Pursers were the front line in this operation closely followed by Catering staff who directed passengers to their cabins. As sailing time approached, things down there seemed to get more and more frantic with the ships broadcast system working overtime. I wanted to get down there and mingle but the other Junior Thirds who were old hands at this, advised me against it. One hour before sailing the Chief Officer broadcast *Would all visitors please now proceed ashore as the vessel is about to sail for Las Palmas* and Deck and Engine departments prepared for sea. When the broadcast *Deck department to stations fore and aft* was made, I proceeded to the forecastle head to assist the First Officer.   I don't know how many passengers were onboard for that voyage but since she had a capacity of about 1400, there were a lot of them and I had to wade through a host to get to my station forward and looking back from the focsle all outside passenger decks seemed to be crammed.   We let go the ropes fore and aft, the tugs started to pull but there appeared to be enough coloured streamers between wharf and ship to hold her alongside.   Shouts, yells, cheers, screams and music   -   what a racket!   Running the gauntlet on the way back from stations I encountered happiness and tears.   Some passengers were drinking Champagne, others pints and others just hugging each other.   I retreated rapidly!

The morning after departure from Southampton there was a passenger boat muster where, at muster stations, the officer in charge would give a brief talk on the ship's safety features,   some of the hazards to be avoided and he or she would then show them how to put on their lifejackets.   From the muster station they would be lead to their lifeboat station where names would be checked off a list.   Since all passengers were required to attend and usually some chose not to, this could be another prolonged exercise. It was the job of the Masters at Arms to gently persuade the reluctant to attend. The Masters at Arms kept their own record book of 'incidents' and I was told that persuading reluctant passengers to attend Lifeboat Drill lead to quite a few entries in their book and that verbatim most of said entries were very rude. In ports such as Capetown when perhaps only fifty to one hundred passengers would join, it fell upon my shoulders to instruct the new joiners on the ship's emergency signal and the emergency procedure and the art of donning a lifejacket. It was not my favourite task. *When abandoning ship, if jumping overboard, always hold on to the collar of the lifejacket* -   Why? I could hardly say 'cos you'll break your bloody neck if you don't.'   There was always some bright spark who would interject - *but when I travelled with* - or - *on such and such a ship they did.*   To attract attention, each lifejacket has a whistle - there would then follow a period wherein passengers looked for and tested said whistle. Also, a water activated light. *But my light doesn't appear to be working* - It won't work until you are in the water. *But I thought we were supposed to be in a lifeboat* - yes, but in case you have to jump overboard. And so on! With some groups of passengers it could be good fun but with others, it could be a definite pain!

The early part of my first voyage I was assigned to the 8 to 12 watch - eight in the morning up to midday and eight in the evening up to midnight - not the most sociable watch to be on onboard passenger ships. By the time I got off watch, most of the venues had shut down, and most of the passengers had retired. Most, but not all! At midnight, I would then have to join up with one of the Master at Arms for a security patrol of passenger decks and the public rooms. This turned out to be another healthy source for entries into the disturbances book. But this was early days, and apart from a few passengers, drunk or sober, who couldn't find their cabins, it was a quiet patrol.

After an early breakfast at the staff table in one of the restaurants, I made my way to the Bridge for my first morning watch. I was then told that it was one of my daily duties to make the

8:30 weather broadcast.   Fortunately these broadcasts had been recorded in a book kept on the Bridge so I had something to refer to.   Anyway, *Good morning ladies and gentlemen.   Here is the weather forecast for today* . Then followed the day, date and current temperature,   my idea of what the rest of the day would be like and finally a brief description of any land in sight or if, deep sea, then the nearest land.   Those on the receiving end of my very first broadcast said that it came over quite well, but I felt that they were just being kind because I was terrified.   As the days went by, I got used to it, and even felt mildly confident. I felt that my BBC accent was quite good, until later in the voyage, a lady accosted me, asked if I was the one who did the morning broadcast and then said how nice it was to hear the Yorkshire accent again.   I felt deflated at first but then   - what the heck.   The BBC would   just have to do without me.   My morning broadcast and the Chief Officer's departure broadcasts were the only two regular broadcasts from the Bridge or the Deck Office.   I made mistakes but I wasn't the only one.   Once or twice the Chief Officer slipped up and said *Would all passengers please proceed ashore* instead of *would all visitors please proceed ashore.* The bulk of our calls were for plumbers, electricians, carpenters, masters at arms or baggage masters.

The blue day uniforms and the evening blue mess-kits soon gave way to the equivalent in whites as the ship moved into warmer climes. The older officers still wore the 'empire builders' but the younger ones sported a shorter, tighter attire. My first Sunday at sea I was ordered to attend church in one of the larger public rooms. The attire for this event was No.10's a white button down the front jacket with a 'dog collar' type collar and long white trousers. It was uncomfortable at any time but once the 'steam queens' had operated on them, they became items of torture. They applied so much starch that a steel ruler was needed to open legs and sleeves so that we could get into them. The Chief Officer would line the unlucky ones up for inspection before the service to make sure that we were correctly attired with 'dog collar' fastened and that we had something to put in the church collection box other than pennies wrapped in silver paper. We would then parade through the ship towards the place where the service was to be held -

looking like angels some said, or like lambs to the slaughter, said by others. Some even expected us to be smitten by heavenly fire!   We would then take up our positions on the front row followed by other unlucky souls from the other participating departments.   I say participating because I can't recall ever seeing any engineers in attendance. Anyway, we had to stand there at attention until the Captain took up position behind the Union Flag which was draped over a table, followed by the Chief Purser.   I must point out that at this point escape was impossible as the four doors were locked from the outside and guarded by the Masters at Arms.   There followed a few hymns, a short sermon and   a Bible reading by the Purser. After that we filed out frantically tugging at the 'dog collars' in an effort to release the bloody things and stop the torture.   It was not my favourite pastime.   There were the odd moments such as when a Purserette's shoe was passed along the line accompanied by furious hisses, or the time when a Hostesses uniform cap went sailing along the line.   But the best one was when one of the officers collapsed and we couldn't get him out of the hall because the Master at Arms, having locked the door, had gone for a smoke.   That particular officer was not required to attend church services from then on, but the Chief Officer stressed that if anybody else tried that one on there would be trouble with a large 'T'. We muttered but suffered.

Apart from church service, the next compulsory attendance required was at burial service which, though not a regular occurrence, was a relatively frequent event. The normal time for a burial at sea was 6:30 in the morning unless there was a rush on when 6:30 in the evening would be added. These early days, being on the 8-12 watch I was required to attend the service on the aft mooring deck. A few Deck Officers and Pursers would be in attendance along with any family or close friends of the deceased. Hats off, the Captain would read the service and then the Boatswains Mates would raise the board holding on to the Union Flag and the deceased would go overboard. This would normally be accompanied by a blinding flash as passengers on the decks above recorded the unfortunates' passage. Later when I changed to the 4-8 watch, this flash would let me know that the service was over, the deed was done and I would signal to the First

Officer who would ring Full Ahead on the appropriate engine. Anyway the sequence was, body overboard, blinding flash, caps on and full ahead both engines. There were one or two variations to this such as when the body was accidentally released at a trial run and a hastily constructed replacement had to be found. I was told that the bulk of this replacement was made up of a carcass of mutton and a large cabbage with a few shackles to weigh it down. Another time when for some reason the vessel was totally stopped. *Normally one engine was reduced to Dead Slow while the other remained at Full Ahead.* Anyway on this particular occasion all went well until the deceased hit the water and instead of sinking the body just bobbed along with us. It was only for half a minute or so, but it felt like an age. Needless to say the blinding flashes were a bit prolonged on this occasion. It took several minutes for us to leave the unfortunate behind. There were no relatives or close friends onboard at the time thank goodness!

I had been onboard for only a few days when I was instructed to go to 'Fluff Ally' to collect monies from all the female officers for some charitable collection or other. I will admit to being slightly concerned at this mission, but proceeded anyway. That was the last time I went down there alone - all future forays would be in a protective crowd. Anyway, I was collared, corralled, kidnapped in one cabin. It doesn't really matter whether it was a Nursing Sister's cabin, the Social Hostesses cabin, the Childrens Hostesses' cabin or a Purserettes' cabin - I was captured, tortured (they forced drink on me) and interfered with me (they partially stripped me and covered me with lipstick) and then fired me out into passenger accommodation. Half naked, dishevelled and distraught and to top it all, without the money I had been sent to collect. Funny really - when I made it back to the Deck Officer's accommodation nobody seemed atall surprised. Subsequently I went down there to the occasional birthday party but never alone. It was alright rubbing knees at the staff table but being caught alone by the pack was a terrifying experience.

Our first port of call was Las Palmas for bunkers and, to let our passengers stretch their legs and their wallets, in the Canary Island sunshine.

There was limited time off for some crew members and the 'bum boat' attendance was much improved to that of my first visit many years before. The Baggage Masters were employed loading fresh produce which was then ferried away by catering staff to the storerooms and coldrooms. The ship was only alongside for a few hours, and then it was upwards and onwards - next stop Capetown. As the junior of the Junior Thirds I was detailed to standby in the baggage hold during the storing operation and was instructed by my immediate seniors to keep my mouth shut if I happened to observe some strange goings on. Cartons of fruit went one way and cartons of something else went another way. Vegetables to the right and cartons of other stuff to the left. I was old enough to recognise a case of wine, a carton of gin, a box of whisky or a keg of rum. It seemed to me that more went left than right if you see what I mean. I was beginning to see why the two Baggage Masters were held in such high regard! Wink, wink, nudge, nudge - alright Third. That night I was involved in the distribution of these goods which had been pre-ordered at the last call. The Junior Third, who I had relieved but never met, had ordered several bottles of gin and whisky and I was initiated into the scheme of things by being allowed to purchase his order. Look not a gift horse in the mouth! I hasten to add that this was totally against company rules but going by the quantity loaded, just about all officers were in on it.

During free time onboard we were allowed to mingle with the passengers and to use the bars. There were two dance floors and off duty officers were actively encouraged to dance with passengers. This first voyage I was on the 8-12 watch so happily missed out on the dance experience but when I changed to the 12-4 and later to the 4-8 I was 'told' to get up. If it was one of the 'festive' nights my lack of dance steps could be covered by the crowd so to speak, but on quieter occasions, it was a pain. I remember trying to do the Mexican Hat dance with one of the Nursing Sisters when she let go at one of the particularly whirling moments and I shot across the dance floor scattering all before me. I was reprimanded for this incident and from then on employed extreme caution when dancing with female officers.

Apart from the senior Radio Officer who was a bit of a dry old stick, the others, of which there were four, were a bunch of characters. As well as normal radio watches, they were involved in onboard film shows, an internal television system and the daily ship's newspaper. The newspaper would contain international news, ship's notices and quite often, a totally trumped up and far fetched story invented by one of the team. On occasion there would be a story, not always trumped up, involving one of the ship's officers. Sometimes vindictive, sometimes flattering but always humorous. They lived 'up top' with the rest of we deck officers, so we saw a lot of them which gave them the opportunity to pick us off, one by one. Usually it was to announce a romantic liaison with one of the least likely amongst the female officers. Or perhaps trumped up birthday announcements. They used to get their knuckles rapped but I don't think it ever stopped them. On the ship's internal television system a face would suddenly appear or a strange notice. I can't remember them doing anything to the film shows but I do know that if they could have done something, they would have done it. They were a good bunch but a bunch to be closely monitored.

The medical team were a dedicated lot. The team was headed by the ships Surgeon, assisted by a Doctor who was working his passage out to the New World or one who was working his way back again, a New World doctor wanting to beat up Europe for a couple of years or one who had nothing better to do than work his passage around the world. Two Nursing Sisters and a couple of orderlies completed the team.. They had an operating theatre, a six bed hospital, a couple of consulting rooms, a dispensary and a sizable waiting room. I heard stories of fine medical and surgical achievements but, on the main, the doctors kept themselves to themselves. However, this could not be said about the nursing sisters, who played fast and loose with the heart strings of most of the junior male officers onboard, then went on to choose amongst us and then to marry the chosen ones. I probably flatter myself by saying that it was a bloody close shave. They were good sports and good fun but lethal when left alone with.

The passage southwards towards Capetown

was interrupted by the 'Crossing the Line Ceremony' which turned out to be a far more elaborate occasion than the affair when I first crossed the Equator. The costumes worn by Neptune and his 'glamorous' assistants were very realistic apart from the fact that said 'glamorous assistants' were mainly bearded or at least, unshaven. One or two 'specially chosen' female passengers would be involved and would be attired in bits of string - just to add some real glamour to the occasion and to encourage those crew members involved in the ceremony. The Old Man would attend but at a safe distance. We Juniors would perhaps get too close to the action and would be thrown into the pool fully booted and spurred to be 'rescued' by aforementioned maidens. Somewhere along the line there was a 'Doctor' and a 'Barber' and assistants involved but by this time people - and I mean passengers and officers - were getting a ducking in the pool. All good fun and the gateway to one or two liaisons! All passengers would subsequently be issued with a certificate allowing them to travel on the high seas by permission of Neptune and signed by the Captain.

I will take just a moment to talk about the Captain. Onboard this, my first passenger ship the Old Man really was Master before God. He was a tall, somewhat staid person with the real aura of command. At 'Captains Cocktail Parties' to which I was required to attend later on, he would put on a sort of 'plastic' smile and shake hands with the passengers as they arrived. During the 'march of the unemployed' or inspection of crew accommodation, he was downright morose and during the sessions wherein crewmembers who had misbehaved were 'dealt' with, he was hatchet faced and severe. Sometime later on I asked him a question and his reply was *'buggered if I know'* and I then realised that underneath he really was human. However, in the Chartroom while those officers involved in taking 'noon sights' and the subsequent frantic calculation of the ship's noon position, the Captain would stand behind us sniffing loudly as positions were compared, some rejected and finally agreed. If things dragged on a bit, the sniffing would increase in tempo and volume and he would start tapping his fingers on the chartroom table. After my one year and a bit onboard he gave me a very good report and for this I will be eternally grateful. I got into trouble a few times on that ship but this man could see through all this - I suppose!

In Capetown, I was one of the Duty Deck Officers which meant that I had to walk around the public rooms and the passenger decks showing my face. At any one time there were also two of the Masters at Arms doing the same thing. On one of the open deck bars I sat down with a couple of passengers and we admired the view over the port, the city and the spectacular view of Table Mountain. I happened to wonder at the rock formation of the mountain and was then subjected to a very lengthy lesson in geology. One of the passengers at the table turned out to be a Geologist. Not only a Geologist but one who really enjoyed his job. His wife, knowingly or wisely sloped off and left me, at first captivated but later, kidnapped. He certainly knew his stuff. It ended when I was called on the ship's broadcast system telling me to *call the Deck Office.* The Senior Officer of the day wanted to know why I hadn't checked in. They were a very nice couple and I spent some time with them on their voyage to the new world but I kept my mouth shut regarding rock formations after that first initiation.

The ship was stabilised and they coped well with the swells off the southern tip of Africa. Even so there was an uncomfortable movement sufficient to 'clear the decks' for a good part of the passage from Capetown to Durban. There were the usual complaints about the sea condition and the ship's movements and why weren't the stabilisers working properly but the Pursers Office withstood the brunt of these complaints while we, Deck Officers, kept off open decks. Well, passenger decks anyway. It was soon over and the pleasures of Durban soon revived passenger spirits. A few passengers left us at Capetown and a few joined. This was the same at Durban. Immediately after departure from both ports I had to do my 'Emergency Lecture and Donning Lifejacket' procedure. I think I did alright but I must have been as red as the lifejacket throughout. I remember one huge Boer nicknamed Beef or the Afrikaans version of same, having some difficulty putting on his lifejacket. The ship provided smaller versions for children but had omitted putting one by for a giant. It didn't fit properly and looked like a necklace when he got it near if not round his neck.   What neck?   He was travelling all the way to Europe on the ship so I got to know him quite well.   He was a gentle giant but I wouldn't care to have met him   face to face on the rugby field.

On the long passage from Durban to Fremantle the passengers had to be entertained and, among other things morning Bridge tours were organised.   A maximum of twenty-five passengers were allowed on these tours which took place at 10:30 and 11:00 in the morning   -   my watch.   Mostly they were quite gentile affairs and I would show them the radars (always popular), the steering and various other instruments.   Many of them just wanted to look out of the wheelhouse windows or to peer over the side from the bridge wings.   The chartroom was another popular venue as they could see our position and where we were going to and any other bits of land around.   There were occasionally, those who had done some research and who tried to ask awkward questions and there were those who took it all in and then complained later.   On one occasion, in answer to their question, I explained that the nearest ship could be over thirty miles away. That night we ran into fog and had the ships whistle going all night until it cleared with the sunrise. Two elderly ladies went to the Pursers Office and complained about the whistle blowing if there wasn't another vessel within thirty miles. The Purser passed this on to the Captain who cornered me in the chartroom and told me to *be careful what you tell them.* There were also Engineroom tours, but we Deck Officers, were not involved in these. I was told that at one particular point of the tour, if an attractive young lady stood on a particular plate a red light would start flashing. They were then told that it only flashed if a virgin stood on the plate. I never witnessed this but I do know that the buggers got away with it!

There would be music in one of the bars at lunchtime provided by the ship's 'orchestra'. Dancing in one of the lounges in the evening accompanied by the same 'orchestra'. Perhaps a quiz or a show in the theatre and one 'festival' evening in the main lounge and theatre. On the 'festive' evenings passengers were encouraged to dress up to the theme of the evening. They were usually very popular with the passengers and it was on these occasions that we were 'encouraged' to get up and dance. The uniform on these occasions was white long sleeve shirt with epaulets, black trousers and cummerbund, finished off with shining patent leather shoes. At the start of these evenings we would file into the lounge in starched dazzling white shirts and wearing trousers with creases you could probably cut yourselves on but by the end of the evening we would be dishevelled shadows of our former selves scattered around the lounge at tables occupied by young lovelies. Always we would be told by our seniors, to *circulate* but by the end of the evening, who cared. Liaisons were made and, where possible, the 'bus was run' but at this particular time on the passage across the Indian Ocean, I was on watch so missed the fun.

I suppose, by a rough count half the passengers would disembark in Australia and the other half would disembark in New Zealand. These would be replaced by young Antipodeans wanting to beat up Europe for a couple of years before returning home to settle down. And it was here on the passage from Australia and New

Zealand that the fun really started! A lot of the outward passengers were 'assisted immigrants' heading for a new life in the New World or Mum and Dad going out to see how young so and so was succeeding in the New World. We even had a few passengers who joined for the whole three month and twenty day round the world voyage. Gluttons for punishment! There were also a few passengers paying their own way out such as my geologist friend and his wife. Generally a good mixture but I do know that the Masters at Arms were kept busy. One of their main tasks was to stop crewmembers getting into passenger accommodation. Another one was policing passenger feuds and there were a few of these. Throughout the night there were fire patrols where 'nightwatchmen' would have a selected route around the whole ship and where they would indicate their position by inserting a 'pin' into fire alarm boxes. This registered the time and their position and these were checked daily to make sure that fire rounds were being done properly. There were very few nights when there were no additions to the 'disturbances during the night' book. On one of my first patrols, the Master at Arms and I caught a couple of passengers 'at it' in one of the ironing rooms.   Another incident when we had to 'rescue' a near topless maiden who was much the worse for wear and was found staggering around the Boat Deck.   When we managed to get her off deck and into the care of a Nursing Sister I realised that she was from my home town in Yorkshire. She kept her head down after that so I never saw her again.   Then again there was the odd drink induced fight or drink induced love affair.   There were robberies but fortunately only a few.   There were liaisons, separations, near divorces, near marriages and near suicides.   For the latter the ship had room in the hospital for reflection and recovery and if violent there was always the padded cell.   There were near riots.   One particular incident comes to mind when a sailor who was washing down the open wooden decks decided to poke the hose through one of the lounge doors   and hosed down the lunchtime dancers. Separating the hose party from the dance party took some time.   They were all, the hose party, marched up before the old man and summarily logged!   There was seldom a dull moment

Fremantle and Melbourne passed by very quickly, and then we arrived in Sydney, where we were to stay for two whole days. I managed to get a bit of shore leave here and caught up with a few old friends, but then it was onwards again across the Tasman to Wellington. Before departure, and on a sunny Sydney morning, we had a full crew Boat Drill where the offside lifeboats were lowered to the water with a full complement onboard. As was usual, the boats with flemming gear just went round in a circle and back to ship. However, the motor boats and the launches were instructed to go for a good run round the harbour. Since I was in charge of the boats at this time, I took them for a run by way of one of the Sydney sailing clubs that I used to frequent in the past. We enjoyed a pleasant lunchtime and then returned to the ship, where I ran into a storm of trouble. I stupidly, tried to claim that one of the boats had experienced an engine breakdown, but this excuse was not accepted. Somebody had been ordered to climb the mainmast to look for us. We were spotted neatly tied up alongside said sailing club and that was that. I received a severe bollocking for that and was never allowed to take the boats out 'en masse' again. But back to the passage across the Tasman, because of the large number of newly embarked passengers we had a full

Emergency Drill and it was at this drill that I realised that the atmosphere was changing. The Brits had been relatively orderly on such occasions but the Aussies were more of a caustic rabble who mercilessly took the 'piss' out of us 'Poms'. It was mainly good natured banter delivered by both male and female of this good looking young crowd and made the outlook for the passage onwards very appealing.

We did our thing in Wellington and then coasted on up to Auckland where we were again scheduled for a two day stopover. Here we had another boat drill because this time we were the opposite side to alongside the terminal and every opportunity had to be taken to exercise the offshore lifeboats. I was not in charge of the boats during this exercise because I had been moved from the 8-12 watch to the 12-4 watch. This meant that I would be able to enjoy some of the action during the evenings but I was warned that I had to be in bed by a reasonable hour. No partying until midnight and then going on watch. It was possible to evade detection but then I'd get it in the neck from the 2nd Officer who was senior on my watch. Mind you - he did it a couple of times but, I kept my mouth shut.

From Auckland we sailed for Raratonga. Now this was the stuff of dreams and I hope Grandma was not watching me. Rarotonga is only a small island without a harbour so the ship did one full circle around the island for photographic purposes and then hove to so that the show could begin. A barge full of dusky maidens wearing not much more than grass skirts would pull alongside the galley 'gun port' door and they would clamber onboard and for a couple of hours they danced, sang and gyrated erotically to entertain the passengers. My job was to see them safely onboard and to then inform the bridge that they were all onboard and without casualties. This was because the sea swell off Raratonga could be very big and if the ship leant into it, as it did a couple of times, then the sea would readily flow through the galley causing chaos. I was at the gun port door one time when this happened, flooding the galley momentarily to about two feet and apparently, on being informed of this, the Old Man stamped on his uniform cap. But back to the dusky maidens. They say that rubbing noses is a sign of greeting. Well I had just about everything else rubbed and thoroughly enjoyed the experience. I was told by the other Junior Thirds that manning the gun port door at Raratonga was a popular duty - I could see why. They were a really happy bunch of girls and ,when, on a subsequent voyage we had to bypass them because of heavy weather, I for one was very disappointed. After embarking the girls, we then took delivery of piles of Palm fronds, from the barge, which were to be used to decorate the lounges for South Pacific Night.

South Pacific Night was the most popular festive night of the whole voyage. The lounges and bars were decorated with the palm fronds and the passengers were encouraged to dress up in grass skirts and colourful Hawaiian shirts for the occasion. Even we were encouraged to wear the traditional Tahitian 'lei'. When I say that we officers were 'encouraged' to wear the lei I really mean that as we entered the lounges we were grabbed by a posse of female officers and passengers, had our noses rubbed (noses only this time) and had said lei placed around our necks. There were tables of food with a colourful South Pacific appearance and the music and entertainment for the evening was based on a South Pacific theme. The show would go on till midnight and the bars stayed open till around two in the morning. You could dance till dawn if you liked recorded music. All in all, a bloody good show. However - that voyage, I was on the 12-4 watch so I had to go to bed early. He he! As this night was held after the relatively short hops around Australia and New Zealand and shortly after the Rarotonga experience it was where our Antipodean passengers really got going and let their hair down. I forgot to mention that the restaurants produced a South Pacific gala menu for the occasion. Even the staff table benefited from this though the service didn't improve, but more on this subject later. The senior officers, be they deck, engine, purser, radio etc all had tables of their own and were able to entertain the passengers at table with bottles of wine that they just had to sign for. The staff table had to buy their own! The hangovers had just about disappeared by the time we docked in Tahiti.

Tahiti - this was another place known for the entertainment. As the ship manoeuvred alongside we were entertained by several grass skirted maidens swaying provocatively to a rhythm beaten out on hollow logs by some large, hairy blokes. The, Boat, Promenade and Sun Decks were awash with passengers enjoying the scene. Again it was time for a crew boat drill but this time one of the boats would remain in the water. After lunch, those officers wishing to, could board the lifeboat and sail out to the reef for an afternoons swimming. Booze was not allowed but it somehow found its way onto the boat. Passengers were strictly not allowed but we usually managed to 'find' a couple on the way. Funny how they always came fully kitted out with swimming togs and other necessary accoutrements. I remember when I went along a couple of times we used to tie up under a Sunderland flying boat which was at anchor in the harbour. There you could sit in the shade or swim off the floats. Great fun!

Earlier on in this tale, I mentioned notorious bars around the world associated with seamen. Papeete had its very own world renowned sailors pub - 'Quinns Bar'. One voyage I was taken there and had a very quiet drink watching some of our crew baiting some Legionnaires. We left before trouble erupted which of course, it did, and my money was most certainly on the Legionnaires. One voyage - it may well have been that one - we had to man the fire hoses and hose down a hostile crowd of locals while others shepherded passengers and crew back onboard. Fortunately, our by now, mainly Antipodean passengers thought this was hilarious. I recall one well travelled passenger saying that she never enjoyed such entertainment with the other liner company's. Anyway, we escaped - we always escaped - but usually we had to leave somebody behind. In jail or in hospital.

And whilst on the subject of 'notorious bars'. Off duty we were allowed to mingle with the passengers and to enjoy a drink in any one of the bars. It wasn't until my second round trip when I moved from the 8-12 watch to the 12-4 watch that I was told about the vagaries of the bar staff. Spirit tots were served in silver measuring cups, where, with a cunningly inserted coin in the bottom, the measure was reduced thus increasing profits. So, for a gin and tonic, you received a reduced measure, a lot of ice and a splash of tonic. The tonic would therefore last for three servings and of course, three payments. Once I found out about this, I made sure that I took my tonic with me. It was that or beer -   and there were rumours about watering that down too! I am absolutely positive that there were other devious doings that I didn't get to know about. All this reminds me of a film comedy called 'The Captain's Table'   and I thought they were joking! The bar staff were a happy bunch -   no bloody wonder!

Onwards again towards Acapulco via a slow cruise past the French atoll of Clipperton Island. Not a great deal to see really.   A very small island surrounded by a large reef with the odd   clump of palm trees growing along it.   The sea, dark blue outside the reef and a very pale blue inside. There was obviously a way in because we occasionally saw yachts at anchor in the lagoon.

At Acapulco the ship had to anchor in the large bay and passengers wanting to go ashore were ferried in ship's lifeboats.   The rigging of the gangway and setting up of the pontoon took some time and then the command boat would go in to establish a landing place for our boats only.

The company flag and the red ensign were used to mark 'our' spot and with a couple of Junior Pursers armed with walkie talkies we were ready to go. I must add that our spot was marked and manned because there would normally be at least one other passenger ship doing the same exercise. Each lifeboat was manned by a Junior Third officer, a Boatswains Mate or a Quartermaster and a couple of sailors with the Third Officer in overall charge. Walkie talkies, first-aid kits and umbrellas were deployed and off we merrily went. The younger passengers had no problems jumping off at the quayside, but bouncing up and down in the choppy waters made it hazardous for others. Getting them back later in the day was even worse, because even the sure of foot would have partaken of the local hooch and could topple into the bilges. Perhaps the alcohol helped because nobody seemed any the worse for wear after the experience. The last boat back was always the worst one and here the Third Officer and a couple of Masters at Arms would be added to the compliment. It was always a mixture of passengers and crew and all the worse for wear. During the day when halfway across the bay heading for the ship, it was not unusual to hear *why are we going to this ship* and to find that somebody else's passenger had managed to sneak onboard one of our boats.   It happened both ways and after a short deviation and a lot of hilarity we would deliver them unto their own.   On one voyage we actually went alongside a sort of passenger quay and I managed to get ashore escorting a beautiful New Zealand girl to the hotel where the 'performers' dive off a cliff face into a very narrow bay.   We drank expensive cocktails, mooched until dawn,   danced through the Mexican national anthem and then got chucked out.   There were tables at different levels on the cliff side and I spotted a few of my comrades also there to the last.   But back to the lifeboat operation.   On one visit, we were caught in a torrential rain storm, and I do mean torrential. My boat was alongside the town quay when the heavens opened and within minutes the water was cascading off the quay like a waterfall.   The quayside tables with their colourful umbrellas were washed or blown away and the local shops were flooded.   Those passengers on the quayside tried to get onboard the lifeboat but this was now a hazardous and very wet move.   The wiser passengers found shelter in the boardwalk bars.

Our lifeboat was an open boat and our only defence against precipitation was a few umbrellas and a manual bilge pump, a couple of buckets and a bailer. The latter appeared on the statutory list of lifeboat equipment as a 'bailer' but it resembled a small 'wok'. Reviewing the situation, we had torrential rain, a very strong wind, a very choppy sea and water pouring onto us off the quayside along with much detritus. By the time we managed to rescue those passengers foolhardy enough to choose the lifeboat as their means of escape, we were in danger of inundation. Fortunately the lifeboat engine was unaffected by the level of water in the bilges and we headed back to the ship with all hands, and I mean all, frantically bailing out. Boat operations were suspended until the downpour passed and the sunshine returned.

From Acapulco, we made our way southwards towards the Panama Canal. Before the daytime canal transit, the ship tied up on the Panama City side of the canal for a night of entertainment for passengers and crew alike. But, at this point I will concentrate on the canal itself. The transit started at daylight and with two

American pilots on the Bridge and another American seated on the Monkey Island with a microphone as we proceeded towards the first set of locks. The commentary started as the ship passed under the 'Bridge of the Americas' which carries the Pan American Highway from Canada down to Chile. Bye now the restaurants and bars were empty and the open decks were crammed with passengers trying to see what was going on. The ship then made a slow approach to the two stage Miraflores Locks where the 'mules' put their wires onboard and started to slowly tow the ship into the lower chamber of the set of locks. Passengers watching the rope men as they threw the heaving lines from the lock approach jetty's would cheer and clap in admiration at their accuracy. I was told that these men held annual competitions for height, length and accuracy. Safely secured in the lower chamber, with not a lot of space on each side of the ship and the huge gates closed astern, the ship would then slowly rise to the level of the second chamber. The commentary continued through all this with a full description of what was happening, how it was happening and the history of the canal construction. And the commentator had plenty to talk about.   Clear of Miraflores the ship made its slow approach to the one chamber Pedro Miguel Lock where another set of 'mules' safely guided the ship into the lock.   From there the ship manoeuvred through the Culebra Cut at the highest point in the transit with sheer rock faces seemingly only a few metres away.   In the history of the building of the canal, it was this part of the construction that cost the most lives.   Then moving from the cut into the Rio Chagres part of the canal where the Panamanian jungle reached the waterway sides.   I must admit that I preferred this part of the canal on a night transit because of the magical scene created by the lights amongst the trees.   However, at this time, passenger ships and ships with hazardous cargoes enjoyed a daytime transit and all others passed through at night. Onwards again and out into Gatun Lake and finally to the approaches to the three tier Gatun Locks. Passengers up on the Monkey Island above the Navigation Bridge could look down the lock steps out over the harbour at Cristobal and into the blue waters of the Gulf of Darien in the Caribbean Sea. After dropping down the three tiers to the level of the Caribbean and after a short   stop at Cristobal the ship would move out into the Caribbean with a mostly satisfied bunch of passengers and a relieved bunch of deck crew.

I have always found this part of the Caribbean to be a bit breezy but after the heat of the canal transit this was welcome. The next part of the voyage was to Curacao in the Netherlands Antilles. It was for a short bunkering stay at Caracas Bay, a picturesque bay with a small beach, a few oil storage tanks and not much else. Those passengers who were that way inclined, could use the small beach for sunbathing or swimming but they were advised to be extremely careful when in the water because of sea anemones. If you step on one of these creatures their spines penetrate the foot and break off. I am told that it is virtually impossible to remove these spines and that they are very painful while embedded in the foot. Passengers were advised to wear some sort of footwear while bathing but, as always, we had to carry one or two of them back to the ship and down to the surgery. Fortunately, it was only a short stay.

Onwards again to Port of Spain, Trinidad, where the ship would be greeted by a steel band.

Not just a steel band, but a one-hundred piece steel band. The music was fantastic - traditional to classical. The local shop-keepers eventually complained, on the ground that they were losing trade because nobody ventured ashore during the performance. After that the band would just greet the ship and then disappear. But this time they stayed until late in the evening and the passengers lined the open decks enjoying the music and drinking from the ship's bars. Many chose to take their drinks onto the wharf to get even closer to the band. I repeat myself, they were fantastic. Port of Spain was another port which had its very own notorious seaman's bar. This was the bar at the Hotel Miramar known for the erotic dancers and wild parties. It is the only place where I have seen a naked coloured girl doing the 'limbo'. Amazing athleticism - really! I recall that we were asked to join in but I, for one, found it more enjoyable being a spectator. Some did join in but they lacked both athleticism and attraction. A few passengers made it to the Miramar and we all had an enjoyable evening.

The next port of call, and one which still rates as one of my favourites was Barbados. By this time I was on the 4-8 watch with the First Officer so I was able to take advantage of the evenings onboard entertainment without being sent to bed before midnight. I managed to get ashore in Barbados with a group of fellow ship's officers and some of the passengers. I can't remember the name of the hotel that we ended up at, but I do remember that it was set back from a beautiful white sandy beach separated from the hotel by a few palm trees. I ended up 'skinny dipping' with a New Zealand girl around midnight. We were thoroughly enjoying ourselves until we found that someone had removed our clothes. It is amazing how quickly one can sober up when finding oneself clothes-less, moneyless and naked. We eventually found that the bastards had left us just enough to cover our modesty but when we got back to the ship we had to sneak onboard via the crew gangway. The rest of our clothes were returned the next day. Amazingly, the whole ship seemed to know about our misfortune.

Shortly after departing from Barbados, on the long Atlantic passage to Lisbon we had a Pirates Night. Another of the festive evenings where passengers would, this time, be encouraged

189

to dress up as pirates.   They put on this festive night while the outside temperature was still relatively high and before we would be affected by any North Atlantic storms.   Even so, passengers remarked at the movements of the ship - even with the stabilisers out -   and dancing was a little more precarious.   If you have the feel for the ship you can feel that the ship wants to roll - say to starboard -   but then you can feel the stabilisers doing their stuff so instead of an easy roll it turns out like a bit of a shudder.   Anyway, it affected the purists dance steps and probably added a little something to mine.

The overnight stop at Lisbon allowed the partakers of flourishing onboard romances one last night ashore together.   The restaurants, bars and cafes in the old town must have done a bustling trade that night.   On my last voyage on the ship, the First Officer and I drowned our, and our partners sorrows in a bar in Lisbon.   In fact so much so, that we couldn't pay the bill. Fortunately, we were bailed out by one of our passengers who was at an adjacent table. It is amazing how well the old Mateus Rose slid down. We had a few bottles -   can't remember how many   -   but quite a few.

And so back to Southampton.   Passengers disembarked   -   a frantic weekend preparing for the next lot   -   passengers embarked and off again.   I had done one voyage but this second one I started off as Senior Junior Third Officer. Elevated to the top of the bottom   so to speak, and all in one voyage.   Upwards and onwards.

One of the safety matters that I have not yet mentioned was the twice weekly testing of the watertight doors.   On the two lower passenger decks at intervals that, in an emergency, would divide   the   ship   into   separate   watertight compartments, were fitted these heavy steel sliding 'watertight doors'.   On the Bridge there was an indicating panel showing each door open or shut, plus the remote operating switch for these doors. As I have said, they were made of steel and necessarily very heavy and hydraulically operated. Once the closing mechanism was operated there was no way of stopping them.   They could be opened manually at each door   but only after they were closed.   They scared the living daylights out of me.   They were tested at 8:15 am after several broadcasts warning passengers to *keep clear of all watertight doors.* Each door was supposed to be manned by a steward who's duty it was to make sure passengers didn't try to pass through the activated doors. I heard tales - in fact read about them in the 'disturbances' book - about women passing children through the doors or trying to jump through themselves. Horrifying! I mean, it was not as though they were trapped - each section had an alternative way 'up'. They held this exercise at 8:15 in the hope that most if not all passengers would be in the restaurants enjoying breakfast. God - I would hate to experience a real emergency!

I talked briefly, earlier on, about the service at the staff table. Service should have been excellent because the table was just outside the swing doors to the galley so, if it was distance that counted, we were number one. However, this didn't appear to make any difference and we were regularly subjected to lengthy periods of waiting between courses. This often caused frustration as some amongst us were on strict schedules needing to be at a particular place at a particular time or to relieve a particular person at a particular time.   The person who bore the brunt of all this pent up frustration was the table steward and on one particular occasion I asked for an explanation. Well   -   it appeared that at the start of each voyage, the table stewards were expected to pay the galley staff a backhand to ensure that they would be served as fast as possible.   The steward at the staff table being the lowest of the low and receiving no 'tips' could not afford to bribe the galley staff so was always at the back of the queue. Whereas the stewards at passenger tables could expect good tips and could afford to spread it around a little.   The internal workings, machinations of the catering department were traditional , well embedded and hard to break and at times, bloody vicious.   We complained to the Senior Catering Officers but it made no difference. The only thing our complaint achieved was to have our table steward threatened.

Then there were the moneylenders. Amazingly, most of these characters appeared to be engine room ratings.   We talk about loan sharks today, well, these people were past masters. Of course it was banned onboard, but we all knew it went on in the dark shadows below decks.   It had disastrous effects on some of the borrowers. Spent on under deck gambling and unable to pay the lender back at the end of the voyage.   No money to take home to wife and kids   -   they would have to sign on again in the hope that they could and under threat if they couldn't, pay back the loan.   A vicious circle and one very hard to escape from.   The sharks would be dismissed if caught,   but   apparently,   there   was   always somebody else to take over the 'firm'.

And talking about 'below decks'.   Where we deck and radio officers were perched high up in the fresh air and sunlight, others were 'down below'.   The engineers accommodation was relatively light and airy.   Even 'Fluff Ally' could get a glimpse of sunlight or a view of a starlit night sky.   But down below in crew accommodation where the bulk of the force lived   -   things were a bit different.   The bottom of the rung catering boys lived twelve to cabin with one small porthole to let in a bit of light.   Some were in inside cabins with no natural light. Others were six, four or two to a room depending on their position on the ladder.   All was painted steel, formica or cracked lino.   The 'facilities' were big and bare with absolutely no privacy.   It was grim down there and at times the smells were ghastly -   sweaty socks and armpits!   The deck and engine ratings lived either right forward or right aft and in much better conditions.   But back to the pits   -   a twice weekly inspection of this accommodation did little to make it any more habitable.   Some of the 'more effeminate' members of the catering staff kept their quarters clean and attempted to make their own areas a little more homely.   Deep down there amongst this squalor was the 'Pig' or the crew bar, recreation room.   It was necessarily large and kept decorated by the crew with flags, pictures and all manner of nauticalia.   It was strictly out of bounds to all officers and passengers except by invitation and believe it or not, these invitations were much sought after by passengers. Once a voyage they would put on a nights entertainment and this was the time when invitations were at a premium.   The show would include comedy, music and dancing with the lavish costumes of the 'ladies' and their outlandish performances being the highlights of the show.   I seem to remember it being a free drinks night and bloody hilarious!   They deserved a night like that to lift the gloom of that 'below decks' accommodation.   No wonder they kept trying to escape into passenger accommodation though I must add that, at that level, there wasn't a great deal of difference.   Passengers were six, four or two to a cabin down there.   The fittings were better mind you.   Some of the passenger inside cabins had an artificial window which lit up with an automatic sunrise in the mornings.   In the equivalent windowless crew cabin they had strip lighting.   It amazed me how they used to turn up for duty squeaky clean and in crisp white uniforms.   No doubt there was a Catering Officer at the 'door' to make sure that they were presentable.

Now as Senior Junior Third   I was on the 4-8 watch with the First Officer and therefore able to attend evening functions.   The other two Junior Thirds were new to passenger ships and were experiencing the rapid learning curve that I had experienced only three months and twenty days before.   However, they were company men having joined as Cadets so, at least, they had an inkling of what they had let themselves in for. The 4-8 watch was the star watch in that when possible, star sights were taken to fix the vessel's morning and evenings position.   When the First Officer was satisfied that I could be trusted to take star sights and to produce an acceptable position, he used to leave me to it.   I was under strict orders to call him if anything untoward happened or if there was a sniff of the Old Man approaching. He got away with it most of the time but I experienced a hairy moment when the Old Man phoned to say that he would be up on the bridge shortly to discuss something with   the First.   He wouldn't answer the phone so I left the bridge to put him on the shake only to find him in bed with two women   -   mother and daughter.   He made it to the bridge in pyjamas and dressing gown which produced some harsh looks and heavy sniffing from the Old Man.   It wasn't so much that he wasn't allowed a lay in but as there was only one set of sight calculations to be seen   - this was frowned upon.   My watch mate was never late again!   I have sailed with a few characters during my time at sea and First was one of them.   He also led a charmed life and in doing so charmed some of the best looking girls onboard. I didn't exactly bask in his shadow but I managed to enjoy myself.   On the ships open market his 'little black book'   was a much coveted item.

He left at the end of the voyage and went on to greater if quieter things. But we still had a few near scrapes and adventures over the next three and a bit months.

And so my initial passenger ship period progressed. I don't think that I distinguished myself in any way but it was a great experience and one that I would not have missed. Being a Junior officer had its perks and its disadvantages. Up to now I have concentrated on the more pleasurable side of things but there were other times and incidents that were not so humorous. The time when the stabilisers failed on departure from Wellington stands out in my mind as one of the major incidents happening during my time on the ship. We sailed from Wellington with the usual amount of ceremony and streamers and moved out into severe weather in the Cook Strait. The ship was bound for Auckland so, on leaving the shelter of Wellington Harbour with the stabilisers out in readiness, the vessel made a major alteration of course to port. It was during this alteration that one of the stabiliser fins failed so instead of compensating for any movement, the remaining fin over-compensated causing the vessel to heel over violently.   I was in passenger accommodation at the time, on my way back from departure 'stations'.   Without warning, the vessel heeled violently to starboard throwing any movable objects, and I mean furniture and passengers,   into a heap on the starboard side.   I was in a wide lobby with access to the lifts and a stairwell to other passenger decks plus a door to the stairwell leading to Deck Officer's accommodation.   I managed to hold on to, hang on to a rail but the easy chairs, the armchairs, settees and tables along with their occupants, were thrown across the ship.   Those passengers or crew caught without anything secure to hold onto were thrown across the ship. Some of   those passengers or crew who found something secure to hold on to were swept away by the mass of sliding furniture. There were one or two major injuries to passengers and a lot of minor injuries to both passengers and crew.   The list of damage to furniture and equipment was long and detailed and included every department but the Catering Department bore the brunt of it.   The incident was over in a matter of minutes and the ship resumed its upright status and proceeded on the passage towards Auckland.   Regarding the injuries, it was deemed

that all were treatable onboard and this was agreed
to be better than trying to reverse the course and
return to Wellington.   The weather at the time
was as severe as it can be in the Cook Strait as the
wind funnels between the North and South Islands
of New Zealand.   The clear up took some hours
but by then all was back to normal.   There were a
few more bandages and slings to be seen around
and a few passengers missing from the bars, but all
was seemingly back to normal.   Apart from the
normal passenger discharge at Auckland I seem to
recall that one or two others chose   to call it a
day.   Choosing to proceed no further!   But with
the influx of young blood at Auckland, the
atmosphere onboard was soon restored and the
incident forgotten.   Of course there were internal
enquiries into the incident but as Junior Third I had
no knowledge of the outcome.   I do remember
that during our two day stopover at Auckland, the
ship was crawling with 'suits' rapidly dispatched
from Head Office and that we were a bit short on
'free time'.   One last word.   If the incident had
happened during the evening meal with hot food
and wine on the tables and waiters weaving
amongst the tables carrying trays piled high with
food   -   the outcome doesn't bear thinking

about!

Another incident or series of incidents involved a 'friend of a friend of my family'. Not nearly as bad as the 'stabiliser' incident but never the less, disturbing. An elderly Aunt asked me to keep an eye on 'friend of a friend' and to see that all went well for him. He joined at Southampton to do the full round the world voyage. Apparently it was to be his second cruise but nobody thought to mention that his first one was as a repatriated prisoner of war from Singapore. The first mistake was his choosing an 'inside' cabin in the bowels of the ship. This triggered memories of his wartime incarceration. I endeavoured to get him moved but it was impossible. Anyway - this started a downwards spiral. He did not like his cabin. He did not like being incarcerated onboard ship with another fourteen hundred souls plus crew. He didn't like the people at his dining table. He did not like the food. He was an elderly gentleman but when he started hurling food and plates around, he had to be physically restrained. The medical staff kept him under some sort of sedation for a couple of days and then he appeared to be back to normal. This didn't last for long and he went berserk in one of the lounges. Again he was restrained. This happened a couple more times and then 'restraint' became 'restriction' and he was locked in the padded cell. This of course did nothing for his psychological state, so under sedation he was landed at Capetown. So ended his second cruise. Afterwards the Aunt admitted that both she and the friend of the friend, knew about his problems and I vowed not to keep any eyes on anymore friend of friends!

Another painful incident which happened later on during my days onboard this ship, was when I felt the wrath of a 'Legionnaire'. I was off duty on a sunny Pacific afternoon walking on the open decks when an agitated female passenger grabbed me and said that her friend was being attacked. When we arrived on the scene, sure enough, there was a man attacking a girl. I put my hand on his shoulder and told him to back off and he then turned his attention to me. By the time the Masters at Arms arrived, I was black and blue from the waist upwards and, I was very pleased to see them before my assailant could transfer his 'operation' to the rest of me.

Fortunately, all this took place not far from the stairwell leading down to the 'brig', our padded cell, so his transfer from freedom to lock up did not take long. I followed the Master at Arms as they 'gently' threw him down the steel ladder and then persuaded him into the brig using boot and fist. He remained incarcerated until arrival in Southampton when the police escorted him ashore. I was told later that he was a German legionnaire proceeding on leave. True or false I know not but I was certainly no match for him in a fight.

Then there were incidents ashore. One weekend in Southampton I flew home from Eastleigh. I enjoyed the couple of days at home and then made my way to the airport to fly back only to find that the airport was fogbound. The airline then put me into a taxi and transported me to Manchester airport where I and one other passenger joined the flight back to Eastleigh. Two passengers on an aircraft that must have been able to carry at least fifty. Anyway, it was one way of getting individual attention from the crew and as the aircraft circled low over Southampton there was my ship below us. I pointed her out to the Stewardess who was sitting beside me and she said something like *what, that puke coloured monster.* Oh well, you either loved her or loathed her - the ship I mean.

The Balboa end of the Panama Canal was always a popular run ashore with both passengers and crew. We were only there overnight but that was long enough to get into trouble. On one occasion I went ashore with one of the junior Pursers and a couple of Australian girl passengers. We started off at the bar of the casino and later progressed to a nightclub in Panama City. All was going well. The show was good, the food was good, the drinks were plentiful and the girls were gorgeous. It was when the purser and I surreptitiously pooled our resources and found that we were a bit short! As a way out, it was agreed that the purser and his girlfriend were to leave and go back to the ship for funds and then he was to return to bail me and my girlfriend out. Meanwhile we were to continue as if nothing was wrong. This went on and on and though I may have imagined it, the waiters seemed to be hovering. It appeared that our rescue mission had failed so drastic measures had to be taken. The Aussie girl that I was with was game for action, so she went to the toilet then headed out into the street.   I gave her ten minutes then ran for the exit and hurled myself into the back of a perfectly positioned taxi which immediately 'took off' only to pass the purser in another cab just entering the club car park.   Apparently they manhandled him a bit and made a few 'additions' to the bill   but eventually parted best of friends.   We chuckled over that one for a while.

To a more serious subject.   Taking noon sights was a bit like the burial at sea ceremony but without the blinding flash.   This was replaced by the sound of camera shutters being operated.   We four, we happy four,   would line up on the Bridge wing armed with sextants preparing to 'shoot' the sun to enable the calculation of the ship's noon position.   There would be a little pre noon banter as we compared sextant readings, but on the order 'ready' from the Navigating Officer we would prepare ourselves.   When the Navigating Officer said 'mark' we would all troop off into the Wheelhouse taking note of our sextant readings. While all this was going on, the passengers above us on the Monkey Island would be recording this routine for their photo albums.

Back inside the Chartroom we would line up at the chartroom table doing our calculations. With the works completed, the noon position on the chart and the day's run calculated, the noon broadcast would be made. Position, speed, day's run, total run and the distance to go to the next port. To some of the passengers, the days run had added importance because there was a daily competition where passengers were encouraged to guess this distance. The prizes weren't great, but it was fiercely contested, and to this end we were sworn to secrecy and any 'guesswork' with favoured passengers was strictly forbidden. All this sounds a bit petty but there were recorded incidents where passengers offered 'rewards' for fixing the day's run. Sometimes there were complaints and our calculations would be taken away and checked by a Senior Officer. But that is another story for another ship.

One thing I found a bit odd when I first joined this particular passenger ship was the inter-departmental animosities. Traditionally deck and engine have had their differences - oil and water -

but to find that the engine department actively disliked the purser and catering departments was a little unsettling.   Everybody loved 'Fluff Alley' - but from afar, and the Radio Officers were always thought to be good fun, but there was a bit of an 'apartheid' atmosphere between the large departments.   I first came across this when, one evening, I announced that I was going to a party in the Engineers accommodation.   While stuck in a hotel in Southampton I discovered that the only other person at the bar was one of my future shipmates and an engineer.   Anyway, when my fellow Junior Thirds heard my intentions it was as though I was about to commit some cardinal sin. I went to the party anyway and enjoyed it and vowed to do my best to break down the inter-departmental prejudices.   By the end of my four round the world tours of duty I like to think that at least deck and engine got on but the feud between engine and purser departments was a no hoper.

At this point perhaps a few words on 'Flag Etiquette' should be included.   At 0800hrs every morning all the flags would rise in unison.   This again was a ceremony much photographed by early rise passengers.   Taking the flags down in the evening was always timed for sunset but had the added attraction of a Bugler playing 'taps' from the height of the Monkey Island. The bugle call was broadcast throughout the ship and always caused a few moments of silence and reflection. I, for one, always enjoyed the sound and the spectacle. In port on special days such as 'Anzac Day' or Christmas Day, the ship would be dressed 'overall' with flags and lights strung from aft to mainmast, from mainmast to foremast and any other place where a few flags and lights could be rigged. This 'rigging overall' was a major task, so these flags did not come down with the bugle call. We did have the odd hiccup when a halyard would jam or a flag would catch onto or wrap itself around a wire mast stay - bugger!

I'm getting closer now to the time when I realised it was time to move on. It was on my fourth round trip that I was informed that my sea time was not counting to the time required for me to sit for my Masters certificate. I talked to the Captain and he arranged for my relief at the end of that voyage. I had enjoyed my time onboard and had learnt much. Had fun! I even had hopes of promotion to Third Officer but without a Masters

Certificate that would be as far as I could go on passengers ships. It was time to move on. I regretted leaving - I had met a lot of people and made some lasting friendships but if 'command' was my ultimate aim, then it had to be. There had been a time when I thought that a career onboard passenger ships could be the way ahead. I had been conditioned to the 'bull', got used to the 'buzz' and - at times - thoroughly enjoyed the company. But the road to the top appeared to be a bit distant - J3O to 3/O to 2/O to 1/O to C/O to Staff Captain and then the dizzy if distant height, Captain. On the freighter service it was a shorter road to the top - 3/O to 2/O to C/O to Captain. Now I look back at my time as Junior 3rd Officer and I smile. It had been good fun - mostly. Later, I was to return to passenger ships for a while and as I climbed the ladder there were more perks but there were more pains too!

My next appointment was to a very different type and size of vessel. This was a refrigerated cargo vessel employed mainly on the New Zealand to the UK trade. General cargo out and frozen lamb and mutton back. For this appointment I had been promoted to Third Officer so with 'upwards and onwards' in mind I joined my first 'Pommie Meatboat'. She was berthed in London docks loading a general cargo for Auckland, Wellington and Lyttelton. It was a depressing bloody place at the best of times but at this particular joining, the docks presented themselves in their wettest, dreariest colours. The ship itself was alright - she wasn't that old. I soon learnt that the main difference between ancient and modern in the company's reefer fleet was a rounded funnel and a slightly raked bow. The accommodation was comfortable and clean and light and airy and not a steam winch in sight. I had a forward facing window looking out over a steel hatch cover to the impressive foremast and a slightly concerning 'heavy lift derrick'. There were other derricks of course but having been away from them for well over a year, I viewed them with caution. However, in London docks, cranes were being used and the derricks were swung out of the way, out over the offshore side. A seemingly tangled mess of wires, ropes, shackles, blocks and pulleys. Anyway - I'm getting ahead of myself here. I managed to climb onboard from a large pontoon twixt ship and shore, the latter to allow barges to position themselves under each hatch, clambering up a floating or swinging gangway and onto the main deck.   At the top of the gangway and strategically placed was a large coir matt with 'welcome' on it.   I remember thinking that this was quite a nice touch but over the following months this matt was to give me a lot of grief.   Anyway, I made way to the Chief Officers cabin and was then pointed in the direction of my own cabin which was just along the cross alleyway.   All well so far. Having dumped my suitcases in the cabin, I was then shown around by the officer I was relieving. The Bridge was small and, apart from the radar and one or two other bits and pieces, rather antiquated.   The up to date equipment had all been added later and seemed to be scattered around haphazardly.   Somebody had put some thought into how to keep the watch keeper moving.   The VHF was on the port side, the radar on the starboard side and the telegraph in the middle. The echo sounder was in the chartroom along with the internal telephone system.   It was in the chartroom that I was introduced to the file containing all, including the current, cargo plans. It was to be my job to create these colourful artistic masterpieces as Third Officer onboard.   The general cargo plans looked complicated and colourful but the refrigerated cargo plans were something of multicoloured modern art. Still, I had the passage out to New Zealand to study their intricacies. My learning tour continued out on deck peering down the open hatchways. I would have to learn about the folding MacGregor hatch lids. Unlike the other cargo ships that I had served on, the holds, instead of being vast caverns, on this ship were broken up into 'Tween Decks' and Cargo Lockers. Upper Tween, Lower Tween and Orlop decks were about to become familiar names. Chuck in the Bridge Space, the Fore Peak and one or two other strangely named dark cargo places and there you have it. The accommodation layout was split with Deck, Catering and Radio forward of No.3 Hatch and Engine and Electrical aft of the hatch. The deck, catering and engine room ratings were on the deck below the Engineers. Here I interject that I was to sail on several 'Pommie Meatboats' in this company, some ancient, some relatively new but with the layout about the same. This means that I won't have to go through all this again!

Back to the cabin and a quick beer before

being left on my own to unpack and dress for the occasion. I remember my first meal onboard mainly because of the silver service with company logo and the beautiful wood panelled bulkheads of the Saloon itself. It was very well done and the different types of timber were all labelled. Starched white table napkins and brilliant white tablecloths. I didn't meet many people that first evening but I was impressed. Things were looking good.

The following morning I signed the ships articles in front of the Purser and thus committed myself to the forthcoming voyage. The 'articles' actually stated that, should the ship remain out of UK waters for two years, I would have to stick with it - but I didn't envisage this. I was reliably told that a 'double header' was the longest period these ships stayed away for. A 'double header' was when a ship would load for Australia or New Zealand and then load a cargo for the USA or Canada then return to New Zealand to load a cargo for home. So, signed on and suitably outfitted, I started my first cargo watch. Armed with notebook and biro, I wandered from working hatch to working hatch making rough drawings of where specific lots of cargo were being stowed such as whisky in a Deck Locker or cars in the Bridge Space. Cases of whatever for Auckland separated from bags of whatever for Wellington or drums of whatever for Lyttelton. Fortunately on this first day, only three of the five hatches were being worked so I was being broken in slowly. By now I had met the Chief Officer, the Second Officer and the Junior Third Officer but I had yet to meet the Captain. I met the Boatswain and the deck crowd as they opened or shut the cargo hatches or rigged the tents over the hatches for the brief periods of rain or for smoko or lunch. I can't remember why they were not working nights but I was thankful for small mercies. Since the ship was tied up not far from the 'Dock Office' we were visited by many superintendents, usually at lunchtime when the bar was open. The Chief Officers cabin and the Pursers cabin seemed to be favourite watering holes for our bevy of interested superintendents. The rest of us got together in the Officers Bar. This was a properly equipped bar with beer on tap or in cans. Spirits on optic, soft drinks and ice machine. It was colourfully decorated with small national flags, company flags and sailing club flags from

Australia, New Zealand and South Africa, a haven at sea and, at times, heaven in New Zealand. But back to the plot. It was later that day that the Captain came onboard and as duty deck officer, I first ran headfirst into the wrath of God. I was 'found' by one of the sailors and told that my presence was required at the gangway. He walked away grinning. I ran into a storm. A short, stocky, greying and very irate person met me at the head of the gangway and flew into a tirade of abuse because the coir welcoming mat that was supposed to be at the top of the gangway was missing. Although in civilian clothes, I knew instinctively who this was and I thought 'oh bugger'! No introduction, no pleasantries, just a lecture on how and why the coir mat should be at the head of the gangway and as duty deck officer, it was my responsibility. It was found, shaken and put back in position. The first person to apologise was the Purser, his men had been loading stores and 'the mat' had been removed for safety reasons. The next person to apologise was the Chief Officer who said that the Third Officer who I had relieved should have told me about 'the mat'. This two foot by three foot , one inch thick coir mat was rapidly gaining a reputation way above its station but a station very obviously supported by the 'Old Man'. I simmered for a while then forgot about the thing, but it was to bite later in the voyage.

And so I was 'introduced' to the Captain and I have to say that our relationship continued much the same throughout my time onboard. Remember way back in the beginning and that 'bloody Yorkshire tartar' well we had another one here except that this one was a southerner.

We sailed for New Zealand via the Panama Canal. A fairly long passage but one which enabled me to get to know my new ship and shipmates. I don't recall anything special about that outward trip other than being very wary when the 'Old Man' was in the vicinity. I enjoyed my 8-12 watch apart from the time the Captain came up to fill in the 'Night Order' book. If there was any conversation it was always very brief and humourless. The Second Officer and I took morning and noon sights, calculated the ships noon position and worked out the days run and the average speed. All this under the 'old mans' watchful and baleful eye. I vowed that when I reached the dizzy height of 'Command', I would be more considerate at these times but, when I did get there, it was all push button and instant readout stuff. Not the same really.

The arrival in Auckland was a much quieter affair than my experiences onboard the passenger ship but at least I was able to really appreciate the approaches to the port. Past Rangitoto, the extinct volcano, and turn to starboard into the harbour. When the ship was tied up and cleared by customs and immigration, the hatches were opened and the discharge began but this was what we were here for and so we started cargo watches. Being New Zealand and this being many years ago, cargo work was a daytime and weekdays only operation. Very civilised! At 5 o'clock the wharfies would pack up and leave and the crew would then close the hatches for the night and secure any derricks. Those crew members lucky enough to be off duty at this time would then race ashore to the pub for the 5 o'clock swill. This was the name given to the period up to pub closing time which was at 6 o'clock. However, if you were in the know and in the right pub, it was possible to get locked in - oh joy - and to enjoy a party.   It was either that or buying a few bottles and moving on to somebody's house or flat. The other alternative and one that I discovered on my first night in port was the shipboard party.   I think the first phone call to the ship was from the Nurses Home wanting a party.   This was a very popular form of onboard entertainment enjoyed by all except the Captain.   The crew had their own bar and parties but it was not uncommon for the two to get a bit mixed up.   It was the Chief Officer's 'duty' to look after the Matron and to keep her happily entertained.   To make sure that she couldn't or even better, that she didn't want, to look at her watch.   I was to enjoy this challenge later in my career!

As the discharge continued and cargo spaces were emptied, these spaces had then to be cleaned and prepared for loading frozen carcases of lamb or mutton for the UK.   The discharge of general cargo and the parties continued at Wellington and then Lyttelton where serious loading commenced. As each compartment was emptied, cleaned, battened and frozen down they had to be surveyed and passed before loading could commence. When all was ready a train would arrive and the wagons would be opened. It was then the ship's Refrigeration Officers turn to inspect each wagon and to check the carcass temperatures. Then the carcasses would be taken from the wagons and put into slings before being lifted onboard where the carcasses would be taken out of the sling and stowed in hold or locker. I earlier mentioned the colourful cargo plans and this is where it started. Each consignment of lamb or mutton had to be shown on the plan with consignment number, port of loading and port of discharge. Some consignments were as small as twenty carcases, some were many thousand but all had to be accurately shown on the cargo plan. They were works of fine art! But back to loading - wagon to sling, sling to ship - we used to consider how much quicker the operation would be if we just picked up the wagons and stowed them onboard. It was only a few years later when some bright spark introduced 'containers' and in doing so, ruined our New Zealand way of life.

Lyttelton is a beautiful South Island port in New Zealand's version of a fjord. It also had one of those notorious seamen's pubs - part of the worldwide chain. The British Hotel was very popular with the crews of all the shipping companies on the meat run. It was a pub where it was easy to get a drink and easy to get into trouble. Once or twice I was sent to get crew members back to the ship for sailing and it was never an easy task.

From Lyttelton we moved on to Timaru under the meat loaders. Again some bright spark had invented these monstrosities in an attempt to speed things up. When functioning properly these devices would throw carcasses at you at quite a rate making the planning part of the operation difficult. The carcasses still had to be stowed by hand but even so, checking the consignment and discharge ports was difficult and at times, hazardous. As I recall there were two of these contraptions in operation at Timaru so hopping from hatch to hatch trying to keep up with things was a feat in itself. But here the coir mat cropped up again. Carcasses flying out of the loader like machinegun bullets - well not quite, but it felt like that - and I was called to the gangway. Here, red in the face and jumping up and down I found the Old Man. Somebody had removed the mat. Probably some New Zealand wharfie who considered it a safety hazard!   Anyway, as duty Deck Officer I got hauled over the coals, again. He went on and on about the bloody thing and it being my responsibility to make sure it was in position.   How you can go on and on about a mat, I can't remember, but he managed it somehow. When I pointed out that while he was going on about the mat I was probably missing many consignments of frozen carcasses thus making the ship's cargo plan a waste of   bloody time, things got even more heated.   The Chief Officer was called to the scene and appraised of my discrepancies, my shortcomings and my blatant insubordination.   The Captain then stormed off. Those in the immediate vicinity who had witnessed the scene, both Kiwi and Brit, thought this was immensely funny.   Me, I eventually found the f-----g mat and put it back in position. I did two voyages on that ship and I cannot ever recall hearing a word of encouragement or humour to anyone pass his lips.   However   -   I survived!

One other time that I witnessed his fury was when the 'Inspection' team found a 'ringbolter' in the crew bar while we were at sea.   A 'ringbolter' was   the name given to any young lady who would 'join' the ship at one port and leave at, not necessarily, the next port.   Strictly forbidden by both ship and shore - it still went on.   On this particular incident the young lady was found seated at the bar drinking and smoking.   Legs crossed, net stockings - get the picture.   When she told the Old Man to *f--k off,*   after he asked what she was doing there, the shit hit the fan. Fortunately I was on watch at the time but it seemed that every off duty officer was called to the scene.   The 'bar steward' who was of a different persuasion and could not therefore be accused of smuggling a moll   onboard for a trip around the coast, was reduced to tears under the barrage. The senior petty officer, the Boatswain who was a very large person, was summoned and apparently stood there like a stranded goldfish as the tirade continued.   By this time I had been relieved, and primed, by the Second Officer and proceeded to the scene of the crime.   I could hear the commotion well before I arrived at the scene. The 'sailors' alleyway which led directly to the Crew Bar was filled with interested crewmembers trying to look innocent but failing miserably.   To me it seemed as though the Captains voice went up one octave when I arrived but maybe that was just my imagination.   Anyway the result of the matter was one 'ringbolter' to be strictly guarded by the Boatswain until arrival at the next port while the rest of us had to search the ship for any other illicit passengers.   I knew that the Boatswain could be relied on to do his job properly because I knew it was his girlfriend.   I also had a feeling that there was more than one 'ringbolter' onboard but we didn't find any.

The next port of call was The Bluff which is about as far south as you could go on South Island without getting your feet wet.   Apart from the cold store and meat works and a few fishing boats there was not much there.   A few houses, the essential 'pie cart' and one pub.   In all of the New Zealand ports that we visited you could always find a pie cart somewhere in the vicinity and if we were fed up with ships food we would delegate somebody to *go up the road* to bring back supplies. This was a very popular pastime with the Engineers who would be released from the Pit for lunch break and instead of changing to eat in the Saloon, would lounge around on deck in the sunshine eating Kiwi hamburgers.   I emphasise the Kiwi hamburgers because I still consider them to be the best in the world.   It was not uncommon to find the ships cook in the line up at the pie cart. Actually, as I recall, the food onboard wasn't atall bad   -   just a bit repetitive.   Mostly you could tell what day of the week it was from the menu.   I say mostly because on the voyage back to the UK we seemed to be fed on mutton alone and since we were virtually sitting on top of thousands of carcasses of the stuff, it made one think. Anyway, back to the Bluff.   It always seemed to me to be a cold, windswept, God forsaken kind of a place but one good place for shipboard parties. We had to be a little careful after the 'ringbolting' affair but we still managed to enjoy ourselves. The ladies mostly came from nearby Invercargill so it was either early to bed in which case a fleet of taxis would have to be called, or early to bunk in which case the taxis could wait for the morning. It all depended upon the Chief Officer and his relationship with the Matron.   And from the Bluff we sailed back to the UK.

I did two round voyages on that ship as Third Officer and by then I had sufficient seatime accrued to go ashore to college before sitting for my Masters Certificate.   For this exercise I chose to go back to Hull.   Too many pubs in South Shields   -   I would just have to resist the parties in Hull.   I got the positive results of the examination just before Christmas so I enjoyed the Festive Season at home and then phoned the company with news of my exam results.   They were a bit miffed at me for not advising them of my exam results immediately but they soon started planning for my next appointment.

It was back to passenger ships for me but this time as Second Officer.   My appointment was to a passenger cargo ship carrying just over 500 passengers and with a crew compliment or about 250.   I joined in London shortly before sailing for South Africa, Australia and New Zealand. No more rubbing knees with the Children's Hostess or Purserette at the Staff Table, now I had a table of my own with which to 'entertain' eight passengers. But I'm jumping ahead here.

After quite a lengthy handover I was left to find my way around my new ship.   I remember being quite impressed with the public rooms and the passenger accommodation. I was also impressed with my own quarters - en suite at last! Again I had a host of new faces to put names and ranks to but there were one or two familiar faces. I don't recall much about the cargo operations or the passenger embarkation day. The glamour of the 'boat train' was missing this time because we were in one of the Royal docks in the Port of London. I don't know how the passengers got to the ship but arrive they did and once onboard we sailed.

After the usual initiation drill for the passengers we settled down for the outward voyage. My first shock was when the Social Hostess asked me to prepare a clock schedule for the whole voyage. She must have registered the shock on my face because she then launched into an explanation of why it was necessary, to enable the pre-planning of all onboard entertainment for the voyage. Not only for the entertainment schedule but also for the printers, the pursers, the passengers - in fact every department had an interest. As Navigating Officer it was up to me to deliver. It took a while but I managed to get it out and printed in time to satisfy all departments and to my amazement we managed to stick to the clock schedule without deviation for the whole voyage. My next shock to the system was my 'table'. I say shock but it was really just a few moments of nervous anticipation. After the Maitre d' introduced me to the passengers at my table we settled down to enjoy our first meal together. Again the passengers were a mix of those emigrating, those going to visit those who had emigrated and those doing it for fun. My lot were a mixture of the latter but all doing it for fun. One of the perks of the job was that I was able to order wine for the table, again under direction from the Maitre d'. I didn't have to pay anything for this pleasure, just sign for it. I do recall being pulled up before the Captain later in the voyage for exceeding my allowance - substantially - but got away with it after being supported by the Chief Officer. He said something about me entertaining a particularly lively table. I did and they were but I had to tow the line after that!

The navigating part of the job I thoroughly enjoyed but I still felt a moment of relief followed by exhilaration when our first port, Las Palmas, appeared exactly when it should have done and exactly where it should have done. The noon calculations were a cause of some pressure but only so that the Noon announcement could be made giving the ships position and the speed and distance over the preceding twenty-four hours. Onboard this ship the announcement was made from the Pursers office so at least, I didn't have that to worry about. The 12-4 watch was a good one. Relatively quiet in the afternoon watch and usually very quiet in the morning watch. Quiet but restrictive as I had to be 'off decks' by 11pm thus missing some of the fun. But not all of it!

But back to the noon announcement of speed, position, days run etc. Passengers could wager on the daily outcome and the winner was awarded a cash prize depending on the number of entrants. Some bright spark complained to the Purser's office that there was collusion between the Bridge and some favoured passengers. Some jealous sod was bent on revenge. This caused an almighty stink and those officers upon whom the calculation of the noon position depended, had their noon sight books confiscated. As Navigating Officer and therefore the principal 'calculator', my book was closely inspected all the way back to day one.   Suspicion was not completely allayed and we 'merry three' were questioned and lectured. I even think one or two passengers were also questioned.   Anyway, our books were returned and things quietened down but we made sure that our 'friends' made no further wagers on our calculations.   Guess, yes - wager, no!   This was not the only time during my passenger ship stints that some passengers, feeling miffed with other passengers tried to drop us officers in the *'sierra, hotel, india, tango'!* Internal politics could be quite interesting at times. Anyway, names cleared   -   wink, wink. Normal service was resumed!   After all these years I cannot recall daily happenings onboard these ships but I do remember that there were plenty of daily happenings, mostly amusing or pleasurable but others, painful.

I did one and a half voyages on this ship and was then transferred to a ship in New Zealand and promoted to Chief Officer.   Upwards and onwards.   She was only three thousand tons but she was a ship of immense character and some comfort and another ship that I remember with great fondness.   The Chief Officer who I relieved had been hospitalized after an accident at sea. He had been on deck checking lashings when the ship took a green one which hammered him against a steel hatch coaming doing him no good atall. However, it got me one more rung up the ladder so!

The trip was from Auckland to Napier, Wellington and Lyttelton. From there she sailed up to Fiji, onwards to Honolulu and then across to Los Angeles. After LA she moved up the coast to San Francisco, Tacoma and Vancouver. And then, via all those ports, back to New Zealand. What a run! From Kiwi northwards the cargo was mainly frozen with a bit of general, and southwards it was mainly but not all, US military cargo. To a young newly promoted officer it was a dream.

We loaded boxed, frozen crayfish tails for the USA in tweendeck lockers. In the holds we loaded frozen lamb for the USA. There were small parcels of general cargo and mail for Fiji and some general cargo for the USA. Southbound we loaded some general cargo from Vancouver and bits and pieces of military cargo in the mainland

US ports.   Occasionally we would put into a small port on Vancouver Island to load newsprint for New Zealand.   Very picturesque if you enjoyed looking at forest and piles of lumber. The fact that the place smelled of damp paper gives you the full picture.   The smell reminded me of the outside Loo at my Aunts farm in Lincolnshire. At Honolulu we loaded chilled pineapples in the tweendeck lockers.   There were the odd times when the usual cargoes were supplemented by more exotic stuff.   A timber wolf from Vancouver to NZ,   two brown bears from Tacoma to NZ and a mountain lion from San Francisco to NZ.   There was one voyage where we loaded a few cars on deck from Vancouver for Auckland and when they opened one of the cars up in NZ, several weeks later, a cat jumped out. This caused a major rumpus in New Zealand because of their exceedingly strict attitude to imported animals or foods.   It resulted in the poor old moggy being shot but not before it managed to scratch a female official.   By way of a return match we loaded 23 wallabies for some port in North America.   They were kept in cages on the Boat Deck and when we got to San Francisco some sympathetic wharfie let the buggers out.   I was watching TV in the lounge with one of the cadets when we felt another presence.   One wallaby sitting between us also watching TV. This caused something of a panic but with   all hands armed with bed sheets we eventually managed to capture the lot of them   -   I think. Great fun.   I remember George the timber wolf with great fondness.   He was friendly-ish and would quite happily play but when he gripped your arm he was not sure when to let go   -   or   when to stop gnawing.   The brown bears were identical and one liked his ears being scratched and the other certainly did not.   You had to be very careful deciding which one did and which one didn't.   He that did not was very fast with his claws!   The mountain lion was fed and viewed from a safe distance.   I sailed with many animals during my time at sea   -   mostly of the furry kind but with a few humans thrown in.   Of the furry kind I have very good memories apart from one polo pony but that tale is for later on in the story.

But back to George the timber wolf.   When we arrived at Auckland the boarding officer was quite shocked when George walked into the ship's office especially when having asked what type of dog was that and was told it was a timber wolf. Put him right off his whisky   -   for a moment.

They were a good crowd on that ship.   The officers were a mixture of Kiwis and Brits and the ratings were Hong Kong Chinese.   Of the Brits, I think the Captain and I were the only ones not residing in New Zealand.   Apart from the Old Man, I was the only Gweilo without a beard and I was urged to follow suit.   So to blend in I sprouted a beard and have it to this day though now it is a different colour.   And there you have it   -   with a ship like that, a trip like that and a crew like that   -   who could fail to enjoy the posting.

I joined the team just in time to enjoy a weekend getting to know my new ship and shipmates as the Kiwi wharfies still did not work at weekends,   One or two had wives visiting and most of the others had girlfriends onboard.   I think it was in the 2nd Officers cabin on the Friday evening that the Flying Angel padre   -   beer in hand   -   issued a weekend absolution for those cohabiting and those wishing to cohabit.   I remember the old padre with affection   -   he was the seaman's champion. He fought our corner many times and, although I didn't see it, I believe he table thumped on our behalf during a TV interview. Anyway - blessed and absolved my fellow shipmates set forth to enjoy the two day break. I was the new boy in the team as they had been together for some months by the time I arrived on the scene but it didn't seem to take long to blend in. I just needed to find a girlfriend to take advantage of the 'heavenly' free pass.

On one voyage we carried the 'Pineapple King' and his wife from New Zealand up to their home in Honlulu. I don't think that they were overly impressed with the accommodation provided - the ship really wasn't intended to carry passengers - but I think they enjoyed the experience. By way of thanks they invited all off duty officers to their luxurious hose on the north shore of Oahu where we enjoyed a splendid pineapple based meal and some exotic pineapple based drinks on a balcony looking out to sea to the great rollers breaking onto the beach below.

Actually, we had some good times in

Honolulu.   Some of the hotels provided excellent entertainment and in those that didn't, we provided our own.   One hotel bar had one wall made of glass giving an underwater view of the outdoor swimming pool.   It was not unknown for one of our team to swim past fully booted and spurred but eventually the management took a dim view of this sport and we were banned.

In Los Angeles there were many places of entertainment which we took advantage of when we managed to get time off.   One such place was called something like 'Apple Annies' and had machine guns and other weapons, hopefully decommissioned, on the walls.   We visited bars in Los Angeles, Long Beach and Hollywood and had some enjoyable moments.   We worked hard and when possible, we played hard.   We were a long way from head office so, perhaps, we played a bit harder than we would have done under closer supervision.

Of course there were more serious moments. One voyage we arrived in San Francisco and tied up astern of a German ship which was on virtually the same service as us.   Her hatches were open but there was no sign of any work being done. Our agent told us that when the San Francisco wharfies had opened one of the hatches they had found what appeared to be a dog turd on one of the hatch bars. It turned out to be a plastic imitation turd but it was enough for the Americans to reject the whole meat cargo. Some joker down under must have put it there and the result was that the ship had to take the whole refrigerated cargo back to New Zealand. The Yanks would accept the Crayfish Tails but when it came to Kiwi lamb carcases they would use any excuse to reject them. The meat inspectors were much feared! We were told that they were strict in an effort to protect the home grown product. The Refrigeration Engineer and I as Chief Officer, sweated a bit! Fortunately, we managed to get by without any great problems in this regard during my time onboard.

One Christmas in San Francisco a fleet of cars turned up at the ship and took all the off-duty officers away to a number of homes to enjoy an American Christmas and a very hearty American Christmas dinner. This all happened because the 2nd Officer and I spent a very pleasurable

Christmas Eve in a bar in the financial district of the city. How we ended up there I can't remember but we were made most welcome and the following day being adopted three to a home, was also very enjoyable. We ate too much, drank too much and were returned to our ship, happy. We even made the local radio news this time. Same city, different time, we managed to get into the Playboy Club and again, had an enjoyable evening. I do remember dancing with one of the Bunnies on a strictly 'look don't touch' order. I also remember that there was plenty to look at! Before we left we had a group photo taken with a bevy of Bunnies just to remember the occasion.

The coastal run from San Francisco up to the Juan de Fuca Strait which separates Vancouver Island from the US mainland was memorable for sealife spotting. What would appear at a distance to be driftwood, would turn out to be a colony of seals on close approach. Just lying on their backs apparently waving at us. Another wonderful sight was our occasional glimpse of the sea otter. Neither otter nor seal seemed perturbed by us as we swept by but we enjoyed watching them. Porpoises and whales were also present on this leg of our voyage just to add to the list. The Strait and then the Sound as we approached Tacoma were enjoyable for the vista of dense pine forest but with green clearings with dazzling white painted lighthouses or dwellings. Small fishing villages dotted both shores along with the occasional logging settlement. As I mentioned earlier, part of our cargo for the southbound voyage was huge rolls of newsprint from one of these logging settlements called Port Alberni destined for New Zealand. One voyage we passed close by a huge WW2 battleship at anchor in the Sound. She was still in commission so according to 'flag etiquette' we dipped our ensign as we passed. The pilotage from Tacoma to Vancouver was equally enjoyable as the ship manoeuvred between islands and through narrow channels. It was all very beautiful on a summers day but it was definitely raw during the winter months. We saw it at its best and at its worst. Viewed from the warm interior of the Bridge it was at times spectacular in the snow but it was a pain having to go out onto the bridge wing to take compass bearings! They told me that the climate in Vancouver was relatively mild because of its position in the Fraser Valley and that may be so but the moment the ship passed under the bridge which joins the city to the North Shore the temperature seemed to plunge. The call at Port Alberni remains in my memory as piles of timber, steam rising from the processing factory and the smell of wet paper. Apart from going ashore to read the draft before sailing we made no forays into the township. Anyway, it was only a short stop as we loaded only a few rolls of newsprint in the lower holds. We did not call at Tacoma southbound so after leaving the Juan de Fuca Strait we headed south towards the sunshine.

Southwards again from Honolulu we would see the Pacific at its very best with magnificent sunrises and sunsets and flat calm seas that nearly blended into the sky on the horizon. The Navigating Officers noon sights were sometimes impossible to take as the horizon would be virtually invisible as sky and sea were the same colour. As Chief Officer I was on the 4 to 8 watch so I was able to enjoy the sun popping up or dipping down during my 'working' hours. The 'green flash' was a phenomenon that I observed many times, envied by some, disbelieved by others. Again in seas like that, if something showed itself above the surface it was visible for miles and we would see huge schools of porpoises heading towards us and they would surround the ship and leap and dive alongside us for miles. They were always a wonderful sight especially standing at the bow and watching them sweep back and forwards across the bow-wave. One voyage we spotted what appeared to be a line which stretched from horizon to horizon moving southwards towards us quite rapidly. When it swept by us it was a single line wave about 30 centimetres high. It had obviously been caused by some large sub-sea disturbance way up to the north of our position so the Radio Officer immediately broadcast a 'tsunami' warning. We heard no more about it so presume it either just petered out or caused no damage when it reached land.

Another thing that could be spotted from great distances were rain clouds and rain showers. These could easily be avoided if painting on deck or aimed for if the decks needed washing down. We did not enjoy the luxury of air conditioning in those days so the showers were sometimes used to cool things down a bit. Observed from a distance we could navigate dryly between showers or get thoroughly wetted by aiming for the dense part of the downfall. The islands that we passed on the run down from Honolulu to Fiji were dots of green in an ocean of blue or, in the case of reefs, dots of disturbed white water in an ocean of blue. The lush foliage and colours of Fiji afters days at sea were a welcome sight and the passage around the island from Suva to Lautoka inside the reef was spectacular. I often thought about the Australian 2nd Officer on my first ship who had the dream of one day owning a schooner and trading copra amongst the Pacific islands. I wonder if he ever got there.

Onwards again to New Zealand and our first port of call at Auckland. Always a welcome sight as we steamed past Rangitoto into the port to be met by office staff, port officials, wives and girlfriends. Being a small ship we didn't stay for long in any of the ports unless we managed to time it for a weekend in any of the New Zealand ports of call. I did several happy voyages on that ship but time came to move on and in the port of Napier I moved on in unusual fashion by falling overboard. Careless you will say but it was

Chinese New Year! Anyway, after a short spell in hospital and a couple of weeks touring in a hire car, I was put onboard another of the companies vessels for the trip back to the UK.

I did a couple of relieving trips around the coast then while the company decided what to do with me. I was on one ship in Liverpool which was about to sign on the crew for the deep sea voyage. The Chief Officer who I was standing in for had particularly asked me to take care when choosing the next crew and to this end I spent a few hours in the Shipping Office in Liverpool interviewing prospective crew members. I managed to select about five but the following day a full crew signed on including those I had rejected the day before. It was out of my hands but I apologised to the regular C/O when he returned from leave. I spoke to him months later and was told that I had been right in trying to weed out the bad ones because they had a troubled voyage which included a lot of crew trouble and even arson.

For my sins I was then appointed Chief Officer of another passenger ship. I tried to protest but I was given the choice of 'take it or leave it' - I took it - reluctantly. Fortunately, it turned out to be just another way of getting me back to New Zealand and I was relieved at Auckland in a direct swap with the C/O of the ship I was about to join. Back to the small ships. This one was the twin to the earlier one but this traded between New Zealand and Japan. I joined her in Gisborne as she continued her Kiwi coastal loading for small ports on the east coast of Honshu and for Muroran and Otaru in Hokkaido.

I have never seen snow as deep as it was in Otaru. You had to walk or slide through narrow paths to shops or pubs with the snow well above head height. In some places it was actually a snow tunnel. Amazing how good a glass of warm Saki tastes on a day like that! The locals were obviously used to this so work onboard, loading and discharging, continued unabated. One particular but not snowy visit, we were having some repairs done on deck and down the engine room and on completion the Captain, the Chief Engineer and I were presented with wonderful wooden carvings of the Hokkaido bear. The Captain's bear had a salmon in it's mouth but the other two were fishless. The next voyage we were told by the repair people that this was to be our final visit to Japan. It came as a bit of a shock and wasn't confirmed until we got back to New Zealand. However, it was not the end of things - we just transferred to the Fiji, Hawaii, USA and Canada run. We had enjoyed the Japan run but switching to the other run was no pain.

One thing I didn't mention about the other ship was that she was a regular for holding shippers parties. The agents in the ports would arrange for shore caterers and then we would entertain those people who put their cargoes in our safe hands. This chore was taken over by us on the replacement vessel. The incident that stands out in my mind was the one where a lady visitor wanted to use the toilet and there being a queue for the one in the lounge, I said she could use the one in my cabin. She emerged drenched. Instead of the flush, she had operated the shower lever and got thoroughly wet. I forgot to tell her that you could s--t, shower and shave without moving position. She was a small ship, but very nice. Explaining to her husband was a little difficult! Then there was the incident in Tacoma where during a small apres shippers party gathering in the Captains cabin, the Old Man shot a hole in the wooden bulkhead while inspecting a visitors hand gun. It had a sobering effect! Again, it didn't last for long and I walked down the gangway in Lyttelton and up the gangway of the ship on the other side of the quay. Again a direct swap.

This ship I was to serve onboard as Chief Officer for nearly two years and although she was an older vessel I remember her with great affection. The Old Man was a character. We had met before and I liked him from day one. Of course we had our ups and downs but overall it was a good partnership. The ship was loading in New Zealand for France and the UK and after completion we set sail for Panama. I have to mention here that the Old Man had his brand new wife with him and this was to be her first voyage and first visit to Europe. She too was a character and fortunately, she was also an ex nurse.

On the long passage to the Panama canal our first casualty was a sailor with suspected appendicitis. He was put in the ship's hospital and with instruction from Gorgas Hospital in Panama, pills and potions from our dispensary and ice packs from the 'freezer control room' we managed to control the condition. I must admit that the thought of putting him under the knife scared me as much as it did him. Our next casualty was one of the stewards. While serving breakfast he complained of abdominal pains but by the time I opened the dispensary at 0900 hrs he was in agony. He was put in the hospital which was now full. Between the Old Man, his wife and I plus the Shipmaster's Medical Guide we had no idea what was wrong so we again got in touch with Gorgas Hospital in Panama. Under their instruction we prodded and probed. Under their instruction we tried to insert a catheter and under their instruction we starting giving him shots of morphine. The Captain's wife and I took turns in sitting with him so he was under watch for 24 hours a day. The hospital had told us there was nothing we could do but watch, hope and apply the morphine as directed by them. We had moved the appendicitis sufferer back to his cabin during all this to avoid distress both ways. Anyway, shortly after I took over being with him he died and we were still several days out from Panama.

Under normal circumstances we would have buried him at sea but on this occasion we were ordered to carry him on for an autopsy in Panama City. We landed him on arrival in Panama along with the appendicitis sufferer who survived the ordeal.

In a situation like that there is not much of humour to add but in this case one little part of the story need a mention. For the days prior to arrival at Panama the body was stowed in in the freezer pipe room and when it came to removing him to be taken ashore much difficulty was encountered getting the now deep frozen corpse around the intricate pipework of the chamber.

The Captain had been standing my Bridge watch during the emergency and now things started to get back to normal. When we docked at Curacao for bunkers, the Old Man decided that the three of us should go ashore for a meal other than mutton and we enjoyed a run into Willemstad. When we arrived in Dunkirk to discharge our cargo of baled wool, I decided that it was my turn to take them ashore one evening for a meal. I investigated and found a good French restaurant and we enjoyed a relaxing meal and drinks. The Maitre d' made some reference to my intake of French fries but hey - I was paying. By this time the Old Man was in mood to carry on and since some enterprising person had slipped a card under my cabin door advertising a pub called 'La Frigate' we decided that this would be our next venue. After a short taxi drive and some peculiar looks from our driver and we were there. The bar was very dimly lit and the soft music was unusual for a pub. By the time I had ordered drinks we new we were in a brothel - I was intrigued, the Old Man was interested and his wife thought it was hilarious! We had a wonderful evening there talking to the girls and the owner and in the end it was the boss who drove us back to the ship. The Old Man and his wife had enjoyed it so much that they invited the owner and his moll onboard for lunch the following day. They duly arrived and the lady was wearing a split up the front dress that had the gangway watch drooling. I think in all my months onboard that ship it was the only time that we had a full complement of Deck and Engineer officers in the saloon!

My following appointment was triggered by

a major shipping accident between two ships on the River Plate. An associate company vessel was tragically lost with all hands - crew, passengers and pilot - after colliding with a tanker. The company decided to replace this ship on the South America run with a ship from the Australia, New Zealand trade. Along with all hands, a mass of chains and other equipment we flew on a charter flight from Luton Airport to join the ship in Bremerhaven. We left Luton a couple of hours late which was fatal as the crew managed to fill tanks in the airport bar. By the time we got to Bremerhaven the crew were drunkenly morose and when we arrived alongside the ship, the departing crew were beating each other up. No bloody wonder the Old Man chose to fly out under his own steam. It took some time to get the departing ratings onboard the recently vacated bus and by the time we managed to bring things under control it was late at night. Oh yes - I forgot to mention that all those previously mentioned 'chains' had to be unloaded from the accompanying truck and then stowed onboard the ship and guess who had to do that. Handovers were left to the morrow. However, it seemed the departing senior officers had miscalculated the number of cabins required for the joining officers so most had to bunk down in the mess room and the hospital. I had a cabin of my own whose main use was as storage for the aluminium beer kegs used in the bars. I managed to work my way through to a single bunk without a mattress and spent the night thinking up ways of retaliating! After profuse apologies and a brief handover, the departing Chief Officer and I parted amicably and as we were all new to the ship we started finding out what we had let ourselves in for. By this time the Captain had boarded having spent a comfortable night in a hotel in Bremen. Our education was about to begin as the Old Man was the only officer familiar with the South American trade.

While all this was going on, the ship continued discharging its cargo from New Zealand. This gave us time to read up on the South American port information which had been in boxes amongst the chains on the charter flight from Luton. I was told at this time that on arrival in London docks we would be berthed next to a regular on our new route and that the Chief Officer on that ship would come onboard to give me a full briefing on what to expect.   We did dock in London and there was a regular South American trader berthed ahead of us but the 'briefing' turned out to be a one liner delivered about five minutes before we let go to commence the voyage.   There follows an unabridged quotation of the 'briefing'. 'Don't fuck up the perks'.

But back to the cargo operations in London. Amongst cases and cases of general cargo, we loaded more cases of whisky than I had carried in all my previous voyages.   The lockers were full of the stuff and the overflow had to be in open stow in the ship's holds.   Now I had previous experience of loading this stuff in London and knew that it was going to be something of a challenge stopping the wharfies filling their boots so to speak.   I set about the task.   Or rather I placed Deck Cadets in strategic areas to set about the task.   Even the Superintendents said I was on to a loser   but I had to make some effort.   We lost a lot of whisky but the Cargo Superintendents seemed happy with the final tally.

Another thing that surprised me was when loading ship's stores.   Of course there was the usual amount of beer, spirits and cigarettes for crew consumption but along with this was a large amount of perfume, ladies make-up and a few more personal items.   A separate order of whisky, brandy, gin and cigarettes was also loaded at this time.   I asked the Purser who was in close attendance throughout the loading of these items what it was all about as the whole batch was to be stowed separately in the Pursers lockup.   I forgot to mention that he was a man of the South American trade.   We sat down in his cabin and had a pre dinner gin and tonic and he put me straight as to some of the quirks of the run. Apparently, these 'special' items were for the sweetening of port authorities, agents and pilots. When we were at sea and again over a gin and tonic but a lunch time one this time,   he put me straight over the '*don't fuck up the perks*' episode. Apparently the ship had to order timber dunnage for flooring out the holds and lockers in Argentina prior to loading cases of frozen meat.   This was normally done in Santos,   Brazil on the southbound leg of the voyage.   I would be approached by a number of timber merchants who would give me a price for the quantity of timber which I had to calculate, would be required for the reefer cargo. Apparently there was a lot of guess work involved in this calculation but the big thing was not to under order. During negotiations with said merchants individually, they would offer me 'perks' in the way of a cash bonus. The darker side of the South American trade was discussed at great length and over many gin and tonics on the southward voyage.

Apart from having to order the timber and then get the ship's carpenter to batten out the holds or lockers as required, pre cargo plans had to be submitted at irregular intervals. I say irregular because the cargo bookings were frequently changing and as they went up or down, I was required to do another plan. These were quite large sheets of paper and I went through a lot of them. Big changes could amount to two or three new plans a day, smaller amounts were a little less urgent. But from planning to preparation. As each compartment was emptied of general cargo, the deck crew would go in and clean up the space. They would be followed by Chippy who would lay and secure the timber which would support the cartons of frozen meat and allow air circulation around the cargo. When he had finished and I had inspected the space we would then 'bomb' the space to kill off any bugs or spores. By 'bomb' I mean newspaper wrapped potash dropped into a bucket half full of formaldehyde. Chippy and I would plan our retreat carefully. Drop the potash, run for the ladder or door. First one up or out slam the door or drop the plug as soon as the second person emerged. When 'bombing' a large space such as a lower hold, three or four bombs were necessary and because the chemical reaction was instantaneous our retreat had to be rapid. Chippy and I would then retreat for a beer - any excuse! After that Chippy would seal around the door with paper and paste and put the date and time of the operation so that the cargo surveyor could see exactly when it was done. He and I would be the next ones into the space so it was rather important to get it right. The space would then be frozen down to the desired temperature which as I recall was -18 degrees centigrade for frozen cargo and something like -1 to -2 degrees centigrade for the carriage of chilled cargoes. When a cargo space was deemed ready for survey, Chippy would open the space and then the surveyor, the reefer engineer and I would enter. If the surveyor was satisfied we could start loading immediately.   If he didn't -   then there would be hell to pay as usually there would be a line of reefer trucks waiting in anticipation.   I think it only happened once on my watch and I think it was something simple such as sawdust.   We did have difficult moments when a space prepared for frozen cargo suddenly had to be surveyed for a chilled cargo.   I must say here that the chilled cargo was the most valuable and carried a much higher freight charge than the frozen.   It was also the most difficult because if the temperature dipped by more than half a degree it would be deemed to be frozen and the freight rate would be reduced. Also frozen meat was more valuable freight wise than frozen concentrated orange juice. The most valuable cargo carried in those chilled chambers was horse meat.   Large hanging sides of horse meat destined for discharge in Rotterdam to be then distributed around the horse eating nations of Europe.   Chilled hanging donkey meat again for discharge in Rotterdam for onward transportation to either Denmark or Italy.   I have enjoyed horse meat and I still enjoy salami.

One voyage we carried a small consignment ginger root from Buenos Aires to London and as all spaces were fully booked I chose to put it in an empty Forecastle storeroom.   I read up about the stuff in the bible of cargo stowage   -   Thomas's Stowage   -   and soon realised that the author didn't know much about this stuff either.   When we left Argentina the ginger root was as you would find it in your local supermarket but when we arrived in London and the space was opened up, you had to beat your way through the foliage.   I was told it was a freight loss of £10,000   - ouch!   The company tried again   some voyages later and on a different ship but this time I made sure that the consignment was stowed in an accessible space with space not only for ventilation but also for inspection   -   daily by me.   This time it was successful and during the homeward passage, if I saw any sign of green, I removed it. It was a large consignment and all concerned were satisfied and I was much relieved.

I did three voyages on this ship learning the ropes and actively not 'fucking up the perks' and then transferred back to the New Zealand run.   I think I've been through most of the ins and outs of this trade so the interesting bits of this voyage were in Europe.   We loaded a full cargo of frozen lamb and mutton for Alexandria, Famagusta, Piraeus and Genoa. The Alexandria cargo we discharged at Port Said. We then bypassed Famagusta and went to Piraeus. Now this change of port rotation created a problem in one cargo space because the Cyprus meat was stowed on top of the Greek meat. This would mean having to dig down through the Cyprus cargo and finding some temporary frozen facility ashore for the displaced cargo. This was deemed impossible so at an urgent meeting onboard, I suggested that minimal amount of moving could be achieved by by digging down at the hatch entrance ladder to the space below where the Piraeus cargo was stowed. It also meant that the Cyprus cargo being moved could be re stowed onboard as it was such a small amount. To my amazement this idea was accepted and the whole of the Greek cargo was passed - carcase by carcase - up the hatch ladder. I even received a bit of money by way of reward for thinking of a way around the problem. This really led to a bigger problem - for us. As the cargo was for the Greek military and because they had no appreciable reefer storage facilities ashore - they used us for storage and only took what they wanted each day. This meant a lengthy stay in Piraeus and a lot of angry words between London and Athens.   During one period of discharge and during a lunch break things got even worse.   The Captain and I were enjoying a pre luncheon drink when the ship shuddered and there was a loud bang.   We moved rapidly.   Out on deck we met the Boatswain heading rapidly in the opposite direction. Anyway -   he took us to No.2 Hatch and we peered over the hatch coaming into the empty space below.   There we could see the cause of the 'bang'.   The thick tweendeck coaming had fractured and the deck plating was split nearly to the ships hull plating.   I could hear the superintendents boarding the plane in London. They arrived within hours and along with surveyors, engineers and agents -   stared gloomily at the damage.   The Piraeus sunshine and an outside temperature of +40 centigrade and the lower tweendeck temperature of around -18 centigrade had caused the 'temperature' fracture. It did speed up cargo operations somewhat and the space below the fracture was soon emptied.   After that, the fracture was patched up pending a major repair and we sailed for Famagusta.

For some days prior to this the Refrigeration Officer had been voicing some concern about frozen space where the temperature was showing some abnormalities.   When the space was opened up for discharge at Famagusta a block consignment was found to be showing signs of decay.   The whole consignment was immediately condemned and questions were asked. Fortunately the rest of the cargo in the space was alright.   The inquiry led to the conclusion of 'inherent vice'.   Something in that particular shipment had caused the meat to heat up. Fortunately, the reefer engineer had kept notes during the loading and had tried to reject the consignment before it was loaded.   He was overruled by 'someone' ashore but the ship was cleared of any responsibility.

We were all relieved at Genoa and from there I was transferred to a ship to have my first experience with containers.   Box boats were rapidly taking over and I opted to try 'stacking bricks'   on a small ro-ro containership trading between the UK and Norway.   She was on a weekly run between Newcastle, Felixstowe, Stavanger,   Haugesund,   Bergen,   Mongstad,

Alesund and Trondheim. A bit of a work up but a great experience. I walked up the stern ramp in North Shields just as a container of glass was prematurely released from the ship's crane, letting it plunge down the hatch guides until it reached the lower deck level when it stopped with a horrible crash. I thought briefly about turning around and retreating but I didn't. The mess cleared up, I was shown up the spiral stairs to the accommodation. She was a small ship with a small crew and therefore small accommodation. The wagons carrying the containers to be loaded drove up the stern ramp and through a tunnel above which was the accommodation and the Bridge. The 'legs' of the accommodation contained the entrance stairs, the engine room access and on one side the funnel and on the other, the vent for the generator. She was interesting.

This was by far the smallest ship that I had served on up to this time and on arrival at Felixstowe I realised really how small she was when we berthed in close proximity to the big boys. I am going back many years and these monsters appeared to be just that, however, later on I was to serve on even bigger 'box boats'. The huge cranes, the straddle carriers and endless stacks of multicoloured containers were all new to me at this time.   I had seen these ships in the distance in New Zealand and had passed them or rather, been passed by them, at sea but close up, they were quite something and I looked forward to moving up the scale.

The run across the North Sea to Stavanger was punctuated by passing the huge oil platforms. Visible for many miles with their waste gas burning like a vast torch above them.   We saw oil rigs, exploration rigs, accommodation platforms and a host of guard vessels and oil support vessels. We passed within a reasonable distance from these installations   and   listened   and   sometimes answered the VHF warning calls instructing us to 'keep clear'.   I find the North Sea a grey, monotonous stretch of water so the visual contact and occasional radio contact served to break it up a bit.   At least we were going somewhere whilst they were stuck out there in all weathers.   Some of those guards boats were very small and to be stuck out there for days on end in everything that the North Sea could throw at you, did not appeal!

Because of the size of the ship our chance at exploration in the Norwegian ports of call was severely restricted. She only carried approximately one hundred containers and since the ship's crane was used in most ports for loading and discharging and as it was six hours on and six hours off driving it between myself and the 2nd Officer, our runs ashore were virtually nil. The crane would lift the container and then a truck would reverse up the stern ramp and the container would be 'gently' lowered into position. Our scheduled arrival at Haugesund was midnight local time and apart from the ramp adjustor we saw no one. At this port we drove our own 'Ottawa' tractor and put the containers onto a low loading trailer called MAFI's. We then drove these into a side street in Haugesund and left them behind. Any containers to be loaded were already sitting there on MAFI's waiting for us to drive them onboard to be stowed. The ramp adjustor adjusted his ramp, we lifted ours, a quick wave and off on our way again. Bergen was a very attractive place seen through the rain but as said earlier, apart from arriving and departing, we saw little of the place. The next port of call, and I use the word port, carefully, was Mongstad, This was a large lump of rock on which a number of people were employed building an oil storage installation. Here we delivered the odd container but mostly it was huge earth moving equipment, cranes and other types of machinery used in the construction business. Normally we would drop one anchor and then back up to the quay and secure with a couple of ropes from each quarter. This was secure enough to drive off the voyage consignment. One voyage we had just one large truck to discharge and with everything fired up, we just backed in and lowered the ramp. Truck off, ramp up and off again. That particular call lasted less than five minutes and still stands in my record as the shortest call ever! The men on the rock were a bit disgruntled that time because on any normal visit we would sell them whisky at UK prices. I think the island was supposed to be dry but even if not, Norwegian prices for whisky were monstrous.

Onward again to Alesund where our berth was in the town bus station. We would back into position watched by people waiting for their buses and before our stern ramp could be lowered I would have to wave at them to move aside. We were only a small ship but that ramp with its heavy steel fingers could do a lot of damage. And talking about damage - on one call at Alesund we were involved in a collision between us and a removal van. In manoeuvring into position we managed to lift up the rear of the van and then drop it. The van driver was a bit shaken but there was no damage to his vehicle. The Old Man in reporting the incident asked whether he would lose his Masters Certificate of his 'no claims bonus'. It was an interesting stopover and as there were a few shops surrounding the bus station we were able to get supplies. Again, it was up to us to discharge the containers and we had the occasional near gridlock with buses and MAFI's.

After Alesund we moved onwards again to our final destination in Norway - Trondheim where we tied up not far from the massive submarine pens left over from World War 2. Trondheim always seemed to be a bigger, more bustling town than the others further south. On some of our voyages we would load ancient, old or broken down tractors on deck surrounded by a protective wall of containers. What they did with them after discharge in Norway I do not know but we carried a lot of them.

From there we sailed back across the North Sea to the Tyne. On one particular voyage we had loaded a 40 foot container of frozen seafood at Stavanger for discharge at North Shields. When we berthed at North Shields there was a line of refrigerated vans and trucks waiting to unstuff this container after discharge but when opened it up on the quay it was found to be empty! We completed our discharge and went straight back to Stavanger to pick up the full container. There were shouts, yells and screams but we only loaded what we were told to load.

The passage across the North Sea from Trondheim to the Tyne was unbroken by points of interest such as oil installations but it was not without incident. One voyage during my dawn watch, I watched with some trepidation as a surfaced submarine seemed to home in on us, veering away at the last moment. I could see men on the Conning Tower looking at us through binoculars so they knew what they were about but I put our ship into hand steering just in case evasive action had to be taken. I was not aware that we were at war with the Soviet Union so it was unlikely that they would do anything drastic to us. In the end they approached us from astern and then passed close by to starboard with a few hands on deck and a few on the conning tower all waving cheerily. Great fun, in reflection.

The coastal run inside the islands off the Norwegian mainland and the run up the fjords was both beautiful and spectacular. After the grey drabness of the North Sea, the clear calm waters, the sheer rock faces the waterfalls and the forests stretching upwards towards snow capped mountains was something to see and enjoy. The small colourful towns, the little wooden hamlets and the brilliant white lighthouses set against forest or rock made these passages some of the most pleasant that I can remember. By law we had to carry a Norwegian Government pilot and the company also put onboard a privately hired pilot so, although the position of the ship had to be charted at regular intervals and at course changes, we had plenty of time to admire the scenery. Plus with two pilots we had a running commentary on what we were seeing, what we were about to see and when to have camera or binoculars ready. The ports we called at were nice, what we saw of them, but the star of the voyage was the Norwegian coastal and fjord scenery! We waved to minute figures way above us perched on top of sheer rock faces. We passed fishing villages where the smell of the catch wafted out to us as we sailed by. I joined the ship in August and each voyage we could see the difference as the snow line moved slowly down from the high peaks. Manoeuvring at night in the close confines of channels and fjords watching the navigation lights on rocks and headlands and nasty things just below the surface of the waters was an interesting experience and I well remember the multiple light sectors on some of the lights. Sectors of green, white and red. The general idea was to keep well out of the red sectors. Unfortunately, the voyage after I left, she hit a rock when the Bridge party failed to register one of these red sectors. The ship was badly damaged but after a spell in dry-dock she was back in service.

My next appointment was to another container ship, a bit bigger than the last one. Upwards and onwards! However, one would have thought otherwise when I joined her at the Victoria Deep Water Terminal on the Thames close by the Blackwall Tunnel. The gate security guard pointed me in the direction of the ship but I could see nothing until I got to the edge of the quay and there she was, below me. It is the only time that I have joined a ship by climbing down a ladder onto the Bridge wing. Even at high tide, boarding was still via a ladder but this time to the main deck. I have already mentioned the security guard on the gate but that was just a start - there were guards everywhere. The ship was on charter to ZIM Line of Israel and was loading containers for Israel. It was also the time of one of their brief but eventually victorious disputes that Israel enjoyed with her Arab neighbours. We sailed into a storm - but not the Arab/Israeli storm. Our passage across the Bay of Biscay was turbulent to say the least. I have sailed across 'the Bay' in much worse weather conditions but on much larger ships but in the confused swell and high seas of this particular passage, being a small ship we took a bit of a hammering. At one time the ship fell into a trough and the oncoming swell crashed down on the foredeck. We knew we had suffered some damage but it was impossible to get forward to have a look because of the weather. Later, in the relatively calm waters off the Spanish coast we were able to make our way forward to survey the scene.   The forward two tiers of containers were smashed open and the contents were scattered along the main deck.   Now rightly or wrongly, I was under the impression that, though sympathetic, Britain was not exporting arms to Israel.   The scene that greeted us after the storm was of crushed and open containers and many long wooden boxes with rope handles.   All the boxes had survived the impact so we were unable to inspect their contents but to me they looked very much like boxes containing guns. Here, I hasten to add, that I am not an expert in such things but at the time it did add something to the atmosphere onboard. There was no further excitement on the outward passage until we approached Israel   when a gunboat took position off our quarter and escorted us into Ashdod.   It picked us up someway out and then quietly and efficiently herded towards our destination.   On the final approach to the port entrance we were told to wait for the signal that the boom defence had been opened and then we were to enter at speed.   As we passed through the entrance two inflatables raced past us to port and starboard dropping some sort of explosives into the sea each side of us.   Boom, boom, boom and we were in and the boom defence was closing behind us.   All through our stay these inflatables cruised around the port dropping these anti personnel devices. Slightly disturbing at night but we soon got used to it.   Even noisier were the aircraft from a nearby military airfield   which took off in groups and roared, seemingly, at just above mast height, over the ship.   They left with wings dripping with missiles and then returned a short time later without the appendages.   The theatre of war seemed to be very small.   The workers onboard were prisoners and the foremen and women were armed to the teeth.   It was all very interesting. When we sailed from Ashdod the operation was the same.   Boom open, boom, boom, boom and full ahead.   On the voyage up to Haifa we reported an unidentified radar echo off our port quarter but we were later told that we had reported our submarine escort. Oops!   Same operation entering Haifa.   Boom, boom, boom and in we went.   At Haifa I was sent to the port hospital for a due re-vaccination and in a car with blue covered headlights is was escorted through the blacked out port.   What a greeting I received when I got there. The Doctor was originally from my home town and wanted to know how things were back there. I have to say it was the most pleasant and amusing vaccination that I have ever received.

Apart from discharging whatever, we started loading chilled containers full of Jaffa oranges and the shipper placed two or three cases of these oranges in our accommodation for us to enjoy on the voyage homewards. I don't think we were in any danger at any time but we were treated very well by those Israelis that we met. Shore leave was not allowed but this was understandable and anyway, small ship and not much time in port.

When the time came to depart from Haifa and to leave Israeli waters we were instructed that we would proceed in convoy with escorts towards Cyprus. After that we would be instructed on what passage we should take up to the Strait of Gibraltar. Three ships left Haifa in that convoy with one Israeli gunboat as escort. When we reached the point where were instructed to scatter, one ship headed for the Adriatic and we and a small West German container ship headed westwards towards the Strait. We were ordered by NATO to go north of Crete while the German ship went to the south of the island. We were told not to communicate with any other vessel and certainly not to say where we had been. Most of us found this highly amusing as we were two high on deck with containers clearly marked ZIM Line. Each day until we passed safely through the Strait of Gibraltar a NATO aircraft would fly past at mast height to make sure that we were alright. All very exciting! After that the remaining part of the voyage back to London was tame. Even the Bay of Biscay had calmed down and allowed us across with minimal rock and roll. After that it was a change of ship and back to the New Zealand run.

I joined my next ship in Liverpool just before Christmas - never a good idea. She was scheduled to sail for Auckland just a couple of days before Christmas with a 'pool crew' and at that time of year it usually meant every desperado who couldn't get a job elsewhere. The Petty Officers, the Boatswain, the Carpenter and the Cook were all company men but the rest. The 'scrapings of the barrel' as it was often referred to. It was shortly after departure that we found out that the ship was to be handed over to the Kiwis when we got to Auckland and knowing this did nothing for the atmosphere onboard. However, after a rather unpleasant voyage out we finally arrived in New Zealand and handed her over to her new company. Myself and one or two others were transferred to other ships around New Zealand and the rest were flown home. I joined my latest vessel as Extra Chief Officer just a few days before she sailed for the UK. The 'Extra' bit is not to be recommended as I was neither here nor there. Just another watch keeper really but the passage home was soon over and I was back to the minute container ship previously enjoyed on the Norway run.

Now, patched up and repaired, she had transferred to the Caribbean where, now with a crew of Barbadians and seemingly lockers full of Tabasco, she was employed on the run from New Orleans to Puerto Cortes in Honduras, Puerto Barrios in Guatemala, Kingston, Jamaica and then back up to New Orleans.

I joined in New Orleans at a berth out on the Industrial Canal well away from the tourist or cultural part of the city. She was berthed amongst light industry and a mixture of bars and fast food outlets virtually under the bridge that carried the Chef Menteur Highway into the city. The passage down or up the Industrial Canal was nothing to write home about as it passed through industry, flatland, scrub and swamp and finally out into the Gulf of Mexico. The flatland, scrub and swamp seemed to be infested with large, biting insects who were determined to attack our ship or at least, the warm blooded operators thereon. Somewhere along the canal we passed the battle ground made famous by the song that included the line 'we fired our guns and the English kept a coming'. Obviously the American war of Independence but that's all I can remember about it. It was not picturesque and it was not pleasant and it was very hot!

The voyage southwards to Puerto Cortes was uninspiring. After clearing the oil platforms and the run southwards across the Gulf there was just a distant hazy glimpse of Mexico as we passed through the Yucatan Strait which separates Mexico and Cuba. Onwards passing Cozumel Island and then keeping well clear of the reefs off Belize until the final approach to Puerto Cortes. On arrival the pilot/harbourmaster would board us and take us to our anchorage or berth.   I remember my first visit and first impression and that impression did not improve over the next few visits.   There were a few white houses, a bit of industry, one bar/brothel and a rail head.   There was a semi decent restaurant but it was a taxi drive out of town.   It was very hot and very humid!

We discharged our containers onto a convoy of very colourful but very rickety trucks.   Each one owner driven by large, swarthy, dark browed and sweaty individuals reminding me of old pirate films. Only one or two were designed to carry containers while with the majority, the container just balanced on the back.   Some with a large overhang.   The pilot/harbourmaster who just happened to be the ship's agent, was in attendance throughout and showed no concern as to the plight of our cargo.   While watching a container being lowered onto one of these sagging trucks I spoke to him about this but he said that this was the way of things in Honduras and that apart from the odd accident, they usually managed to get by. He was a jovial Dutchman who seemed to be involved in all matters regarding ships, cargoes, crews and wharfies and the purchase of stores, spares or provisions. Engine spares had to come from Germany via Tegucigalpa, the capital of Honduras and it was necessary to oil the wheels of government to expedite the delivery of same. Our Dutch friend saw to these matters.

The short passage from Puerto Cortes to Puerto Barrios was in a narrow-ish channel between the mainland and a line of reefs. On a calm, clear daylight passage it was quite something looking at the line of broken, boiling water that marked the reef line. In the dark or in bad weather it was not so pleasant and great care had to be taken. Head in radar and a keen lookout on such occasions. Once round the corner and into the Bahia Amatique the pilot would board and take us to our berth. Apart from one voyage which I will talk about later, we never seemed to meet up with any other sea going ships. Fishing boats, government gunboats and the occasional coaster were our only companions in this area. Puerto Barrios was much the same as Puerto Cortes but with a bit more lush vegetation and possibly, even a bit steamier. Again, apart from the local bar/brothel and a few white houses there was nothing to write home about.   Perhaps a bit more industry and the odd oil storage tank.

From there, the passage to Kingston, Jamaica was a very pleasant break.   A passage to enjoy the calm blue sea and a bit of a breeze. Fresh air at last.   Apart from bad weather or the Hurricane season, this breeze was mainly the wind of passage but after the close, steamy confine of Puerto Cortes and Puerto Barrios it was pure luxury and we used all manner of means of directing that breeze into our cabins.   Apart from the former pirate islands of Utila and Los Fuertes to the north and mainland Honduras to the south, once clear of them it was a clear passage to Kingston.   We would enter via the Eastern Channel and pick up the pilot off Port Royal. These names, Port Royal, Spanish Town still conjure up pictures of pirate ships and swashbuckling seafarers.   In our white shirts and shorts we definitely did not fit into this scenic vision.   Nor did we go ashore and revel in rum soaked premises full of loose women.   I have been to Kingston quite a few times but apart from getting ashore to read the draught, I have seen nothing beyond the dock gate.   The company regularly employed a local engineering firm as our 'Mr Fixit' and he would regularly offer to take us ashore for a meal but it never happened. Either he was too busy or our time was too short. However, he did supply us with fresh fish, vegetable and fruit each time. He was a very jovial, hard working Jamaican and he must have done quite well because his son was at a public boarding school back in England.

From Kingston it was back up to New Orleans passing close by the Cayman Islands which, apart from the buildings, appeared to be little more than sand bars. Up through the Yucatan Strait but this time close into Cap San Antonio on the western most tip of Cuba and across the Gulf of Mexico to the mouth of the Mississippi where we would pick up the pilot for our passage up the Industrial Canal to our berth in New Orleans. And that was our round trip on a ten day schedule. Admittedly, this schedule was only loosely followed but it was there as guidance. It was much later on in my career where the god 'Schedule' was to become an angry god.

It was on the second voyage that thing

started to deteriorate. I was doing my six hour stint in the crane in Puerto Cortes when I noticed that cargo operations had come to a halt. There were often breaks in the proceedings as we waited for trucks but this time I could see a line of them waiting to drive up the stern ramp and offload their containers. Eventually I decided to climb down from my lofty perch and to go and investigate. I met with a lot of waving arms and loud voices on the ramp and found the Captain refusing to let the lorries onboard. When I asked him why, he didn't appear to have an answer so when I challenged him, he just walked off and went to his cabin. We carried on loading and then sailed onwards. Unfortunately, this became a regular happening but we couldn't find out why he was doing this. Things continued going down hill and during the following voyage I seriously thought of releaving him of his command. Finally, he totally lost the plot going up the Industrial Canal so in the end I didn't have to do anything because the US pilot reported him and the charterers and the ships agent had him removed in New Orleans. He was removed under medical grounds and was eventually repatriated back to the UK. Shortly after he left I had a meeting with the charterer and the agent in the Captains cabin and when the agent said 'can you take her to sea boy'   I jumped at the chance.   My first command was to be only a temporary appointment but I thoroughly enjoyed the experience.   It was a shame that it had to be achieved this way but it was an experience that I would not have missed.

In Puerto Cortes we had some serious crane problems and the New Zealand Chief Engineer spent many hours in the close confines of the crane machinery space.   I was standing by this leg of the crane when his head appeared out of the manhole and he was physically sick onto the deck. In the end we had to wait for spare parts to be urgently air lifted from Germany.   These bits were dispatched rapidly and our Dutch friend 'oiled' the necessary wheels in Honduras to get them cleared and delivered to Puerto Cortes.   It took two days for the parts to arrive but long enough for the Chief Engineer to have a recovery break.   On one evening I took him ashore to the restaurant for a meal and drinks.   At the next table was our Dutch friend with some of the local dignitaries who remarked with pleasure, how good it was to see that some of us (seamen) visited places of repute other than the Bremerhaven Bar which was the local brothel. We ended up there for a nightcap anyway and finished off a very pleasant evening. When the bits arrived, the Chief Engineer was back up to speed again and the crane was soon back in operation.

We were now well behind schedule so when we approached Kingston I decided to take the Western Channel to save a few hours. It is a bit tricky winding between islets, reefs and with some shallow places. We got through alright and saved a few hours but both pilot and agent tut tutted and recommended that I didn't try it again. My brief command ended here as the new Captain was waiting on the wharf.

The following voyage was something of a trial for the new Captain as we ran into Hurricane Fifi between Puerto Barrios and Puerto Cortes. We were tracking the storms approach while alongside in Puerto Barrios and in the end we were ordered to sea by the Harbourmaster. The hurricane hit Honduras while we were virtually hove to between the coast and the reefs to the north. I remember the peculiar colour of the sky, the torrential rain and a very nasty, confused sea. Later, as we approached Puerto Cortes we saw the wreckage of timber buildings well out to sea. We were ordered to make our own way into the bay at Puerto Cortes and because we appeared to have the only working radio communication centre in the area we were to be used to relay messages and appeals to the outside world. We were empty having abandoned cargo operations in the previous port so the main deck was a large, open, flat area which was used as a morgue for a couple of days with bodies lined up on deck. Amongst these bodies was that of a cat which after a few hours lying out there, suddenly came back to life. It stayed with us for a few ports but then 'jumped ship'. Our position as centre of operations was over when two much larger container ships arrived to relieve us. From there we were ordered directly back to New Orleans to load a relief cargo. We loaded containers full of fresh water, food and medical supplies. Local expatriate Hondurans filled what little space we had in our accommodation with parcels for their families back home. From there we retraced our steps back to Puerto Cortes. Things appeared to be much better on our return and we were able to ascertain that at the height of the storm the waters were tit height when standing on the bar at the Bremerhaven. Puerto Cortes got off relatively lightly but the death toll for the whole of Honduras was very large. We rejoined our scheduled port rotation after that.

Earlier I briefly mentioned the food onboard this ship and made reference to the Tabasco store. Our Barbadian cook and crew were very fond of spicy food and by the time I left, my taste buds were numbed for months. Whatever we had, be it fish or meat, it was liberally doused in Tabasco. Now, I do enjoy spicy food and I do like Tabasco and I did enjoy the meals onboard this ship but it did take a long time for me to properly regain my sense of taste. But, it was back to the UK for me and I left the ship in New Orleans for the flight back to London. My Caribbean adventure was over for now and I went home with my seriously impaired taste buds.

My next appointment was to the sister ship of the last one but this one was trading in the Eastern Mediterranean and the Red Sea. I flew out to Ravenna on the Adriatic coast of Italy to join and spent an uncomfortable night in a 'no star' hotel waiting for the ship to berth. It was that evening that put me off Italian pubs. On one side was a bloke eating ice-cream and on the other, a bloke eating cake and if you made any noise you were hissed at by the locals watching TV. Anyway, that experience was short lasting and I joined the ship the following morning. She was on charter to an Italian company and was full of their brightly painted yellow containers. The handover was brief as the ships were identical. Only the places on the voyage were different and I would find out about these during the voyage. However, my first job was to escort about half a dozen crew members to Rimini for vaccinations - me included. It was an enjoyable ride down the coast road to Rimini which, to my view, appeared to be much superior to Ravenna. We arrived at the medical centre where I made sure that I was first in the queue. I was not totally trusting the medical team and no second hand needles for me. Back to the ship and almost immediately back up the crane for my six hour driving stint. The loading and discharging procedure was much more efficient than my Caribbean experience so our port time was not very long. A representative of the charterer was on hand throughout and this bloke wielded some power so there were no disputes or delays.   So off we went.

The port rotation was Ravenna, Piraeus, Beirut, Port Said, Jeddah and then back up to Ravenna.   This was my first run through the Corinth Canal and I thoroughly enjoyed the experience.   I enjoyed the passage through the Gulf of Patrai, through the Gulf of Corinth and finally the Canal.   The sheer sides of the canal and the few bridges across it were quite something to see.   We were only a small ship but there wasn't a great deal of space on each side so we steered 'carefully'.   Little did I realise that later on I would get a much closer look at these canal sides!   From the Corinth Canal to Piraeus was only a short passage where we backed up to a dust ramp in the middle of a dusty, rock strewn field. The efficiency of the operation here was somewhat less than at the last port and certainly a lot grimier. The container trucks arrived in a cloud of dust which gently settled over our ship. It was very hot but to keep the accommodation clean, we had to batten everything down.   Away in the distance I could see the buildings of the town and I knew that there were some excellent bars and restaurants around the marina but too far and too little time.

Onwards to Beirut. This was to be a first time for me but I had seen many pictures of the place on TV and in newspapers as it was in the middle of a civil war. In the following months we came to judge the state of play at Beirut by which floor of the Holiday Inn was on fire. The entry to the port was a narrow channel between two finger piers which then opened into quite a large port area. Our berth at the ramp was just inside the finger piers and well away from the port buildings and the main gate. The latter meant little to us as shore leave was not allowed because of the troubles. To me it was much like any Arab port and if you wandered too close to the stern ramp you would be instantly accosted by individuals trying to sell you, watches or cameras etc. The shore security would not allow them onboard but they were a persistent bunch and would remain 'in waiting' throughout the daylight hours. When the bullets started flying they would disappear rapidly! It was mainly at night when we really got some idea of what was going on ashore. We could stand on the Bridge wing watching tracer bullets arching 'gracefully' over the town, or watch the glowing fires as buildings ashore went up in smoke.   When spent bullets started landing on deck we would retreat to the safer internal parts of the ship.   The noise of battle and the howling of sirens was constant throughout the hours of darkness.   On occasional nights things would be relatively quiet but then things would flare up again and smoke would pour out of another level of the Holiday Inn.

As I have said, we were not allowed ashore but we were allowed to walk around the port area during daytime.   One afternoon when cargo work had ceased for some reason, the Captain and I went for a walk along one of the finger piers out towards the Mediterranean.   Standing at the end of the pier you could look out to sea or turn and look towards the town and the high rise buildings overlooking the port.   This particular afternoon there was a small Soviet freighter actually berthed on the finger pier and some of the crew were enjoying kicking a football around on the pier itself.   We stopped to watch and we only realised things were going badly wrong when with shouts and yells the Russians ran for their gangway.

When we heard the 'cracks' and saw the spurts of concrete dust we realised that we were under fire and we rapidly fled the scene. The Old Man was in uniform while I was in overalls so he kept trying to duck behind me as we raced back to our ship. Olympic records may well have been broken on that short run. Incidentally, when the last Russian got onto the gangway it was immediately hoisted so there was no refuge there. Brotherhood of the sea went out of the window that afternoon. Anyway, we raced up the stern ramp and into the accommodation to safety. Shore security had also taken cover onboard and they told us that we were being shot at from one of the high rise buildings. We didn't stray far from home base after that. Each morning we would have a tally of the bullets which landed on deck and as I remember, our record 'catch' was around fifty.

From there it was only a short but refreshing run to Port Said and the Suez Canal. Here security was a little difficult because the bumboat men could virtually step down from their craft onto our main deck. Fully loaded we did not have much freeboard so they could get onboard anywhere and with a small crew, we had difficulty controlling them.   Everything had to be locked up and if you couldn't lock it up and it was movable, they would try to take it.   Our main concern was the lifeboat stores, the pyrotechnics and lifebelts. We would manage to herd one lot off and turn around to find another boarding party behind us. I did not like the Suez Canal from day one but I really learnt to hate it on this ship.   The passage through the canal was a relief after all this but still the 'gimme gimme' went on.   It was a relief to clear the canal at Port Suez but we did not have much to look forward to at Jeddah.

Once formalities were over at Jeddah and the boarding authorities were satisfied that anything remotely alcoholic was locked away and sealed we then had to face the arrogance of the locals.   Shore leave was banned and I had to ask permission to read the ship's draught prior to sailing.   One call we were berthed behind a large animal carrier and watched as it discharged camels.   Injured ones were mercilessly whipped and the dead or dying were just dragged off by chain and tractor.   I didn't like the place and really have nothing more to say about it.

Back up the Red Sea to the Gulf of Suez and another canal transit. They did not improve! Then back up to Ravenna, south of Crete and up the Adriatic. On one voyage we entered the Gulf of Patrai and suffered a major machinery breakdown. With the main engine out of action and the main generator out of action we were in a dangerous spot and drifting towards the rocks near the town of Patrai itself. With power now supplied by the emergency generator we had radio power so we managed to relay our plight to our agents in Piraeus. I told them of our plight and that we were drifting in towards the rocks but the agents just kept asking when we would arrive at Piraeus. I shouted at them but they still didn't get the message. Eventually a female voice from another radio station butted in and I told her what was happening. I then listened in to a short sharp conversation in Greek where she forcefully passed on our message. I can't remember who she was or what radio station she was with but I thank her. The salvage tug grabbed us just before we made contact with the rocks. I must add though. It wouldn't have been a crashing contact, more of a nudge really because the sea was flat calm and there was hardly any wind. By this time I had been on the radio to the company back in London and I must say that Portishead Radio realised the emergency and bent over backwards to get us through to the necessary superintendent. Who just happened to be enjoying life onboard one of the passenger ships berthed in Southampton. It was late by then so we probably interrupted his after dinner brandy and cigar. By the time we had run him down the tug was attached and we were being towed to safety. And that too was an experience. The transit of the Corinth Canal started with the salvage tug towing and a small tug attached to our stern to control the swing as we still had no way of steering. We were much photographed this time as we swung this way and that. Touching the sheer side here and there and piling loosened rock on the Bridge wing. It didn't do the paintwork much good either. Anyway, we eventually arrived safely in Piraeus and enjoyed a few hours of relative quiet before being descended upon by superintendents, surveyors, insurance representatives, repair engineers, representatives of the engine and generator builders and Uncle Tom Cobbley and All! Since most of the visit was concerned with the engine-room, the Captain and I had only to answer questions regarding the procedures we had taken and since all our distress calls had been recorded by the Greek radio station there was not much else to tell.   We could do nothing but sit around until we got power back and were eventually moved to our load/discharge berth. From there we carried on with the voyage.   Beirut seemed a bit tame after all that.   And that was the scene of my last incident onboard that ship.   It was daytime in Beirut and I was standing on the stern ramp negotiating the price of a watch that one of the Arab vendors was offering.   He wanted too much and I was offering too little.   Somebody opened fire on us   -   he grabbed my offering, I grabbed the watch and we both fled in opposite directions.   And still smoke poured out of the Holiday Inn.   On our return to Ravenna I was relieved and flew home to return to the Australia, New Zealand trade for a few months.

My next ship on the Antipodean run was the same one that I had learnt my South American lessons on, only this time she had a name linked with the South American trade.   That and the change of funnel colours were the only differences that I could see.   The Captain, officers and crew were all Kiwi and Aussie originals so it was virtually back to the old times. She was loading general cargo in London docks for Australia and then she was scheduled to go to New Zealand to load frozen lamb for the UK. The general cargo was just the usual mixed bag apart from one special consignment which was a Rolls Royce jet engine designed for the Concord. This and a host of other things that went with it was destined for the port of Mackay in Queensland where, I believe, it was destined to become an emergency generator for some large hospital. It was lifted onboard by a floating heavy lift crane at London but it was to be our creaking heavy lift derrick to discharge it in Mackay, our last Australian port. Now the Australian ports could be a little difficult at times regarding ships lifting gear and all the necessary attachments. Each part had to be clearly marked with an identification number and this had to tally up with the corresponding certificate showing Safe Working Load etc. If it didn't, work would stop until a properly marked and certificated piece was found. Now this happened in most ports around the coast so for Mackay with this very valuable heavy lift I feared the worst and had every certificate laid out in the office on arrival. Each moving part of the heavy lift gear had been checked and greased - nothing could go wrong. I was greatly relieved when the foremen and union representatives came into the office, took one glance at all the certificates laid out neatly in front of them and said something like 'OK mate you can bugger off to the beach, we'll see to this'. I did and they did and I enjoyed my short stay in Mackay.

On most voyages from the UK to Australia or New Zealand we would carry dogs and the occasional cat. The owners would go by plane or passenger ship and the pets would follow on a freighter. As I remember, the voyage out was considered to be quarantine by the Australians but the New Zealanders applied a stricter rule and they would be quarantined again on arrival. As we sailed from our UK port there would sometimes be ten to fourteen cages on the boat deck each containing one animal. By the time we got into the Bay of Biscay all these cages would be empty as deck and engineer officers adopted an animal and moved it to their cabin. I have to say that in most cases this would be dogs as cats were much more difficult onboard ship. Born escape artists whereas the dogs just needed and wanted company.

On one particular voyage sailing from Liverpool into very bad weather, I found that there was just one cage on the boat deck where the occupant had not been adopted. It was a very large cage, with a small wired window and a notice saying that *this animal should be exercised on two chains*. I peered through the little window but all I could see were amazingly white and large teeth. I decided then that this was going to be a two person task so I called on one of the Cadets for assistance. Chain in hand I told the cadet to open the cage door and to remain safely behind it until we could see what we were dealing with. Out came one of the most beautiful dogs that I have ever seen but, at that time, one with an exceedingly bad attitude. It took one look at me standing there and lunged and those beautiful white teeth snapped onto the gold bars of my, relatively new uniform. It could have been worse but I was backing off rapidly at the time. My immediate reaction to my arm being held in a vice like grip was to kick as hard as I could and in the ensuing melee I managed to get a hold of the collar and engage the chain.   We now had a bit of a tugging and worrying   match and again the odd kick.   It took some time but in the end 'she' calmed down and after a while I was able to stroke that huge head without getting a dentists eye view of those molars!   Sitting up there on a rain swept, windy boat deck, it took a while to gain her confidence but after that I had made a friend of the only Alaskan Malamute that I have ever had the pleasure of meeting. And what a pleasure she was to be with over the next couple of months! The cadet closed up the cage and carried her bowls down to my cabin and after that Tina never left my side.   Where the others ate dog food, this animal had a special meat diet which had been put onboard at Liverpool.   I forget exactly how much her daily meat ration was but I seem to think it was around five pounds of raw meat per day,   There were other things but the meat was the staple. There were instructions on exercise as well.   She must be walked at least twice a day on two chains. Rubbish, she just followed me around day and night on no chains.   She soon learned the lunchtime drinks round and would sit amongst us without a problem.   There was a bit of a problem with the other dogs which she appeared to view as just another part of her diet.   Most would keep well clear but there's always one little bugger who will try and give it a go or at least stand his ground.   A Main Deck dog walking rota had to be devised!   If somebody knocked on the cabin door she would move but not bark and as long as I spoke to her all was well.   When I was called for my watch at half past three in the morning where before it was a loud banging on the door now it became a telephone call.   Then I would get up and wash and together we would make our way up to the Bridge for my watch.   Here she would pad up and down with me or just lay down in a corner. On the odd occasion she would sit on her haunches put her nose in the air and let out a long lingering howl.   The hairs stood up on the back of my neck when she first did it and the look-out nearly wet himself but we soon got used to it.   I could imagine that sound across the mountains and forests of Canada or Alaska or across the Siberian tundra. Her origins were from up there somewhere as I believe the breed originated from the cross between a wolf and a husky.   I was told that there were only thirty-five of her kind in Britain and that she was destined for the United States forces in New Zealand as a breed dog for their sledge animals in Antarctica. She had the most beautiful intelligent big yellow eyes and a really thick silver grey coat. She was also very stocky and powerful - not a bit like the timber wolf I had sailed with earlier. Needless to say, she didn't much enjoy the Tropics so monopolised the air-conditioning unit in my cabin. Anyway, the time came for her to leave in Lyttelton and I admit to being very distressed. I had returned her to her cage the night before arrival and she had not been impressed with that. When it came to her turn to go she threw herself about the cage in a fury and in the end I took her out and led her to the gangway. I felt like Judas. Here a proportionally large American Master Sergeant picked her up without protest and carried her down to the quayside where she walked off without looking back.

On one voyage, after a few days at sea, a large brindle Boxer was alone in it's cage having failed to be adopted. I had already taken pity on a very small dog which was apparently terrified by the whole experience and just stood in its cage shivering. Once in my cabin it soon settled down but unlike Tina, once in the cabin she wouldn't budge. However, back to the Boxer. The reason that nobody had adopted him was his constant barking and excessive drooling. He was friendly enough and enjoyed his daily walks but once back in his cage, the barking and drooling would start again. In the end I decide to see what would happen with two dogs in my cabin and magic, he stopped barking, he stopped drooling, he made friends with the little dog and he took over my cabin security. Where before the little dog had to be forced out of the cabin for exercise and toilet, the two now happily (for them and me) walked out together. The Boxer did the lunchtime round and he enjoyed his walks around the main deck but once back in the cabin, he was on duty, on guard. The little dog went back to his owners at Fremantle so now he, the Boxer, really was king of the castle On one occasion, in Melbourne, I came out of the shower to find him holding an Australian policeman at bay. It was just a routine call and after we shook hands, the Boxer let him in. Just one of the many four legged characters I had the pleasure to sail with.

Then there was the unfortunate incident with somebody's beloved Spaniel. This time we were outward bound to New Zealand via the Panama

Canal and we were experiencing a particularly hot spell as we approached the canal. One of the engineers had adopted the Spaniel and it was showing some distress in the heat so in an effort to cool the dog down he threw a bucket of ice water over it. The poor thing died instantly.

Then there was the occasion when one of the engineers accidentally knelt on the tail of his adopted dog and it turned and bit him cheek to jaw making a terrible gash. Again this was on the approach to the Panama Canal, so we were able to get him ashore to hospital without too much of a delay. He rejoined in New Zealand sporting a huge scar.

Or the time we reintroduced a lovely natured Alsatian to his owner in Auckland prior to the animal being landed into quarantine. We left and went around the coast loading our usual cargo of frozen lamb and wool and then returned to Auckland as our final port some weeks later. On arrival the lady owner of the Alsatian came onboard and asked us to take the dog back to the UK as she and her husband had decided to split up and she had booked passage home on one of the passenger ships.   That poor hound had spent a few weeks in kennels in the UK prior to a months passage to New Zealand, then a few weeks in quarantine kennels in Auckland and was now heading for another month at sea and quarantine in the UK.

Not all were paying passengers. Somewhere off the south coast of England we were joined by a racing pigeon who decided to hitch a ride.   He was quite used to humans and although we couldn't pick him up, he would strut amongst us quite happily - inside or outside of the accommodation.   We thought he would stay for just a few hours but as we left sight of land he was still with us.   He was out for adventure and would fly off and circle the ship daily.   Returning to eat the scraps left out.   You could be walking along one of the long internal alleyways and he would fly past at head height.   You could sit out on deck and he would land close by and wait for something edible to be thrown in his direction. He became a topic of conversation on the lunchtime round with the Old Man worrying about the Australian authorities attitude to the stowaway. The closer we got to Australia, the more determined became the Captain for one of us to put the bird down. It never happened and after staying with us from Fremantle, to Adelaide, to Melbourne he made his choice and was last seen circling with a host of local pigeons.

I had enjoyed my three voyages to Australia and New Zealand but now I was to visit new territories on a new ship. Well not exactly new, but certainly new to me. She was a small general cargo ship running between London and Libya, the Lebanon, Syria, Turkey and Cyprus. I did mention to the powers that be in London that some of my documents were clearly stamped by the Israelis and that perhaps, this was a bit too sensitive for some of the places I was about to visit. They said that they didn't think it would matter and anyway, I should keep shush about having been to Israel. They were right in the end, the Arab states made no fuss about it but I was banned from going ashore in all of them. Even to going down the gangway to read the draught!

The first port of call was Benghazi, Libya where the boarding authorities after clearing the ship and sealing the bonded store plus banning my shore leave, proceeded to stuff their diddy bags with whisky and tobacco and then happily made there way ashore. The drinking of alcohol while in port was strictly forbidden but knowing this was about to happen, a few cases of beer had been stashed around the vessel. A few cold beers were available at any time but had to be drunk behind closed doors with curtains drawn. We had to be a bit careful as there was a guard onboard at all times and he would just wander around ad lib. One evening while enjoying said beer there was a nock on the cabin door and the guard walked in. Apparently he had figured it out but his sole purpose was to join us for a drink. After the initial shock we relaxed a bit after that.

The next port of call was Tripoli, Lebanon which appeared to be suffering a lot less than poor old Beirut. No bullets or fires to observe and no shore leave so nothing really to report. Onwards to Latakia, Syria where we berthed in a small basin right in the middle of the old quarter. I have to admit that it was fascinating to look at but the call to faithful in the early morning from the Mosque next to us was a bit much. Our next port was Iskenderun in Turkey where, at last, I was allowed to stretch my legs. I very nearly got into trouble there as I took a walk out of town and up towards the mountains. I was stopped by an army patrol and escorted back to the ship where the agent explained that just about everywhere beyond the city limits was military land and strictly out of bounds.

Onwards again to Famagusta for a bit of a pleasure break. We tied up beneath the walls of the Old City which were still being patrolled by blue helmeted United Nations soldiers. All was apparently peaceful as we went ashore to the hotel and swimming pool owned by our Greek Cypriot agent. I met him again in Limassol sometime later and after the Turkish invasion and he told me at length the story of loosing all his possessions in Famagusta. He was still dreaming of a settlement and getting his hotel back. Without further excitement we sailed from there back to the UK.

After that ship I did one more round the world trip to New Zealand. Outwards via the Panama Canal and homewards via the Suez Canal. The Captain was on his retirement voyage and was as big a tyrant as I had sailed with at that time.

He might as well have banned my shore leave for the voyage because whenever I did step ashore, something would go wrong.   The party in the officers bar would go on too long or crew members were making too much noise.   Where was this and why was that.   I found it very wearing and was looking forward to the end of the voyage. In Auckland with his permission I took a weekend off and went to stay with a Chief Engineer friend and his wife but I had such a feeling that things had gone wrong that I came back to the ship a day early.   I could feel the atmosphere as soon as I got to the top of the gangway and received the summons to his cabin. Apparently he had gone down to the officers bar the night before to complain about the noise and had been roundly abused by a female visitor. This resulted in said bar being closed for the foreseeable future and rumblings amongst deck and engineer officers.   It took some time and diplomacy for me to get him to change his mind but he appeared to blame me for the incident for the rest of our time together.   When we left New Zealand we sailed south of Australia and then up to Jeddah our first port of discharge -   it had not improved.   On that passage I had written the longest letter of my life to my wife. Some thirty five years on she is still waiting for delivery. Later I was told that the agents in Jeddah just dumped the ships mail in the waste bin when they got back to the office. From there we sailed up the Red Sea and the Gulf of Suez and after another Canal transit, onwards to the UK where the Captain retired and I was relieved to be relieved.

After an enjoyable and relaxing spell of leave with my wife my next appointment was to a familiar ship but under a different name and under different colours. We (my wife and I) joined the ship in the London Docks where she was loading for South America. I had sailed on her previously as Third Officer but I was now joining as Chief Officer. On the journey down to the ship I thought it wise to tell my wife that some of the catering staff on this one were females but tempered this by adding that I thought they would be of a more mature age. We got onboard in time for afternoon tea which was delivered to my cabin by a young and very attractive brunette stewardess. When the officer who I was relieving pressed the button to get the cups and plates removed it was done by an equally attractive and young blond in a revealing white uniform.   I say this now   -   Oh joy   -   nothing wrong with a bit of eye candy.   I think this is the modern way of putting it. However, by this time I was getting some enquiring looks from my wife.   Again, however, the Senior Stewardess and the one who would be in charge of my quarters turned out to be an attractive but more mature lady with a military outlook on life.   My wife had to look after my cabin while she was onboard but subsequently this task would be taken over by the Senior Stewardess who applied herself with cold, impersonal military precision.   I most definitely got the impression that she considered her charges to be delinquent boys.   The female staff were made up with said tartar, the two attractive maidens and a large, motherly cook.   I jest about them but they were a good bunch.   The blond was a bit of a teaser and was openly playing the field with the drooling junior officers and the brunette was 'going steady' with an engineer.   They were the ships regulars when they went on leave it was the relieving female staff that were a bit of a handful.   Perhaps I should rephrase that.   Anyway, that first voyage was a bit of an eye opener for my wife as she observed the 'goings on' during her first voyage.

She was dismayed to find that some of the married officers had long standing relationships with ladies in South America. I had my ear bent a few times regarding this subject.

In the saloon the veneered bulkheads remained the same as did the silver service but all was vastly improved by having ones meal served by an attractive stewardess doing a sort of 'bunny dip'.

As Chief Officer one of my duties was to man the ships dispensary from 0930hrs to 1000hrs each day or to attend to injuries or illnesses outside that time. I had not thought this through properly and was somewhat concerned when the brunette was at the head of the queue. When she asked for a tube of K-Gel my mind went into overdrive and I think I must have gone a deep shade of scarlet. After that, apart from administering the normal pills and potions I seem to recall this visit as the only call that didn't spare my blushes. We would have a bit of a chuckle when one of the girls would ask for 'headache' pills. Sticking a needle into a sailors hairy arse was just not the same.

But back to the voyage itself. We were loading a general cargo for ports in Brazil, Uruguay and Argentina and the first port of call was to be Vitoria. On arrival off the port of Vitoria we were instructed to go to anchor until a berth was available. The Captain asked me if I would like to take the ship into the anchorage and I jumped at the offer. I had done it before quite a few times but this was to be my first time on a 'larger' vessel. We were the only ship in the anchorage so choosing a spot and dropping the anchor was a doddle. Later in my career I was to experience much tighter spots in well occupied or overpopulated anchorages. The other incident while at anchor was when the ship took a direct lightning strike during my evening 4-8 watch. It was blowing hard and raining heavily when out of nowhere came the blinding flash, a very loud bang and the subsequent roll of thunder. The lightning flashed, every alarm onboard went off and we found out that the Radio Room equipment was partially demolished. Sparks did not actually appear in a charred pair of underpants but he was as white as a sheet. The power of the strike went to earth, the alarms were re-set and the lighting came back on again but the Radio Room had a tinge of blue and a burning smell.   Fortunately Sparks was able to fix the damage during our stay in port but we were out of touch with Portishead Radio and therefore out of direct touch with the office for a few days.   However, contact with the outside world was maintained via the Agents office through telephone and telex.   There was no way of escaping!   When we finally received our berthing orders via VHF, I was again put in charge of picking up the anchor and taking the ship in to the Pilot boarding station and under instruction from the latter,   to the berth.   The only thing that I remember about this pleasurable incident was passing close to a sheer cliff with a monastery on top.   Quite a sight.   After Vitoria, we called at Rio de Janeiro where I took my wife for a walk ashore where we were nearly set upon by a gang of youths.   Fortunately we managed to stop and jump into a taxi before we could be set upon.   I should have known   better having been there quite a few times   -   around the dock area of Rio - always take taxi.   After a pleasurable run ashore we got back to the ship   -   safely.   I got it in the neck that night!

Onwards to Santos, Montevideo and then

Buenos Aires.   This port rotation was to become the routine for the next three years with occasional calls at Recife,   Salvador,   Paranagua,   Porto Alegre and Rio Grande do Sul.   Great names, great places and some great experiences and, I have to say, some not so good experiences as well. Santos was and no doubt still is, a very busy port with ships being levered into spaces where the bow of one would overhang the stern of another.   We had one incident where being levered into such a tight space, our bow took away the flag and staff of the Soviet freighter   ahead of us.   To prevent an international incident our Captain went onboard bearing gifts.   I recall that it took several hours to placate the Russians but the 'Old Man' returned much the worse for wear but having seen off a relay of their crewmembers.   We heard later that he was held in high prowess having drunk the lot of them under the table.

Another incident was when we had to 'shift ship'.   This was a regular occurrence as one ship would depart and the remaining would shuffle up to make space for another.   Usually we would have the assistance of a tug and, occasionally, our own main engine but on the odd occasion we would have to walk the vessel along the quay using winch power only. The shore side rope men would shift our ropes bollard by bollard along the quay until we were in the new position. Sounds easy and usually things went without a hitch. However, on one occasion during a movement astern along the quay, the flow of the river managed to get under the bow and we ended up well out in the stream. Ropes singing and winches straining and the Captain holding his head in his hands we took a long time but eventually managed to get the ship alongside again and in the new position. The 'Old Man' who had been ashore when we got the order to shift ship and who had observed the operation from the quayside was much relieved and poured the drinks.

On arrival at Santos the crew would always show a great interest as to which berth we would be assigned to as the proximity to 'shit street' was of great importance to them. The aforementioned street was a sailors paradise of bars, brothels, cheap hotels and restaurants and shops selling the usual bumboat stuff. A berth at the seaward end of the port would mean a long walk to the 'street' whereas a berth upstream where the river did a right angle bend was but a stone throw from the activity. There were many, many establishments along the street but the one I remember was the ABC Bar where senior officers would get a discount on their drinks. Discount on drinks only! I remember the reaction of our Storekeeper on his first introduction to the delights of Santos. He swayed onboard grinning from ear to ear and pronouncing that 'all his Christmas's had come at once'. With all these delights just a short walk from the gangway it is amazing that we did not have more trouble than we did but then, most of the crew were old hands on this trade route and therefore knew what to expect, how to handle it and what they could get away with!

On one voyage when I had my wife and step daughter with me, we went ashore one evening under the direction of and accompanied by the Purser. He had been on the South American run for just about all of his lengthy sea career and was a mine of information when it came to local entertainment and local custom. It was he that suggested that we go for a meal at the Hotel Atlantico which was down stream where the river emptied into the Atlantic and well away from the places frequented by the rest of our motley crew. We started by having a few drinks and listening to a fantastic Brazilean drum band. There were a lot of them and the beat was magnificent and changed every time a whistle was blown. From the verandah we moved inside for the meal. I do not remember much about the food but one incident occurred which is still talked about, at home, to this day. My wife and step daughter decided that they would use the facilities and found themselves surrounded by ladies dressed only in 'G' strings and tassels. When they returned to the table they found that their places had been taken by more ladies dressed in 'G' strings and tassels and I was then in deep mire. To this day I am accused of taking my eleven year old step daughter to a brothel. My eleven year old step daughter is now a forty+ year old mother of two and smiles when the subject is broached whereas my wife still talks about it accusingly with great emphasis on the accusingly!

I have to add that it wasn't just fun in the sun and that behind the scenes or at least onboard the ship we worked hard. The wharfies here worked shifts over the whole twenty-four hours. Southbound we were discharging the general cargo loaded in Europe and at the same time, as spaces became available, we were preparing those spaces for loading frozen or chilled cargoes for the north bound part of the voyage.   I mentioned earlier on the 'don't fuck up the perks' - well it all started here in Santos and after agreeing the price, the dunnage was put onboard and hold and locker preparations began.   Each space had to be thoroughly cleaned and then 'chippy'   came into his own and battened out the spaces.   Meanwhile I was deeply involved in pre-planning the stowage of the declared northbound cargo and allotting spaces for frozen or chilled cargoes.   Chippy worked to my plan preparing each space and we had many 'blue' moments when the cargo declaration was changed and therefore the stowage had to be changed.   The carpenter and his team worked long hours and for him, Santos, was just another port southbound.   However, he usually managed to make up for this on the northbound call.

We had two heavy lift derricks onboard - a fifty ton derrick on the foredeck and a twenty-five ton derrick on the aft deck. Because of the move into containerisation these had to be prepared for use in Buenos Aires. The old ship hadn't been designed to carry 'boxes' but we were punished with more and more each voyage. When I finally left the ship the company put a 'proper' containership on the run alongside the old-timers. Anyway, these jumbo derricks along with all their wires, guys, blocks and pulleys had to be prepared and maintained in readiness. On one southbound voyage we took out a fifty ton heavy lift to Buenos Aires. It had been put onboard in London using a large, modern floating crane with plenty of heavy lift capacity. We were to lift it off using our ancient heavy lift derrick at its capacity lift. The winches strained, the derrick shuddered and the lift barely cleared the ships bulwark rails. The ship heeled, the wires sang and the derrick shuddered. Everything was in slow motion. The men driving the winches had been hand picked and they took it softly, softly. It took time but eventually and safely it was landed on the quayside and the Argentinian stevedore and I stopped praying and retreated to my cabin for a drink.

Anyway, back to the natural progression of things. After Santos the usual call would be at Montevideo to discharge and then onwards up the River Plate to complete the discharge and to commence loading. By this time spaces had been prepared, cleaned, battened out and gassed and then frozen down or chilled ready for survey prior to loading at Buenos Aires. A successful survey was always anticipated by the Office in BA and we could see the lines of refrigerated wagons waiting as we manoeuvred to the berth. The surveyor, the reefer engineer, chippy and I would then go round the prepared spaces and as each space got the thumbs up the loading would commence. Boxes of general cargo out and boxes of frozen beef or chilled horse in.

Buenos Aires was a favourite amongst the regular deck and engine officers. The city had everything one could want. Restaurants serving excellent Argentinian beef. Bars with all the necessary entertainments. Good shops for those wives travelling onboard and a city centre with some historic buildings for those seeking a touch of culture. However, the place was under military government and the docks were under the

317

control of the military. We were allowed ashore but with passes and strict orders to procede from ship to gate or from gate to ship without deviating. All the trees within the dock area were painted white up to about six feet as were all the warehouses and buildings. They didn't appear to have spotlights but the dock area was very well lit. Just to add to this there were heavily armed soldiers strategically placed along the port roads. We suffered one casualty. A junior electrician was shot in the leg while 'deviating'. I seem to remember hearing about a crew member of some other ship being shot dead for the same offence. Papers were always scrutinised in and out but once out we were mainly left alone. I say mainly because there was the odd moment when the military would make their presence known. As when my wife and step daughter had to stand to attention on the roadside with armed soldiers pointing their guns at them during a bullion transfer at one of the city banks. A fidgety eleven year old couldn't understand this thus terrifying my wife and annoying the soldier directly in front of them. It was a crowded street and my wife did as the locals did and stood rigidly at attention.

But back to more pleasant things. The Argentinian beef steak is prepared by rolling the beast on its back, cutting off its legs, cooking it perfectly and then putting it on your plate. Or sometimes that's what it seemed to be. Anywat this very large steak would be served up with a few French fries and no vegetable. No room on the plate for the latter. All this we looked forward to each call until the Government invented 'meatless weeks'. This dastardly invention was to preserve the beef production for export only and was viewed by us and the locals with equal disgust. I did see one or two of the reefer truck drivers sitting under their wagon with a small burner enjoying a steak. I was even offered a steak cooked this way but, for fear of the consequences I declined the offer. At these times we had to move our sphere of operation to the suburb of 'La Boca' where we enjoyed some spectacular seafood. On one occasion I was invited to a wharfies 'do' in one of the nearby warehouses. I hasten to add that this was not during a 'meatless week'. I was told to expect beef cooked over coals in old forty gallon drums, cups of raw but powerful red wine and a lot of coarse conversation. The Purser told me that it was men only but when I appeared without my wife I was ordered back to the ship to get her. The steak was prepared over coals in forty gallon drums and was delicious, the red wine was raw and powerful and delicious and the wharfies were a bunch of gentlemen and we enjoyed a very nice couple of hours eating our steaks armed only with knives like daggers. The posh restaurants in the Avenue Florida and the cantinas out by the airport all served delicious steaks but the warehouse in the 'portuaria' beat the lot.

But back to 'La Boca' on a visit we made on one of the non meatless weeks. This particular call was during the Football World Cup in 1978. A few of us from the ship including my wife decided to visit our favourite restaurant in 'La Boca' and sat down at table next to the Swedish football team. They were really enjoying themselves with the food, the wine and a host of beautiful Argentinian maidens. To add to the ambience of the place there was a trio of violin, guitar and accordion who wandered amongst the tables. It was a place of nets and nauticalia with bags of atmosphere. When our meal had been eaten and enjoyed the two tables merged and a very pleasant evening was had by all. The next day we heard that Sweden had been beaten.   I don't remember the team that beat them but I did think that their evenings training in La Boca probably didn't do them much good.   It was generally agreed by those amongst us who had witnessed the scene that the Swedish team had been sabotaged.   That was the voyage where we loaded the   World Cup lawn mowers in London for discharge in Buenos Aires but we were delayed in Brazil so the games were underway by the time they were dug out of one of our ships holds.

I have to intersperse these tales of revelry with stories of a more serious nature.   I have already mentioned that we were ordered to load quite a few containers as this side of the trade was growing.   We were asked to load one tank container full of grape musk for discharge at Rotterdam.   I forget the tonnage of this our first wine container but when our twenty five ton jumbo derrick landed this tank on the aft deck there was a distinct groan from the steel plating.   Enough to have the tank floated again until heavy wooden uprights were put in position in the tweendeck below.   As it was, the tank twisted on the voyage north and developed a small leak.   We managed to control the leak but not before we found out that grape musk was a good paint and rust remover. The container was delivered to Rotterdam minus a few pints of its contents but nobody seemed to mind. Future tanktainers were treated with much care and a lot of heavy timber support. We loaded forty foot containers on the foredeck with about three inches of space between the mast housing and the winches. As I have already said - the old girl was not designed for this sort of stuff.

We had fun with other parts of our cargoes. The lower holds when full of frozen boxed meat had to be carefully pre-planned because of the depth of these spaces. The discharge rotation in Europe was Rotterdam followed by Newhaven so discharging from one should not leave sheer faces for discharge at the next. We had one incident where by discharging the Rotterdam cargo meant that the Dutch wharfies would be working under a cliff of unstable cartons of frozen beef destined for Newhaven. They did not have to cope with 'health and safety' back in those days but all involved could see that a dangerous situation was developing. The result was that the wharfies refused to work in the space until the face was stabilised or reduced. It was an all hands operation on a voluntary basis and overnight we shifted around 700tons of Newhaven beef from the lower hold up to the Tween Deck space above. Two teams passing cases along the line and upwards. We stopped for a break in the early hours to enjoy steak sandwiches prepared by my wife and the Captain. The hardest part of the job was getting the volunteers back down below again to finish the job. At 0700hrs when the Dutch wharfies turned to, we had finished the job and after a brief survey the discharge resumed. That was one of the few occasions when my beard was frozen. I retired to a warm bunk. All hands involved in the operation received a bonus from the company.

Then there was the occasion when we transported nine polo ponies from Buenos Aires to Newhaven. They were owned by Lord Vesty who also owned the Blue Star Line. We pondered long and speculated much as to why he shipped them with us and not on his own ships. The ponies were housed on the aft deck in adjoining narrow boxes where the animal could neither turn around or lay down. They could bite the ones in adjacent boxes and that was there scope for entertainment for thirty-five days. We carried two Gauchos who's job was to look after the ponies but they spent most of the voyage drinking in the crew bar. As with the dogs and cats on the Australia/New Zealand run, we adopted a horse taking on the feeding and watering. The boxes were open at the base to allow for hosing down to remove the droppings and to cool the ponies feet in the tropical heat, a duty taken on and enjoyed by all hands. My personal adoption was a pony called 'Pampero' who had a penchant for biting his neighbours. I should have taken note of this. Each day I gave him his oats and a bucket of fresh water. Each day I would talk to him and gently pull his ears and as repayment for my kindness he bit me in the armpit and lifted me off the deck the day before we arrived at Newhaven. The Electrician who was standing next to me feeding his charge, said something like 'I bet that hurt' to which I was unable to reply. Fortunately it was a cold day and I was wearing a thick Merchant Navy pullover so the skin wasn't broken but it did go red, blue and yellow and lasted for weeks. I know that they were all very frustrated at having to stand for thirty-five days through the Tropics and through some poor weather in the North Atlantic but I couldn't help myself considering the big, black 'Pampero' an ungrateful bastard! When we berthed at Newhaven we found that others were concerned at their plight as we were greeted by Radio, TV and a large group of animal rights protesters. They were discharged safely and successfully and driven away to some green English meadow to recover from the voyage. Unfortunately this could not be said for the racehorse which was being loaded for discharge in Brazil. Apparently the horse had been landed on deck but the lifting chains were lowered onto his back and he kicked out and broke a leg. The ship carried a 'humane killer' so the animal was put down immediately. I was driving down to rejoin the ship after a few days leave and missed this action by about thirty minutes. There was a gloomy feeling onboard until we sailed about twenty-four hours later.

Montevideo was a popular port of call. The food was good, the booze was cheap and the people were friendly. Every time we called there one of the first people to board would be a local shop owner who specialised in leather goods and virtually any by product of the trade in animals. He also stocked the usual souvenir stuff associated with South America. He was also a friend to the ship and would often ferry the lads ashore or meet up with them ashore for a meal or drink. On one call he took my wife ashore for a meal and fed her monkeys brains. She didn't know what they were at the time but after saying how much she had enjoyed the meal, he told her what she had been eating. I have to say, it did not spoil her enjoyment. Sometimes when busy, he would send his assistant down to meet the ship and he would arrive driving a 1928 Chevrolet Open Tourer. One call he asked me if there was anything I would like to buy and I said I would like to buy his car. We agreed on a price and set the wheels in motion. It turned out that this was a business side line of his and he had sold several old cars to visiting ships. Anyway, by the time we reached Montevideo the next voyage, the export papers were ready and in order, my shipping company had given me permission to carry the car back to the UK and with all systems go we got the car onboard and stowed her in the

Bridge Space.   From Montevideo we sailed up the Brazilean coast calling in at several loading ports where I set a round the clock cadet guard on my car.   I recall being a bit paranoid about its safety and visited it every day while we were at sea.   My good deal in buying the car was tempered by the import duty but it was still a good experience.

I stuck it out on the South American trade for nearly three years but then asked for a transfer to a proper containership.   After a bit of leave I was appointed to a container ship employed on the North Atlantic trade between Northern Europe and Canada and the United States.   I joined the ship at Felixstowe and managed to jump onto the gangway as the ship was about to let go.   It was touch and go and a bit crowded on the end of the gangway as I threw my suitcase onboard and the ex Chief Engineer threw his suitcases onto the quayside.   There were a few ribald remarks from the wing of the Bridge but all ended satisfactorily - Chief Engineer off, Chief Officer on.   The Old Man was relieved because he would have had to stand a watch if I hadn't made it.   I found my cabin, dumped my stuff and went up to the Bridge.

Later when I appeared before my new shipmates in my grey uniform I was dubbed 'one of the grey brigade' by the Captain and learned that I was the first member of the parent company to be appointed to this merry band. It took several days to integrate and get rid of the feeling of being an interloper. They were a good crowd and I eventually got on well with them and the Captain.

The ship had been purpose built for the North Atlantic so the navigation bridge was totally enclosed and compared to my last ship, very well equipped instrument wise. There was even an enclosed area with a bunk for the use of the Captain during prolonged periods of fog or very bad weather. My first shock was when I took over my first navigation watch and found that instead of using the good old British navigational charts, this ship used the United States version overlaid with Loran. I won't go into the details of Loran, it is enough to say that the charts were a haze of different coloured lines and numbers criss crossing the chart. That and the amount of detail shown on these US charts persuaded me that I should have my eyes tested as soon as possible. It wasn't exactly a blurr but I did find it difficult.

However, with years of training behind me and the surreptitious use of the bridge magnifying glass, I managed to keep my navigating end up. The ship was a very sociable one where the officers bar was well supported, with regular film shows, quiz nights and social evenings but the BBQ held at sea shortly after departure from Norfolk, Virginia was something else. I can honestly say that I have never enjoyed one like it before or since. It was a BBQ of the usual meats but with a magnificent seafood selection included. It was for all hands, with all hands helping and all hands enjoying. It was just as well that we had the BBQ as soon as we left port because by the following morning we were jumping around a bit in a good North Atlantic storm.

The port rotation was Felixstowe, Halifax, Nova Scotia, New York, Norfolk, back across the Atlantic to Le Havre, Antwerp, Rotterdam, Hamburg and then back to Felixstowe. The seafood for the BBQ was put onboard at Halifax, a fact I was to remember and take advantage of some years later. The agent in Le Havre topped up the cheese and French bread supply and the stevedore in Hamburg tempted us with German sausages and sauerkraut. She was a good ship on a good run and we fed well. When she was first built she would have been amongst the largest of her type in the world. When I was on her she would have been considered to be middle of the range. This was my first experience of life onboard a real containership and I thoroughly enjoyed it. Perhaps being permanently on the North Atlantic run might have become a bit tedious after a while but I wasn't about to find out as I was transferred again after just one round voyage. Transferred to another container ship and transferred back to the New Zealand and Australia run. I have to add that all these transfers were within the group and when I finally transferred to the parent company in Hong Kong, most of those shore contacts and friends I had met in the line of duty in North America and Northern Europe, I was to be reunited with.

However, back to the North Atlantic and experiences thereon. In thick fog on or around the Grand Banks I had spent nearly four hours at the radar surrounded by the blackout screen plotting passing ships and fishing boats. We had been in dense fog for a couple of days. The lookout had been set when I came on watch and the ships whistle was blowing automatically, one prolonged blast every minute. During a quiet traffic moment I left the radar and stepped outside of the blackout curtain to find the ship bathed in early morning sunshine with near perfect visibility and the lookout staring vacantly into the distance. I remember using all sorts of Anglo Saxon words before switching off the whistle just as the Old Man came onto the Bridge. He made some pointed remark on what a fine morning it was while looking at the blackout curtains surrounding the radar. I questioned the ancestry of the lookout again but by then we could see the funny side of the situation. There were a few caustic remarks made at the breakfast table.

This ship enabled my second sighting of the 'Northern Lights' and I enjoyed a wonderful display. Rolling curtains of light much like theatre curtains . However, this was not enough to make me choose the North Atlantic trade as my future but I was to return to the run a few times and on a few ships.

My next appointment was to a relatively

new container ship on the USA to New Zealand and Australia trade. This one had a self discharging facility in that there were two cranes on the foredeck and one on the aft deck. In the major US Gulf ports of Tampa, New Orleans and Houston and in the New Zealand port of Lyttelton and the Australian ports of Brisbane, Sydney and Melbourne, cargo operations were operated using shore based container cranes but around the Caribbean ports of call such as Martinique and Barbados we used the shipboard cranes. Port of Spain, Trinidad had shore based cranes but we seemed to by-pass the place most voyages to discharge their cargo at Barbados. Unfortunately the cargo for the Caribbean ports was usually limited so we didn't get much time in port. The first port of call in New Zealand which was New Plymouth was also a ship crane operation. I freely admit that by now I was fully converted to the pure container operation where the decks were uncluttered by derricks or cranes. A far simpler way of life.

Along with a few other crew members we were flown out to Houston to join the ship. We enjoyed one last night of freedom in a hotel in downtown Houston but we were warned that if we stepped outside of the building we would very likely be shot. We propped the hotel bar up instead. The next morning we were bussed to the ship. There I met the incumbent Chief Officer who had a reputation of being a very flamboyant character. If he ever writes his story it will be hilarious and possibly pornographic. We were to share the ship on a six months on, six months off basis for the foreseeable future except that during the six months off we were usually appointed to another ship to fill in. The powers that be weren't going to let us lounge around on full pay for six months! After the handover and a tour of the ship I was introduced to the Captain, to some of my new shipmates and to the Houston stevedore. My previous containership experience had been with dry cargo containers with the odd self contained reefer box. By self contained I mean a box with its own Thermo-King cooling unit. On this ship the bulk of the below deck containers in the forward holds were of an integral cooling system where the boxes were connected to an air in and an air out system. It was quite a complicated system and prone to one or two gremlins. It was also a bit of a fitness test because the space left over for checking the bloody things was minimal and required something of the contortionist.   Fortunately we carried a Refrigeration Officer and it was mainly his job to crawl around these spaces.   Come to think of it he was quite a tall and slightly portly person but he seemed to manage alright.   We others sweated and cursed and emerged battered and bruised from these hell holes.   But beyond all that we seemed to successfully carry our refrigerated cargoes backwards and forwards without too much bother. The connections to the boxes was sealed and cushioned by an inflated ring something like a car tyre inner-tube.   These would occasionally burst interrupting the air flow to or from the container. They would burst with a very loud bang when the box was being connected or make a noise like a deflating balloon when the box was being disconnected usually because the ring was frozen to the surface of the container.   Fortunately we carried a lot of spares.   Computerisation was beginning to take over!

The outward voyage from the US Gulf ports was direct to New Zealand via the Panama Canal. A strait-forward and relatively pleasant run down to the canal, followed by a sweaty and by now, boring, canal transit and then the long run down to New Plymouth.   I still consider the Pacific Ocean as an ocean of wonders.   Wonderful sunsets or sunrises, calm seas that stretched to the horizon and beyond.   Skies absolutely filled with stars. Wildlife to observe admire and wonder.   My mind wanders to the girls in grass skirts who used to greet us at Tahiti but I digress.   If you want to see the stars as they are supposed to be seen get onboard a ship bound for the central or south Pacific Ocean.   Not onboard a modern overlit passenger ship but a freighter or containership with minimal deck lights.   On a clear night the universe appeares to stretch forever.   Consider standing on the Bridge looking up at the glory of the sky at night.   It makes one wonder why modern youth doesn't want to go to sea.

New Plymouth, Port Taranaki or even the 'Harbour at the Sugar Loaves'   sticks out into the Tasman Sea on the South-Western bump of North Island, New Zealand and as the first port of call after the Pacific crossing it was looked forward to by all onboard.   There was a pub within easy walking distance from where the ship berthed and this coupled with the conviviality of the local ladies made it a good party port. There were one or two Kiwi crewmembers onboard so this was their home port and wives and families were welcome onboard adding to the friendly atmosphere of the place. The only negative about the place that I can recall was that it was a swell port and heavy shore side coir mooring ropes with slip wires had to be used. There were two long breakwaters but any westerly swell would have the ships in port bouncing about a bit. A heavy swell would mean slipping the moorings and proceeding out to sea to wait until it calmed down again. Discharging containers using ships cranes was hazardous with even the smallest ship movement. As I recall this at times meant a longer stay in port than anticipated much to the joy of many. On one voyage we did enjoy Christmas in New Plymouth and I remember it being one of the better ones. A 'fancy dress' party was the theme of the day and, apart from those people on duty, the sprit was entered into with enthusiasm. My wife went as some sort of cube, with arms and legs sticking out of a multi-coloured box. I remember that she had difficulty getting glass to mouth! There were some very good outfits, including 'Jake the Peg' but in the end it was a Steward who took the prize. She was a very sociable ship and when my wife won at darts in the crew bar one Sunday - the contest became a regular feature.   The Boatswain - the Bear - who was well into the six foot - six region, took her under his wing so she was in safe hands down there!   She had a lousy but very effective technique and usually managed to wipe the floor with them.   These occasions were by invitation only and when my wife wasn't onboard, I didn't get invited.   I wonder why.

After New Plymouth the ship sailed through the Cook Strait which separates the two islands of New Zealand and then down the Pacific coast to the port of Lyttelton.   Again another popular port. Situated in a very picturesque fjord on the north-western side of the Banks Peninsula it is the port for the city of Christchurch.   It was only a small port with small population but a host of pubs. One of these, the 'British Hotel' was at that time one of the worlds sailors pubs.   In checking my facts I find that the 'British' was severely damaged in one of the earthquakes that hit the area in 2010/11 and has been condemned.   As it says on the search website where I found out about this 'hang on to your memories'.   Back in the good old days of 'pommie meat boats' we would spend many happy days in port but on this containership time was short.   It was still a good party port but you had to be quick about it.

On one voyage, northbound through the Panama we had quite a serious accident when the ship hit the side of a lock approach and pushed the starboard anchor through the hull plating.   The ship carried on to Cristobal where we berthed and waited for the 'enquiry'.   The Captain, myself and one or two deck and engineer officers, plus the helmsman, were transported back across the Isthmus to Balboa but in the end, after the Captain had been called, the Pilot admitted responsibility, and the rest of us just enjoyed a day out.   One thing I do remember, was the utter squalor of the suburbs of Cristobal and the quiet dignity of the people who lived in the small tidy villages of the interior on the edge of the jungle.   We did some repairs and then sailed onwards but not before meeting a large Australian container ship which had suffered major damage when a deck cargo railway lines had broken loose in bad weather in the North Atlantic and had demolished the surrounding deck containers. Talk about knit one perl one!

I did three six months stints on this ship on the US Gulf ports to New Zealand run but on my last appointment we were diverted to the UK and because of industrial unrest in Panama we went south about round Cape Horn. My wife was with me for this voyage and recalls the run across the southern Pacific Ocean to Cape Horn as being an uncomfortable and unpleasant journey. We pitched and rolled with emphasis on the rolled for the full twelve day crossing. It was my first real experience of synchronised rolling where we would have to put the ship into hand steering and put the wheel over to break the synchronisation. I have experienced heavier rolling and I have again experienced synchronised rolling but because the accommodation on this ship was like a block of flats, it appeared to be more severe at this time. We survived and sailed around 'the Cape' and since that time my wife claims that as a person who has successfully sailed round Cape Horn she qualifies as being able to put her elbows on the meal table, onboard, ashore, at home or in restaurants. I remember being a bit disappointed with the cape as it appeared to be just a smallish rock.   It lies off the southern most headland of Tierra del Fuego on island of Hornos.   However, the back drop was something else as we ran down the south-western part of Tierra del Fuego with its jagged sea battered black rocks, high black cliffs and ice and snow capped mountains.   Cold, wet, very windy and being tossed about like a cork but something worth seeing   -   once.   And all this onboard a medium size containership!   Having rounded Cape Horn, the 'Roaring Forties' released us and by the time we were up around the Falkland Islands we were in a flat calm.   From there up to the Bay of Biscay we enjoyed calm seas and good weather.   As we approached the Bay we listened to and read with some misgiving the weather reports for our run across the Bay and up the Channel.   As it was we sailed across a calm but grey Bay and after rounding Ushant we sailed up a calm but grey Channel.   I emphasise the 'calm' because ahead of us ferry services were being suspended, astern of us ferry services were being suspended.   Ships were reporting being hove to in atrocious conditions all around us. Some ships were in trouble astern of us but we sailed along on a calm grey sea.   The south coast

'Coast Guard' stations were transmitting severe weather warnings, the BBC shipping forecasts from Dover to Finisterre spoke of severe weather but we sailed on in calm grey seas. We must have been travelling in the 'eye of the storm' all the way up to our berth at Tilbury. We anchored off the port because the ship in our berth had been delayed by severe icing. When we berthed on New Years Eve we had missed the bad weather and the ice had gone and we had time to enjoy a New Years party. When we woke the following morning, the new year had started with a real 'pee souper'. The fog was to last for a few days but my wife and I were off home for a spot of leave. My relief boarded ahead of his current girlfriend whose micro skirt was at nose level to our company chairman who followed her up the gangway.

I mentioned earlier that the powers that be wouldn't tolerate a six month break on pay so I soon found myself back at sea and back on the North Atlantic run. Another containership but this a pure one and not encumbered with cranes. Again medium sized and originally built for the Americans, she was built more for quality than comfort but she was a good ship and I enjoyed my three voyages as Chief Officer.   Sometime later as Captain I thought she was the bees knees! However, back to this first voyage.   I flew out to New York to join and after we sailed we ran into a very bad, very large Atlantic storm.   Within two days we were leaping around like a mad thing and existing on sandwiches or broth.   The US radio stations were advising all shipping to keep clear of the North Atlantic.   A bit difficult since we were in the middle of it.   As it was we   diverted to pass south of the Azores trying to get out of the storm.   It was just after sandwiches one lunchtime that the engines failed and we fell into a trough which reminded me of Wharfedale but we survived when the engineers managed to get power back again and we managed to steer into the oncoming face.   That was the one moment in my forty years when I thought it was all over.   We arrived in Southampton a day behind schedule and with ship and cargo intact.   Crew members a bit battered and bruised and cabins a mess but safe. She was a well built ship   -   thankfully.

In another effort to break up the six months away from the US to Kiwi run the company would send me on a course. When they considered that I had endured enough time on leave, personnel department would put their heads together and cunningly find a course that must attend. Just to break things up a bit. The Merchant Navy Fire Fighting course was a firm favourite and I suffered three of these short but brutal courses. The first one in Hull, the second in Leith and the final one in Liverpool. They only lasted for four days but the organisers packed a lot into those four hazardous days. Dispatched by sadists to be managed or taught or tortured by sado-masochists. I say sado-masochists because sometimes the bastards had to get into the nasty situations alongside us poor sods. Don't get me wrong, these courses were necessary, in some ways inspiring, certainly eye opening and because they were so short, necessarily tough. One Fire Officer in a group preamble said that we were to pack into four days what a trainee fireman would have to learn over a few weeks. My admiration for the service and all they do continues to this day but at the time and under the cosh, I wasn't so sure. Another thing adding to the tension of the moment was that it was a 'failure course'. If you didn't complete the course or if you didn't satisfy the course leader as to your personal attitude to the course you would be required to do it again immediately.   It was a Merchant Navy officers, deck or engine requirement.   I'm not sure what happened to your career if you didn't pass   - fortunately I passed each time probably through fear of having to do it all again.   But I did have to do it again.   I do not recall any government instruction saying that this thing was to be an annual affair but it seemed to be that way at the time.   However, those gallant but determined bastards who tried to singe my beard were really to be admired.   On my first course I was forced to wet my beard from a puddle to get a proper seal on my breathing mask before entering a flaming chamber.   In doing this I immediately appreciated how realistic the course would be.   I remember that the first exercise was in a chamber with a fire in the middle.   We entered without breathing apparatus and had to sit close around the fire slowly roasting and slipping lower and lower with the smoke level following us down.   This, we were told, was to accustom us to high heat and to prove that it was still possible to breath with our noses three inches off the floor.   Advantageously, my   nose   found   a   crack   in   a   weld   and pneumatically attached itself. I don't know how long they kept us locked in the hot can but we were a wide eyed and sooty bunch when we finally emerged coughing and spluttering. All the exercises were conducted in steel structures that vaguely resembled a ship, with bridge, engine room and accommodation. Bare, fire blackened steel throughout mind you. We 'fought' fires in the engine room or in the accommodation, entering the areas as we would have to do at sea but exiting the engine room, rapidly, through a door that in real life would have been below the water. The latter exercise being an oil fire, we were fully and uncomfortably geared in protective clothing and breathing apparatus. It was during this exercise that we discovered that underwater escape door when one of our team managed to tear his mask off against some protrusion and one of our minders miraculously appeared from nowhere and dragged him through said underwater door to safety. The door was then slammed shut and we carried on with the exercise. Those of us left behind took extra care only mildly reassured in knowing that our minders were around, somewhere. Washed, scrubbed and back in the hotel bar, the beer intake was phenomenal. I think it was in the hotel bar in

Leith that our nerves were calmed drinking pints of ale in the presence of a humorous lady who was somehow involved in the sale and distribution of 'French letters'. The hotels in Hull and Liverpool had no such distraction. But back to the training sessions. Just holding the hose was a two man job and took some doing. It was not unlike what it must be like trying to hold onto a large, enraged anaconda. Actually directing the jet of water and hitting a small aperture was quite a feat. The breathing apparatus was fitted with a low air alarm which would whistle when the air in the bottle reached a certain low level. We were told that when it went off we would have plenty of time to vacate whatever space we were in. However, when the 'air' or lack of it alarm sounded there was usually a bit of a panic. Three or four men in a smoke filled, flame filled small space and handling said 'enraged anaconda' with somebody's alarm whistle sounding was bound to cause confusion. Was it yours or one of the others. Apart from the noise of the fire, the gushing water, the noise made just by breathing and the sound of that bloody whistle. Each of us trying to find the dial that would indicate that it was you about to collapse through lack of air. On occasion one of our minders would sound the alarm to add some suspense to the situation - they succeeded! They, the minders, used all sorts of underhand tactics to add reality to an exercise. Boot up bum, hand on head, low air alarm, even turning off our water supply - they were all employed for the sake of reality. I look back now and agree with their tactics but it was a little painful at the time.

The Ship Masters Medical Course was another distraction or diversion from the pleasures of home leave. This was another course where it was compulsory to pass and rightfully so. Anyway, we band of company men were assembled at a Liverpool hotel in preparation for four days of medical induction and instruction. I seem to think that we started off by being shown exactly where to stick a needle in a sailors arse and being told what would happen if we got it wrong. After that we spent some time sticking needles in harmless and apparently, healthy, oranges just to get the feel of things. I don't think that there was one amongst us who had not enjoyed quartering a sailors buttock, then applying a dab of some disinfectant to the upper outer quadrant before giving said quadrant a sharp smack then sticking the needle in, usually with some relish! There was one full and disturbing afternoon dedicated solely to childbirth. The afternoon of 'childbirth' started off with the team being full of mirth. The expectation of meeting many pregnant sailors along the way - seemed unlikely! The lecture was illustrated by a film in living colour and loud sound and showing graphical pictures of natural childbirth followed by harrowing pictures of all the things that could go wrong. After this the much shaken participants were then individually required to 'deliver' a baby from a plastic dummy. All this may sound quite simple and straight forward but the graphic detail shown in the movie accompanied by the sound effects, had us all shaking and white faced. As the afternoon progressed, the mood changed, and it was a sombre group who quietly and meekly trooped out of the lecture room. The hotel rule was that we had to order our evening meal during our lunch brake and to a man, we had ordered steaks for that particular evenings meal and to a man, we all missed that evening meal. Rare steak on top of the afternoons activities was most definitely a no no. One of our group had a bottle of scotch in his room which we soon demolished. The same happened to the replacement bottle. The rest of the course was devoted to pumping hearts on dummies or to bandaging each other or applying splints to each other and generally making each other uncomfortable. All this culminated in a written examination that we had to pass. Fortunately we all got through.

Another one off intrusion into my leave space was the Business and Management Course the company decided I should attend at one of the Scottish universities. I wasn't alone as they had obviously been through the list of personnel on leave and had decided that to attend the above was a good idea. This two week stint seemed to be mainly based on the construction of a petrol station and having labour and bits and pieces arrive on site at the right times. It was one of those courses where we were required to sit in a circle and then each one had to stand to introduce ourselves. As we were all from the same shipping company all this seemed fairly pointless. Again, once a day and in the same circle of enthusiasts, we each had to address the group on how we viewed progress so far and insert any relevant suggestions as to how matters could be improved. I say relevant suggestions because we were jointly reprimanded for some totally unrelated suggestions. A load of bull but we waffled our way through it successfully. Another major point was that we had been housed at a teetotal hotel. I for one didn't know such places existed. It caused some distress at first but then we managed to circumnavigate their eccentricities. More communal thought was applied to this than to the whole two weeks course. I have a feeling that as a group we were threatened with expulsion from the university but I can't remember what for. I do remember us all having a meeting with the Bursar and managing to persuade her to let us stay on and complete the course. When it all ended we had a hell of a job getting out of the city as it was the one day of the year when all Glaswegians went on holiday. We ended up hiring a car and enjoying a hilarious trip southwards.

But back to the seagoing bits. In between my stints on the containership on the US to Kiwi run I did two voyages on the North Atlantic and several periods standing by conventional ships in ports around the UK. The latter was not my favourite way of passing working days away but it was a necessary evil.   After this I was flown to South Korea to stand by the building of a new containership, specially designed for the trade from Europe to the West coast of South America. This was my first and only experience of shipbuilding apart from a short visit to a small yard on the Humber during one spell at college. Anyway, when I arrived on the scene loaded down with food parcels for those who had gone before me, the vessel was spread around the shipyard in large prefabricated bits.   The keel and most of the lower ballast tanks had already been assembled in the building dock and over the next few months all the other bits would be transported to and craned into position to be welded to the fast growing ship. Our engineers, electricians and superintendents on the scene had their hands full but I was employed wandering around with Korean quality control officers checking that things were being done correctly and that things were being clagged on in the right places.   Later on there were representatives of companies from all over the world and swear words in English, Danish and German could be heard emanating from all manor of strange holes and heights around the ship.

Now winter in South Korea is fairly brutal with very low temperatures but little snow. The large ornamental waterfall just outside the foyer of our hotel had turned to a block of ice and there seemed to be a constant wind blowing that penetrated our clothing like a knife. The shipyard or to be more precise, the ship, was freezing. There doesn't seem to be anything as dark and cold as a lifeless ship. OK, the areas of work were floodlit and we each carried powerful torches but still, without it's own power, it was a cold lifeless object. We were issued with heavy winter gear but the cold still managed to penetrate and when climbing around or into parts of the ship, most of the outer clothing had to be discarded anyway. The warmth of the hotel was much appreciated but at times we would be called out in the evenings for an on site survey with Lloyds or our own superintendent and leaving a brightly lit and warm bar was painful. These are the main things that I remember about this experience, the bitter cold, the dark cold spaces and the windswept shipyard. The fact that we enjoyed many evenings in the basement club of the hotel surrounded by attractive Korean hostesses made life bearable but still the favourite song down there was 'take me home country road' and the life saving snack was 'digestive' biscuits bought at a local mini-market. We found a Chinese restaurant where we enjoyed a slap up meal once in a while and one of our engineers occasionally frequented the tented 'shit ditch cafes' along the side of the main road. Early on we had to rescue a Norwegian engineer from one of these 'ditches' and that put most of us off these tented places suspended above. It was rumoured that the main course in these places was 'rat' but this did not seem to put off our own antipodean engineer. There were many humorous moments throughout the build, the floating out and the general fitting out of the ship and later during the sea trials. It was towards the end of the build and fitting out where I felt I had some little input into the proceedings. It was towards the end when the pieces were being welded together that I noted, with some concern, that the cabin of the Chief Officer was 'next door' to the Captain's cabin. It was obviously far too late to do anything about this so I watched these cabins grow from mere outlines on a steel deck to completion, with some trepidation. From my experience to date, Captains were far better when living in glorious isolation. I believed that they were better kept away from the day to day running of the ship and should be allowed to interfere or to be consulted only when necessary.   My fears were proven when we finally sailed away from the yard and, to this day, I view it as a less than happy appointment.   I forgot all this when I finally got command but then again, on the large container ships, I was isolated   -   and rightfully thought I! Anyway, the highlights of the time in Korea for me were when the ship was first floated out, when she underwent Shipyard sea trials and finally, when she underwent Owners sea trials.   The testing of the emergency stop procedure was quite something.   Fro Full Ahead to Full Astern, was a crashing, vibrating crescendo of engine noise and alarms.   She failed a couple of times but eventually they got it right.   From full speed ahead at around 22 knots to stop via full astern took a few miles and a terrific amount of vibration!

The maiden voyage of the 'black pig' as she was affectionately called by those who had stood by the building, was from Korea down to Valparaiso, which is the port for Santiago, the capital of Chile.   I didn't see much of the place that voyage, or on subsequent voyages come to that.   On a later voyage, my wife was with me, and tells me that it was a very nice place, when the agents laid on a car tour for her.   However, back to the story.   The passage across the Pacific was uneventful until we reached the South American coast when, the swell grabbed us and tossed us about quite violently.   Being in ballast, with the majority of the water ballast concentrated in the lower part of the vessel, she wallowed in the swell with a movement akin to a pendulum - very uncomfortable!   The outcome of this short - about two days - movement resulted in a lot of damaged crockery and a crane with a scrambled brain.   Our super, state of the art, computerised super-crane was virtually unusable.   The main electrical panel, which also housed the 'brain', had not been properly secured back in Korea and did not take too kindly to being thrown around   at sea.   In Valparaiso, when all the dignitaries arrived to witness this magic machine doing its stuff, they were treated to a display of manoeuvring the crane by hand, demonstrated by the Boatswain.   He did his best, but it had been designed for computer assistance and it's three dimensional purpose did not react too well to a pair of human hands.   The German builders and electronic wizards were already on the plane. The dignitaries may not have enjoyed the demonstration but, they did seem to enjoy the party. Fortunately the main ports of call had proper container cranes, so all was not lost. In the other ports - it was a long job. For the voyage from the West coast of South America to Northern Europe, the ship was designed to carry copper ingots in the bottom of the main holds with containers above - a labour intensive operation at the best of times but even more so without our ship's crane. The German engineers and electrical wizards managed to get the thing going again but, I don't believe it ever operated at full capacity again.

The voyage of the 'black pig' was from Valparaiso to Antofagasta in Chile, to Callao, Peru, Guayaquil, Ecuador and Buenaventura in Colombia. Fro there it was back to Europe via the Panama Canal to Le Havre, Rotterdam, Hamburg, Gothenburg and Felixstowe. I did manage to get ashore at Buenaventura with my wife, one voyage, but under threat of being eaten alive by the natives, I didn't think much of the place. We did get to see the Gold Museum in

Lima but I think the Spanish Conquistadores must have pinched the best bits. There was a wonderful collection of old guns and swords.

On one call in Callao, we had to call a doctor when one of our Cadets threw a wobbler. The ship's agent reckoned that it would take at least two hours for the doctor to arrive so my wife and I went onboard a Soviet fish factory ship to ask for assistance. Their doctor and a minder came back to our ship and had a look at the Cadet. He was pronounced well enough to travel but, unfortunately, that was the end of his career at sea. By way of thanks we then started pouring vodka down their throats and all was well and jovial until a queue of crewmembers wanting medical attention formed up outside the bar and they upped and departed. It was a brief but formidable display of the Russian capacity for the intake of Vodka though! I did a couple of stints on the ship and then decided to move on.

As the fleet diminished and with it the chance of promotion, the time came to consider company loyalty. From the mainly independent company that I had joined many years before, there had been many changes.   It became a part of a major British group where we could be transferred from route to route as I have shown. Then the whole group was taken over by a Hong Kong company.   Later the Hong Kong company sold the much diminished group to a German company.   Before the latter happened I made up my mind and transferred to the parent company in Hong Kong.   Prior to the actual transfer to Hong Kong I did a short North Atlantic voyage on one of their medium sized containerships.

I found myself standing on a wet and windswept quayside in Antwerp at around midnight wondering if I had made the right decision.   Away in the distance I could see the navigation lights of a ship being assisted by tugs in my general direction and hoped that my waiting would soon be over.   I had been met at the airport about four hours before and the taxi had left me on the quayside some two hours before.   When the ship did eventually berth and I made my way up the gangway, I knew I had made the right decision. I did not know anybody onboard but the surroundings were so familiar that   I soon felt at home.   The officer who I was relieving had been instructed to stay with me until he was satisfied that all was well and that I was suitably indoctrinated into the ways of the ship and the company. The schedule after Antwerp was Felixstowe, Le Havre and then off across the North Atlantic to New York. He was anticipating having to stay with me until Le Havre but the handover went so well, he left in Felixstowe. He was pleased and I was relieved. Two Chief Officers is not a very good mixture and anyway, I much preferred to be on my own. In at the deep end sort of thing and it was the deep end. I found out that I was supposed to do a complete stores inventory and stores requisition before we reached and ready for dispatch from New York. Great fun. I made a stab at it and had everything ready to send off but in the end the effort came to nothing. Nothing untoward or outstanding happened on the voyage but after arrival in the United States rumours and rumblings started. Rumours that the ship was about to be sold and rumblings of discontent and threats of industrial action. The rumour of sale was denied by Agent and Captain but the rumblings continued. It was about two days before we returned to Antwerp that the sale was confirmed and then the crew threatened industrial action when we got into port. The atmosphere onboard was not good. When we berthed at Antwerp the quayside was full of Agents, Superintendents, Unions, Belgian Policemen and the Press. Once we were safely tied up the crew downed tools and refused to lower the gangway so myself and the Second Officer lowered it into position. We were called 'strike breakers', 'scabs' and a few unprintable epithets and threatened with all sorts of nasty things. But hell - the ship was sold, job done, there seemed to be no point on dragging things out. Anyway, after a few hours of discussion, the unions and the company officials managed to thrash out an agreement where all members of the crew, officers and ratings would receive a cash bonus and dismissal. Apart from two - the Captain and I. We were offered jobs with the company, operating out of Hong Kong. I gratefully accepted. I never saw the Captain again.

The result of all that was that I was flown out to Hong Kong within a matter of days and after a couple of days of company induction at Head Office, I was placed onboard my first big containership which was employed on the east bound round the world run.   She was a beauty and I thoroughly enjoyed my six months stint onboard.   The run was Hong Kong, Kaohsiung, Osaka, Tokyo, Long Beach then through the Panama Canal to Savannah, Charleston, Norfolk, New York and Halifax.   Out then across the North Atlantic and the Mediterranean to Port Said. Then after the Suez Canal transit, another long run down to Singapore and then back up to Hong Kong.   All in all, a good run.

It was back to a Hong Kong crew but the officers were a mixture of European, Australian, Singaporean and Hong Kong. I knew the Captain from the 'old' company so it took very little time to settle in.   My immediate recollection of that first voyage was taking over the 4-8 watch the morning after sailing from Hong Kong and finding myself faced by the massed fishing fleet of China or Taiwan.   I don't know who they belonged to and I'm glad I didn't find out but it looked like the lights of a small city in my path.   I spent the first hour of my watch weaving a passage through the massed fleet.   I learnt a lesson that morning and in future I would divert to pass clear of the main mass of boats.   It was difficult to make out which way they were going because of their very bright deck lights and spot lights. No doubt used to attract the fish but blinding to those trying to find a path through.   No wonder the worlds fish stock is rapidly declining.   Anyway we successfully cleared the fleet and then I inhaled a couple of coffees.   The next port was Kaohsiung, Taiwan, another first for me.   We sailed up the West coast of Taiwan to pick up the pilot at the northern entrance to the harbour.   The approach is through a narrow entrance channel then between two high rocky cliffs followed by a tight turn to starboard. After that it was a straightforward run down the harbour to the berth.   Seems easy but I was to learn later that it could be anything but.   The only other thing that I can remember about that first call was that if you needed books for technical information or study, this was the place.   Pirated books of course but at a quarter of the price of the original.   On the passage from Tokyo to Long Beach we encountered the Taiwanese fishing boats with nets marked with small buoys stretching out for miles.   There was no way of avoiding them so we just maintained our course. As Chief Officer I spent some time on deck during the Pacific passage as the ship rolled in some mighty swells.

With containers stowed five or six high on deck, the groans and creaks and clangs from the locking bars and twistlocks securing the boxes as the ship rolled caused me some concern.   However we did not then and I can say that I never have, lost a container overboard. Damaged a few mind you! After the long haul across the Pacific the first port of call was Long Beach.   The entrance took us past the 'Queen Mary' then on to the container terminal. Here we were all closely scrutinised by humourless US Immigration officers before cargo operations could commence. I was later to come to the conclusion that the British immigration people must have gone to the same training establishment as the Americans. Either that or they had all had their sense of humour surgically removed. Fortunately the days of the 'short arm parade' had gone but they were thorough.   Detailed crew lists had to be forwarded days before arrival and if there was anything wrong, shore leave would be stopped and a guard placed at the gangway. A guard which the company had to pay for. Another thing was that when trading with the United States we had to have onboard a cargo manifest which would also be closely scrutinised on arrival at each port. On that first call we experienced some cargo delay there enabling the Chief Engineer and myself to walk from the docks into the city. We found a suitable pub and sat down to enjoy a drink or two. When the landlady found out that we'd walked into town she was gob smacked and proceeded to give us a long lecture on safety and then insisted on calling us a taxi to take us back to the ship when we left the pub. According to her we were lucky to get there alive never mind with wallets intact. She rapped our knuckles and told us we were old enough to know better! I don't remember ever going ashore there again. Oh well. After the passage through the Panama Canal the trip up the East coast of the United States reintroduced me to a few old acquaintances amongst agents and stevedores.

Perhaps not on this first voyage but sometime during my stint on this ship I managed to get into a spot of bother ashore in Norfolk, Virginia. Several of us were invited to the office barbecue and after enjoying a good helping of American steaks and sausages a bunch of us went on to a pub not far from where the ship was berthed. I got into conversation with a couple of blokes at the bar who, I hasten to add, were not with our party.   Anyway, the conversation got round to the Soviet Union and when I said that all Russians couldn't be bad, one of them pulled out a handgun and stuck it up my nose. It appeared that saying anything good about the 'enemy' in a major US Navy port was not a good idea.   Anyway, it had a rapid sobering effect.   He was eventually persuaded to put the gun away by a large police presence but it had a dampening effect on the party spirit which broke up shortly afterwards and we all went our separate ways.   I have been ashore there many times since and enjoyed myself but managed to avoid that particular pub.   We laughed about it later but it wasn't so funny at the time.

Halifax, Nova Scotia still remains my favourite port of call on that coast.   The agents there were a young and friendly bunch and the run ashore was always pleasant.   Sometimes very cold but pleasant.   On one occasion it started raining in the morning and by mid afternoon after changing to snow it was lying about two feet deep. Cargo work had ceased because of the weather conditions so the Second Engineer and I decided to risk it and go ashore.   By the time we got to the strip club just outside the dock gates my companion was complaining about frostbite and I found he was wearing a pair of flip-flops. He was a bit of an eccentric but this was plain daft. Having thawed him out at the club we made our way back through the snow to the ship. I used to have a photograph of the ship in Halifax harbour surrounded by ice. It looked very impressive but it was just slush ice which had been blown into the harbour. Anyway, with the Second Engineer now properly booted and spurred we ventured forth again in the still falling snow. Again we used the strip club as a staging post before struggling into town. There's not much else to say other than that the pubs and restaurants were full of happy Canadians so we enjoyed a good seafood meal and some good company before staggering back to the ship. But the Canadians are used to this sort of stuff and it didn't take them long to clear the snow and to get cargo operations going again. I mention the seafood because the place was known for it and our agents used to put onboard either a box of rainbow trout or a box of lobsters. One for each crew member. The rainbow trout were huge and the lobsters were large. The lobsters were enjoyed by all but the Chinese crew members only wanted the heads and tails of the trout so the rest of us managed a few excellent meals out of the 'remainder'. They had to be eaten fresh so by the time we passed through the Gibraltar Strait we were back on ships rations.

Again I found that the Chinese crew members were enjoying fresh vegetables with their meals while we Gweilos were eating mixed veg from a can. I did mention it but as I had no say in the ordering of stores nothing happened. The food was generally good though, with a mixture of European dishes cooked a Chinese way or genuine Chinese food. Again the Chinese cook and his assistants excelled themselves when it came to one of their festivals and again I say, they didn't have enough of them.

I talk a lot about crew members but not a lot about crew numbers. My early ships had quite large crews but now, on the container ships the numbers were much reduced. I seem to remember that the one I am talking about now had a crew of about twenty-two but it varied from ship to ship. The lowest I recall was seventeen. The ups and downs were usually caused by the number of cadets or trainees onboard. I had gone from smallish ships with large crews to large ships with small crews.   Of course automation had a lot to do with this but the crews had been pared to the limit.   Gone were the luxuries of a cabin steward or stewardess, I had to look after my own cabin. Gone were the luxuries of table service, we had a more or less self service in the saloon.   The engine room was unmanned at night thus requiring less engineers.   The fact that the engines were much larger and more sophisticated and with all the additional   equipment   to contend with seemed not to count.   From a Doxford requiring a large team of men to two ten cylinder MAN engines requiring three engineers and one rating. The number of deckhands was also much reduced. Gone were the days of quartermasters, boatswains mates, carpenters or storekeepers.   We now had just enough to work the ship at sea or moor the ship in port.   All large maintenance for both deck and engine were to be done in dry-dock or in port. Gone, or nearly gone on this ship, was the Radio Officer   replaced   by   satellite   communication systems.   The catering department now consisted of one cook.   If he needed any assistance such as for a Chinese festival then some of the deckhands would have to help.   And I'm talking about some fifteen years ago so what its like now!

And talking about cargo manifests and containers and the cargoes carried therein we had more to complain about US stuffed boxes than any other. One particular case comes to mind where a container stowed on deck was found to be leaking some unknown liquid onto the steel deck. The unfortunate person who noticed this and unwisely stuck his finger into the liquid so that he could smell the stuff shortly afterwards developed weeping sores and had difficulty in breathing. On investigation the box was said to contain household goods but later, when opened in a safe area of Sydney container terminal, it was found to be stuffed with drums of nasty chemicals. Badly stuffed too because the drums had moved with the ships rolling and one had burst open. We had reason to criticise the people ashore around the world who stuffed the containers as it seemed that few of them appreciated the difference between a stable area ashore and the movements of a ship at sea. Anyway, the container we are talking about had obviously been declared as household goods because the carriage of dangerous goods attracted a much higher shipping rate. Then again if it had been 'household goods' and the shipper had requested it to be carried on deck, the shipping cost would have been less than the rate charged for below deck stowage. The crew member had to be landed at Tahiti for urgent and specialised medical treatment. He recovered and continued his career at sea. The court case regarding the wrong declaration of goods was still going on when I retired. Apart from the United States where a complete cargo manifest was required to be carried at all times, the rest of the world to my knowledge required declaration of only dangerous cargoes and refrigerated cargoes.

There was   one advantage about being on a large containership intending to transit the Suez Canal. Instead of entering the port to wait for the pilot the large ships anchored off to wait. The anchorage was at times congested with little room to swing and if anybody dragged anchor it was bloody hazardous. Instructions would be received via the VHF as to what time the pilot would board and we should have engines ready and anchor chain shortened for a quick getaway. It didn't always happen as smoothly as the above may suggest but that was the general idea. The pilot boat would come alongside, the pilot would board and be escorted to the bridge and then the pleas for cigarettes would start from the pilot boat crew. Gimme, gimme, gimme. Sometimes we would send down a carton but if they were noisy, troublesome or late they got nothing. Then the boat would follow the ship blowing its horn and with the crew waving and shouting - no chance! This was much better than being in port where they could actually board the ship. Anyway, we still had the pilot's shopping list to contend with! And now we carried two of the blighters! What a relief it was to clear Port Suez out into the relative fresh air of the Gulf of Suez and then the Red Sea.

Down the Red Sea , out into the Gulf of Aden and across the Arabian Sea to pass to the south of Sri Lanka then onwards across the Bay of Bengal to round the northern tip of Sumatra to enter the Malacca Strait. A long and relatively relaxing passage until joining the traffic approaching the Singapore Strait. I have already mentioned the smells and scenes of the Straits and I have only to close my eyes and I can experience both again. There was pirate activity in the area but we reckoned we were too big and too fast to be bothered by them.   We took precautions but didn't lose any sleep.   Later I was to find out that size and speed were not enough.

Approaching Singapore from the West necessitated a ninety degree change of course to port to cross the shipping lanes to the pilot boarding ground.   The lanes were always busy so this manoeuvre was always a time of increased observance and stress.   The eastbound vessels had the right of way so it was up to the crossing vessel to take evasive action.   Not always so easy but with engines down to manoeuvring speed it was a case of dodge one, pass ahead of the next and under the stern of another type of thing.   Once in the pilot boarding ground you were in the hands of the Singapore authorities and so busy was the port that although you may have a pilot booked for a certain time it was possible that you would have to wait anything up to four hours before he actually boarded.   Later on I was to sweat over these hours drifting and waiting with ships passing close by to port and starboard.

Then up across the South China Sea to Hong

Kong and one round voyage completed. I did two round the worlders on this ship and was then flown home for a spot of leave. It was during this leave that I took a job as Mate on a small Irish coaster. I took the job because I wasn't sure what my future was with the Hong Kong company so I thought Id experiment with something closer to home. I joined at Ellesmere Port and sailed almost immediately for Belfast. She was small - less than nine hundred tons with a total crew of five. Captain and mate, one engineer and two general hands. The Captain and I shared the bridge watches doing six hours on and six hours off, the engineer did what he had to do but spent most of his time cooking the meals and the general hands did general things around the ship. In port when nothing was happening, the last one to walk down the gangway switched off and locked up. They were a very sociable bunch and we ended up in their regular watering holes in every port. I say every part but there was one exception. In between Rhyl and Colwyn Bay on the North coast of Wales there is one place where a wooden jetty sticks out into Liverpool Bay. We docked there once to load road grit for the Isle of Wight. Said grit was delivered to the ship by conveyor belt across the motorway and onto the jetty from somewhere inland. Absolutely nothing else there. We docked, loaded and sailed. From the jetty until we rounded The Skerries off Anglesey the ship rolled with the motion of a pendulum and for the first time in my life at sea I felt seasick. The Old Man was violently sick for that part of the passage and later admitted that in any sea he felt this way. He was a few years older than myself and I thought that I would have given up years ago if I felt like that each time we left port. But back to Belfast. As we approached we were stopped and boarded by UK Customs looking for arms and militants. She was an Irish ship but there wasn't one Irishman onboard. Later on the run up the river to Coleraine I was called a Fenian bastard by a group off youths on the riverbank and had to ask the pilot what this meant. It was at Larne where the agent came onboard and told me that the Hong Kong company had offered me command and I made moves to get off. After enjoying the delights of Erith on the Thames the owners of the little ship were good to me and I was relieved at Newport on the Isle of Wight.

It was then back to Hong Kong for another

short induction course and then onboard my first real command. She was a ship I was familiar with having enjoyed two North Atlantic voyages onboard. The name had been changed and the livery had been changed but she was still the ship that I knew. She was on charter from the Hong Kong company to a German company and employed on the westbound round the world service. Again I knew the Captain so the handover was relatively easy and then I was in command and after all those years at sea it was a wonderful feeling. It was a feeling that continued for the following ten months when the company stepped in and ordered me to take some leave. I was employed by a good company on a good ship on charter to another good company and I enjoyed every moment of those months. Well. most of them anyway. It didn't take me long to settle into my new quarters and I was even able to point out the secret drawer in the desk to the departing Captain. Unfortunately it was empty at the time but I soon rectified this. It was just big enough to take a carton of cigarettes or a bottle of whisky.

Unfortunately I didn't have much time to sit at that desk preening myself before time came to sail for Singapore. The ship was a medium size containership with a Hong Kong crew and a mixture of European, Singaporean, Hong Kong, and Bangladeshi officers. Some of the officers and crew were familiar so it was home from home really. The west bound run was Singapore, Le Havre, Rotterdam, Hamburg, Halifax, New York, Baltimore, Norfolk, Wilmington, Charleston, Fernandina, Oakland, Tokyo, Osaka, Pusan, Keelung, Kaohsiung and then back to Hong Kong. The bus stop run. Once away from Hong Kong all orders or instructions came from Germany and I had a thick book of their policies and rules to study before bed. They were an efficient lot and had strategically placed superintendents at key spots around the world. As I remember they had three ships on the westbound run and three ships on the eastbound run, all charter vessels. Four were German flag vessels and the other two were from Hong Kong. We seldom saw each other - ships that pass in the night - but enjoyed a chat when we did.

Both companies insisted on weekly reports and the parent company required a weekly meeting chaired by myself and including various officers to discuss and record subjects such as safety, management and necessary ship work or repairs. I soon learned that it was necessary for me to prompt, prescribe, push and put forward to get any sort of meeting underway. Once or twice I adjourned the meeting and invented the minutes from scratch. Doing those voyage reports all those years before now came into play. It didn't always happen this way but it was generally hard going. After adjourning one particular meeting, the Chief Engineer and I left the conference room and went to our cabins on opposite sides of the same deck. As I entered my cabin I looked through the forward windows and saw the stern of a ship very close - too close. I rushed for the bridge meeting the Chief Engineer who on entering his cabin had seen the bow of a ship close ahead - too close. We made it up to the bridge in time to see the log line of the ship ahead just clearing our bow. We were the give way vessel but the Third Officer was standing there unconcerned. I gave him a short sharp lecture on 'close quarter situations'. The VHF was silent so the other vessel wasn't concerned either. Since it appeared to be quite a large Philippino training vessel, I did wonder. This incident took place on a flat calm sea, on a see forever morning in the Indian Ocean. Anyway, to get on, my Third Officer turned out to be a very good officer and I had no further moments of near heart failure when he was on watch. However, during future meetings I made sure that I sat in such a position as to be able to look out of the forward facing windows. However, to get any sort of view ahead over the containers stowed four high on deck meant actually standing at the window. I could see ships to port or starboard or even right ahead at a distance but the blind spot caused by the block of containers was huge. It was a great deal better from the navigation bridge level but then, as with all container vessels, there was still a blind spot.

Another member of the crew who I had sailed with before and who, in my mind, was destined for better things, was the Boatswain. Apart from being a good worker and also good man at man management, he was a keen, if amateur, engineer. When I first sailed with him I had noticed how keen he was on anything down in the pit to the point that, along with the Chief Engineer, we had recommended him to the company for further advancement. He wasn't reluctant, rather he was unsure if he was capable but I kept on working on him and he had started studying for his first engineering certificate. His deck duties came first, of course, but we got him down the engine room as much as possible. The engineers welcomed him with open arms. With reduced manpower down there, any help was appreciated and somebody as keen as the Boatswain was a bonus. When my ship changed from a Hong Kong Chinese crew to a Philippino crew he went ashore and after some time at college, passed his first engineering exam. I do remember him making a sweeping statement during one of our weekly meetings, telling us Gweilos 'never to marry a Chinese women, they're only after your money'. I was married at the time so it did not apply and I thought better of including the statement in the minutes of the meeting.

One of our ports of call in the United States was Wilmington, North Carolina. After departure Norfolk and dropping the pilot at the entrance to Chesapeake Bay we coasted down past Cape Hatteras where the cold current from the north meets the warm current from the south and onwards to Cape Fear. Rounding Cape Hatteras was marked by the two different colours of the waters where to currents meet and the turbulence along the line of the meeting. I have experienced heavy snow followed abruptly by warm sunshine on crossing that line. Anyway, onwards - Cape Fear sticks out into the Atlantic Ocean from the coast of North Carolina and on its southern part is washed by the waters of Cape Fear River. After rounding the Cape we picked up the pilot and steamed up river to the port of Wilmington. From the river it appeared to be a mainly industrial port with a few familiar names on the factories and warehouses lining the riverbank. It was not much of a port for the thirsty sailor but was sufficient if you just wanted a burger or a tube of toothpaste. Surely it must have had more going for it when it was a pirate haven. However, when we were there it was a modern container terminal so we were not there for very long. Apart from the Zillertalle in Hamburg this was not a run for enjoying the old 'sailors pubs'.

On departure from Oakland, California we were faced with the long crossing of the North Pacific to Tokyo. Using a composite great circle course being the shortest route we would pass to the south of the Aleutian Islands but this would take us through any bad weather up there. To avoid the bad weather in the North Pacific we would head up to the Unimak Passage to pass between the islands of Unimak and Unalaska into the Bering Sea. This was a decision to be made by myself based on the latest weather predictions for the route. I have to say that, for me, the northern route was an easy choice. After clearing the Unimak Passage we would then pass to the north of Bogoslof Island and well to the south of the Pribilof Islands where we would alter course to the west to run north of the Aleutian Islands. By doing this we passed to the north of any bad weather therefore justifying the extra distance of the passage. From the Unimak we would then make course for the Soviet port of Petropavlovsk on the Kamchatka Peninsula. Then, keeping safely outside of Soviet waters we would turn south-westwards running down past the Kuril Islands and Hokkaido towards the entrance to Tokyo Bay. Shortly after this alteration of course we would pass through a Soviet missile testing area which always caused me some anxiety. We didn't tell them that we were there but we passed through safely each time. Who knows who or what was tracking our progress. But back to the Unimak Passage. Sometimes we saw nothing with the land covered in fog and at other times we could see the stark cliffs and the ice and snow climbing to a nearby peak. But what made it even more interesting was the abundance of sealife and the birdlife. Whales, dolphins and all manner of birds. Well wrapped up and standing out on the wing of the bridge was a popular pastime for crewmembers. Armed with cameras they would snap away at the wildlife and, when possible, the views of the land. A slate grey sea under a slate grey sky with stark black rocks and cliffs then ice lines and snow on the apparently barren land above. It was cold up there and on the passage across the Bering Sea we would ice up on the foredeck. But it was worth it and I count it as one of my favourite sea areas. The sea was calm at times and rough at others but we did not suffer the huge swell of the Pacific just a couple of hundred miles to the south. The traffic up there was a bit scarce but we did see the odd timber carrier usually covered in ice. It was on our first passage across the Bering Sea that the Chief Officer asked me to walk up forward with him to inspect the ice cavern that had formed between the forecastle deck and the front row of containers. It took some days and a few hundred miles south to clear our personal grotto. But back to the passage. When we closed with the Kuril Islands they appeared to be pyramids of ice to my eyes. Then after that quiet run we would turn towards Tokyo Bay to face the traffic profusion entering, leaving or criss-crossing the entrance channel.

On the one Pacific passage where I was actually instructed to take the route to the south of the Aleutian Islands we ran into some of the most severe weather conditions that I was to experience in all my time at sea. Two or three days after leaving Oakland the barometer dipped and the weather conditions went down with it. By nightfall the sea was rough, the swell was huge and just to top it all we were in blizzard conditions. Howling wind and snow being blasted horizontally. When darkness fell we could not judge where the seas were coming from as we were driving blind so to speak. The radars were useless and the bridge windows were snow plastered. The only view forward was through the two clear view screens but then you could only see for a couple of metres.   Bye now we were in hand steering trying to judge the most favourable course to alleviate the heavy pitching and rolling. The engine speed was much reduced to try and limit the pounding.   Twice the inclinometer indicated that we had rolled to its limit of forty degrees!   On one of those occasions the ship rolled to starboard and met an incoming swell and the resulting crash indicated that we had sustained some damage.   The result of the meeting threw the ship violently over to port and anything or anybody who was not screwed down, lashed down or holding on tightly, went flying.   It is amazing how many of these nasty moments happen during the hours of darkness but in this case after about twelve hours, things started to ease.   By the following afternoon it was safe enough to go along the main deck to inspect for damage.   The second tier of containers stowed on deck were badly damaged from the forward block all the way along to the block just forward of the accommodation. We were lucky -   they were all empty.   The tier below were full of vintage automobiles and we delivered them safely.   When we berthed at Tokyo we were boarded by the men in grey suits carrying briefcases.   They asked questions, studied the bridge logbook and our weather recording instruments. Before the ship berthed I had completed a report on the incident and, fortunately, prepared numerous copies. They took note of the engine room recordings and numerous photographs of the damaged containers in their stowed position and again on the quayside after discharge. Then they all trooped off to do what these people do on such occasions and we heard no more. My faith in the Bering Sea route was firmly consolidated. Instead of arriving at Tokyo ahead of schedule as predicted by those ordering me to go south, we arrived two days late. Now I will say this now and I will probably repeat myself later on 'the god of schedule is an angry god' but on this occasion no blame could be put on the ship. I talked about an incident earlier on when on the North Atlantic run I had experienced a close to disaster moment, well, this was the same ship. Same ship, different name. I had great faith in that ship. I found out many years later that she had foundered on one of the islands in the Azores group and, even now, thinking about it I get a lump in my throat.

On one voyage having just left Fernandina

and on the run down to Panama we heard on the radio about an earthquake in California. There were reports of damage all around San Francisco Bay but much of it seemed to be concentrated around Oakland. As Oakland was our next port of call we were concerned but on company orders we were told to proceed as normal. When we got there and the San Francisco Bay pilot boarded we got the full story and started to see some of the damage. After passing Alcatraz we could see that a part of the San Francisco - Oakland Bay Bridge had collapsed and as we approached the container terminal we could see several tilted container cranes. The berth where we eventually tied up at had two working cranes but they were used very carefully because there were cracked wharf piles and deformed rails. We did complete cargo operations but very slowly. Come to think of it, this may have been the reason that I was ordered to take the southern route across the Pacific in an effort to make up time lost due to the earthquake damage.

But back to Fernandina or to give it its full name, Fernandina Beach, Florida. A name much more associated with tourism than steel boxes and ships.   But there it was, as I remember it back then, with a single berth and one container crane butting on to the main street of this very attractive little port.   Situated on Amelia Island and about thirty miles north of the major port of Jacksonville, the small town has a huge history and is famous for having served under eight flags including Spanish, French, Mexican and British flags. Most of the places of interest were along or close by the main street and all this entertainment was only a two minute walk from the gangway. Fortunate really because we didn't get long in port. It was also a fishing port with a sizeable inshore fishing fleet.   Since they were all berthed close by we took advantage of this to replenish our stock. As I have already said, we were never there for long and sometimes we bypassed the place but when we did call in it was very pleasant mingling with the locals and the tourists.   A change from the large container ports to the north.   Another advantage was that the sun always seemed to shine on Fernandina Beach which in the Winter months was very welcome after the cold ports to the north.

Having talked about Oakland I will move on

to the passage from California to Tokyo when I was instructed to sail south of the Aleutian Island chain in an effort to make up the time lost due to the earthquake.   On the face of it the weather forecast for the route didn't appear to be too bad apart from a small depression which we would meet about midway across.   We sailed from Oakland and after passing the island of Alcatraz and passing under the Golden Gate Bridge, we disembarked the pilot and set course out into the North Pacific on a composite great circle course for Tokyo.   This course which is something of a semicircle with a flattened top, took us up towards the islands to the point where we reached the flattened part of the semicircle which put us fifty odd miles to the south of the land.   It was in this area where we, heading west met the depression, moving to the east but by this time it had developed into a full blown Pacific storm.   We were by this time well past the channels leading up into the relative safety of the Bering Sea so there was nothing to do but batten down and carry on. I have talked about the consequence of this ship meeting that storm a few pages back so I will not repeat myself.   Suffice it to say that as a time saving exercise it was not a success and as a personal experience it was bloody awful.

You may think of the sea as just a vast expanse of water and, yes it is, but what majesty and power it has and it is most definitely not an empty expanse. The power of a very rough sea to the tranquil calms - in all states it is beautiful. Spindrift blowing off the tops of waves, an isolated shower stalking across a flat ocean. The different moods and colours of the sea as it reflects the clouds or bursts with the different types of bioluminescence. The long rolling lines of a great swell, the crashing fury of wind driven waves to the gentle slap of a wave along the ship's hull. From the mini wind whorls to the huge, majestic water spouts - there was always something to look at. Sunset, sunrise, the horizon blending into the sky. The green flash as the sun sets below the horizon on a clear, cloudless evening, emitting a piercing bright green flash as it disappears. The colour of the clouds at sunset or sunrise, especially with the red sky in the morning or the red sky at night. From the fluffy small white clouds, floating above a calm sea to the huge towering cumulus, to the very low, ragged scud, fast moving over a grey, rough sea. Back when I was a watch keeper, I found the 4 to 8 watch by far the best for, sea, sky, sun, moon and star spotting but, day or night,there was always something to enjoy or wonder at.

Approximately halfway through my ten months onboard, the company replaced the Hong Kong crew with a Philippino crew.   As the original crew had been a very good one, I was a bit resentful at the Philippino takeover at first. However, they were generally a happy lot and as they had all been through the company training college in Manila, they knew what to do.   It didn't take long to come round   and accept them. The only real changes were that they spoke better English and that the food seemed to have a more western bias.   I had no struggle in getting them to accept the fact that we Gweilos were equally as keen on fresh vegetables as they were.   Where we were constantly trying to stop the Hong Kong Chinese crew spending all there money on gambling and playing marjon, with the Philippinos it was more of trying to curb their seemingly limitless enthusiasm for parties.   They were a happy lot and their outlook on life was based on the 'work hard, play hard'   syndrome.   Of course the reason for changing crews was a cost saving move and the wage paid to the Philippino crew was much less that to the Hong Kong Chinese. Even so, they sent most of their pay home to their families and kept a small amount for onboard spends. That 'little bit' seemed to go a long way and they managed their money well unlike some of the Chinese or British crews I had sailed with. They didn't gamble and there weren't any nasty money lenders to relieve them of their pay. Crew numbers were much reduced onboard these containerships so it was much easier to get to know the individuals, to learn something about their lives and their families. With a total complement of seventeen it was relatively easy to get to know their fears and foibles, their strengths and weaknesses, their like and dislikes. They did have one similarity to the Hong Kong Chinese ratings in that they would say 'yes' to any order or instruction even if they didn't understand the order or instruction. Many times I had to ask if it was a 'yes meaning yes or a yes meaning I don't know what the bloody hell you are talking about but I'll say yes just to please you or shut you up'. When they got used to me they would generally say yes when they should say yes and question me when the answer should have been 'no'.

One thing that most seafarers enjoy but the Philippino ratings more than most, was the onboard barbeque. Just mention the word and they would have everything set up in no time. Due to the lack of open deck space on modern containerships these barbeque were usually held on the leeside bridge wing. Not really the best arrangement and one frowned upon by the company but the only other open spaces were the forecastle deck or the aft mooring deck. One was way up forward and the other, although open at the sides, was under a cargo deck. The officer of the watch was not allowed to join in the festivities but he was allowed to enjoy the food. There on the wing of the bridge, steaks and sausages sizzling and taped music blaring, all off duty crew members would gather to eat and relax in the sunshine. For those other than the bridge watch keepers and the lookouts this was a rare chance to see the sunshine as just about every other bit of space was either covered by or blanked off by steel boxes.

Which neatly leads me into my next

paragraph which is dedicated to said steel boxes. I do not remember having a childhood penchant for stacking bricks but now, onboard these large container ships, I found an enthusiasm for stacking boxes. To this day my wife mocks my 'container spotting' when we cruise the inland waterways of Europe. These days I like to spot my old company's boxes to let those nearby know that my pension is safe. Here you may say 'get a life', my wife does. But back to the containerships that I was serving on. The complexities and machinations of the business interested me. The management and scheduling involved me. Some of the ports of call fascinated me, others appalled me. I like Singapore as a place to visit but the Port of Singapore container terminal as viewed from the wing of the bridge must be akin to 'hell on earth'. The noise of cranes, trucks and the associated alarms along with the dust, the smells and the heat and accompanied by hosts of ant sized humans scurrying on, under and around the boxes, painted a picture of Hades to my eye. Within the dock areas, and I don't just mean Singapore, there was nothing to tempt the seafarer ashore apart from the occasional telephone booth where one could make a noisy call to home. The port that stands apart in this was the container terminal at Europort, Rotterdam where there was a very good restaurant inside the docks and only a short walk from the berth. It was supposed to be a truckers stop but if this is so, it was a very pleasant one. Some ports at least provided a bus service to and from the dock gates. Others such as Felixstowe, left the mariner to navigate his way between cranes and boxes and stackers and forklifts on a dangerous route to the dock gate. Some postcards of Felixstowe show just a black card with 'Felixstowe at Night' written underneath so was it really worth the risk. At Hamburg one had to get across the river to the bright lights. At Le Havre it was miles from anywhere as was Bremerhaven. Of the US ports of call, Fernandina Beach was a bonus but only for the medium size container ships. The exotic eastern ports of Japan, Korea, Taiwan, Hong Kong and Singapore were accidents waiting to happen. If you didn't get eaten by the natives in Kaohsiung or blown up by terrorists in Colombo you could always get yourself poisoned in the 'shit ditch' cafes of Pusan or get yourself mown down by the kamikaze truck drivers of just about any container port in the world. Forays ashore were few and far between.   Still, I did and still do find it all fascinating.

I feel, at this stage, that I should talk about the pilots who safely guided the ships in and out of port.   My first thought is of some of the Japanese pilots, who were still clambering onboard into their seventies!   Fortunately, with the large slab sided container ships, the pilot entry was via a 'gun port' door only a few metres above the sea level and when onboard it was via a lift up the tower block of the accommodation, to the navigation bridge. On the medium size vessels, they still had to climb the pilot ladder up the side of the ship and whether young or old, in a rough sea, this was a hazardous operation.   In Europe, we occasionally had to over carry the pilot due to extreme weather conditions and if we couldn't land him at Dover or Brixham we would carry him on to Port Said. Some quite enjoyed the sunshine trip through the Mediterranean but the fun ended on disembarkation at Port Said.   Pilots came, and probably still do, in all shapes and sizes.   From the young super fit via the large and rotund to the occasional uber mature pilots of Japan.   From the very tall pilots of Europe and the USA to the smaller versions of the Far East.   Some jovial, some grumpy, some arrogant, some positively anti and some positively painful.   On a cold night in a rough sea with snow blowing horizontally who could blame them for the odd eccentricities.   On such a night we could usually bring the most morose pilot around with a cup of cocoa that you could stand a spoon in or a cup of hot soup. Some would race ashore after their stint, others would stop for a drink and a chat and others would join us for a meal.   I suppose it really depended on how busy the port was.   And while on the subject of port operations   -   'where are the bloody linesmen' could oft be heard from me as we waited to depart a port.   They would always be there on arrival but, on departure, they seemed seemed to enjoy winding me up by being late and when the God 'schedule' was clambering, my blood pressure would rise!   The worst port for this was Singapore   -   they would keep us hanging around off the port waiting for a pilot and then, just to get me fully uptight, the linesmen would be late.   It is a very busy port so it is understandable, now   -   but back then!   It used to be that the last man ashore chucked the lines off but latterly they became dedicated teams with bright uniforms and their own means of transport. Progress I suppose   - health and safety, definitely.

But back to the boat so to speak.   I enjoyed my ten months and I enjoyed my first command.   My next move was to a much larger vessel.   Again it was a container ship that I had served on as Chief Officer so the step up to Master was an easy step.   I knew the ship and had been well coached for promotion on my earlier appointment.   This ship was again engaged on the round the world run but this time in an easterly direction.   A chance to unwind.   Back to a Hong Kong Chinese crew again, most of whom I had sailed with before, so no problem there.   Again, I knew or knew of, most of the officers so, again, no problem there.   I joined in Hong Kong and after being taxied to the main gate I experienced the struggle by bus from gate to gangway.   A bus driven by a maniac and full of port workers with me trying to hang on to suitcases and dignity.   I recall holding on to my possessions but being thrown about on the bus, so I'm not so sure about the dignity.   I add this short tale just to illustrate how well we seafarers were catered for in the worlds container ports back then.   But back onboard, the handover was straightforward and now I was in command of a much larger and a much more up to date container ship. The officers were again an international mixture with British, Irish, Indian. Hong Kong and Singaporean deck and engineer officers. I stated earlier that the crew were Hong Kong Chinese but I forgot George, the cook, who was a gigantic Mongolian. He was a good cook and I was to enjoy most of his repertoire over the following six months. He cooked a mean steak and a borsht to die for but his favourite production of what became known as 'chicken arseholes' I found much less palatable. Again and unfortunately, he had adopted the Chinese belief that we westerners only ate tinned vegetables so I had to pull myself up to my full five foot eight inches and tap him on the chest to forcefully explain how this belief was incorrect. Since he was well over six and a half feet tall in his flip-flops some of the dignity was lost in this gesture. However, since I controlled the purse strings, he soon readjusted and we all enjoyed fresh or at least, fresh-ish, vegetables with our meals.

It was onboard this ship that we experienced

a 'major' fire incident.   I can't remember where
the ship was at the time but it was during a quiet
afternoon at sea in the middle of nowhere when the
peace was shattered by the Fire Alarm.   It is
amazing how different they sound   -   louder and
harsher -   when it is the real thing and not a drill.
Anyway, the crew went to their Muster Stations
and we on the Bridge located the area of the
emergency from the Alarm Panel and directed the
Fire and Search Parties to the area.   The first
thing to do in one of these incidents is to make
sure that none of the crew were missing and in this
particular incident, the Radio Officer was missing.
The location of the emergency in this case was
centred on the ships laundry so the Search Party in
full kit and breathing apparatus was instructed to
approach using a fire hose on spray setting.   They
were assisted by the Hose Party, again in full kit
and breathing apparatus.   Behind them but at a
safe distance came the First Aid and Stretcher
Party.   Now, out of a crew of seventeen, and
counting the Bridge and Engine-room Parties there
weren't many spare souls.   The Search Party was
in touch with all the other parties by walkie talkie
so that we on the bridge were kept in touch with
what was going on.   Anyway,   they approached

the Laundry Room and cautiously opened the door keeping low in case of a fire blow back and keeping the hose spray in front of them. They reported 'no smoke, no sign of any fire'. After that the radio communications became a bit scrambled so I decided to investigate. At the seat of the incident I found my 'parties' convulsed in laughter. A room off the Laundry was set up as a drying room and was fitted out with several heaters. On opening the door to the drying room, the Search Party had found the Radio Officer dressed in swimming trunks and sitting on a deck chair. With the heating turned on full he had been using the room as a sauna! He was sitting there reading a book and with earphones on, listening to music. When the laughter had subsided and the 'parties' had retreated, and when I had finished giving him a bollocking, he volunteered to mop up all the water and clean up the area. He was a bit sheepish after that. Personally, I was relieved that the incident did not involve injury or fire!

After a six month stint on this ship and a couple of months home leave I was flown back to Hong Kong to join one of the company's largest container vessels. I keep saying 'onwards and upwards' but this really was it. Again I knew most of the officers but this time there were only three Europeans onboard, the rest being Singaporean, Hong Kong Chinese and Indian along with a Phillipino crew.

This ship had briefly been the largest container ship in the world but in a period of shipbuilding strength and rapid growth in ship size - that claim to fame did not last long. I was to serve onboard this ship for about one year and then transfer to the sister ship for the remainder of my seagoing career. This ship, along with her sister, was employed on the Far East to Europe service, a round trip of fifty-six days. After Hong Kong the ships route was to Singapore, through the Suez Canal, Rotterdam, Bremerhaven, Felixstowe and Le Havre. Then back out to Singapore, Osaka, Tokyo, Kaohsiung and finally back to base at Hong Kong.

I mention Kaohsiung a few times so perhaps a few words on the port are called for. Approaching the northern entrance to Kaohsiung harbour was always a bit tricky but there is a time of day when the Taiwanese smog of industry settles over the bay making the situation even more hairy.   It would always be a head in radar job and if you have ever seen that speeded up video of traffic in the Dover Strait, you will understand what I mean.   Apart from the ships at anchor and the ships approaching the anchorage there were always hosts of fishing boats and work boats criss-crossing the line of approach.   A few blows on the ship's whistle making absolutely no difference atall.   However, the smog would always clear, as if by magic, when the ship was about a couple of hundred metres from the narrow entrance channel. Back into glorious sunshine.   At this point the two Taiwanese pilots would take over the con of the ship.   They boarded some time before they but would generally leave it to me until the smog lifted with a cheery, 'you keep the con Captain'   - thanks!   My wife, when she first saw the entrance channel, expressed the opinion that we would not fit.   Afterwards she said she closed her eyes   -   afterwards I admitted, so did I   -   I jest of course.   Anyway, having done it before, I knew that we would fit   -   just!   Even so it was a bit of a white knuckle job.   Priority was for ships departing and just to add to the excitement, the Port Authority was not entirely unknown for letting us know a little late that there was a ship on it's way out, causing some rapid manoeuvring and some mutters - even from their own pilots.

You may have noted that my description of happy runs ashore have dried up.   Part due to the 'upwards and onwards' and the responsibilities therewith attached, but mainly due to the much speedier turnaround of the modern container ships. From two, possibly three months on the New Zealand coast, to twelve hours here, twenty-four hours there and times in between, in the world's container ports.   Time enough for lunch in a pub outside Felixstowe, an evening meal at a restaurant inside the docks at Rotterdam, perhaps a quick shopping visit to Bremerhaven or Le Havre.   In the Far East, a phone call to home from a noisy dockside phone booth in Singapore, perhaps a shopping spree in Kaohsiung and most likely, sitting tight onboard in Hong Kong, Osaka and Tokyo.   Time in port was both short and hectic. Places such as Rotterdam, Bremerhaven, Osaka and Tokyo were made even more busy, in that they were the ports favoured by the shipping company for 'shippers parties' where we would entertain our loyal customers and local office staff. A couple of hours of canapés and polite chatter. Introducing company personnel from inland offices to the ships they were dealing with. Anyway - in a six month tour of duty - runs ashore were limited and the bright lights were most definitely out! Entertainment or relaxation was now reduced to time onboard at sea - a barbecue, a video evening, the Sunday lunchtime get together or perhaps a good book from the library. Perhaps a game of table tennis or half an hour on the rowing machine.

At least family or friends could visit the ship in a home port. Sometimes they would need permission from the ship's agents but mainly they could come and go as they wished. Nowadays security has been much beefed up and you need to give at least twenty-four hours notice of your intended visit and if permission is granted, a passport or ID is needed, these having been checked when applying to visit the ship. We have terrorists, illegal immigrants and drug smugglers to thank for the above!

Going back to the subject of purse strings,

on this ship I carried in my cabin safe on average one hundred thousand dollars. This was to cover crew subs, the purchase of the above mentioned fresh vegetables and other foodstuff and sundry expenses that might crop up while away from our home port of Hong Kong. Unlike my first command, my office desk did not have a hidden compartment or not one that I could find anyway. And I did probe and kick. I repeat that the company instructions about the cash carried onboard was that I should leave approximately five thousand dollars in my safe and the balance was to be stashed in safe hiding places. So on approaching 'pirate areas' I would stuff socks with dollars and hide them around the 'Captains Deck' in places that I assumed the pirates would not have time to search. In ventilators, on top of deckhead piping, behind the lockers in my personal pantry and so on. Each cache held one sock containing around ten thousand dollars so I was eager to gather them in when we had safely cleared said 'pirate area'. On one occasion I found that I was ten thousand dollars short and showed some concern. My wife who was with me at the time says that I went into panic mode much to her amusement. Strange really because today if I misplace a 'tenner' at home I get into trouble.   But back to the story.   I frantically searched all my usual spots but to no avail.   I searched again and eventually found the missing sock perilously poised above a deck pipe access where, had it moved again, it would have fallen down several deck levels.   That particular hiding place was removed from my list!

My term onboard the first was terminated after an unfortunate and at the time, horrifying incident off Cape St Vincent on passage from the Far East to Europe.   On a calm, clear Saturday afternoon we hit and nearly sank a mini bulker flying the Austrian flag.   In all my time at sea I had only come across two ships flying the Austrian flag and I had nearly sunk the second one !   It was shortly after the change of watch and just after the ship had cleared the 'separation zone' off Cabo de Sao Vicente to give the headland its proper Portuguese name.   The relieved watchkeeper had handed   over   the   watch   to   the   relieving watchkeeper and reported a ship ahead going in the same direction.   The watch changed and I went down   to   my   cabin   to   continue   writing   my 'handover notes' as I was to be relieved when the ship arrived at Felixstowe. About thirty minutes later we hit. I won't go into the morbid details but suffice it to say that I then talked via VHF to a very unhappy German captain. The ship was badly damaged and we escorted her towards Setubal where the salvage tugs took over. Needless to say, messages to the European Headquarters and to Head Office, Hong Kong flew backwards and forwards. Our next port of call was Rotterdam where we were met by an impressive line-up of suits and briefcases. Company, Insurance, Union, Surveyors etc. Alongside I was able to inspect the damage to my ship and found only a few scrapes to the paintwork down the starboard side. The officer of the watch and I left the ship on arrival at Felixstowe. After a period of leave I was then appointed to the sister ship where I enjoyed the remainder of my career at sea without further incident.

Well, not entirely without incident. One incident comes to mind but it was humorous rather than hazardous. It was one of the voyages when my wife was with me. Anyway, on each deck level there was a steel door giving access to a small room full of pipes and ducts and also a chute for garbage which took said garbage down to a room on a lower level where it could be compacted for disposal in port.   On one occasion mid ocean, though I can't remember which ocean, I took a sack of waste into the room and dropped it into the garbage shute.   Simple, however, while I was doing this the steel door slammed shut behind me. There was I, Master of all I surveyed,   Captain of a large container ship, at sea and locked in the garbage disposal locker.   Not ideal but at least there was a single electric light so I could see what I was doing.   I assumed that my wife would eventually miss me and that she would then release me from my prison.   However, I had not told her where I was going and she would probably assume that I had gone up to the navigation bridge to talk to the officer of the watch.   I kept on banging on the door but a bare fist on a heavy steel door does not make much noise.   I think it was about two hours before my wife released me from the locker. She was amused, I was relieved and I made her swear to secrecy about what had happened.   I can't remember what I told the search party. The promise of strict secrecy obviously does not stretch to the river cruises that we now enjoy as my wife revels in telling this and other tales.

Another development during my time in command was an interest in potted plants. I had a very large dayroom and a large desk and the cabin was much improved with potted plants on the desk and around the cabin. I managed to acquire one or two exotic plants in Singapore and on one occasion off Brixham the North Sea Pilot boarded with the usual newspaper but also with a couple of buckets containing a variety of plants. My garden was underway! I eventually branched out to growing tomatoes and chilli peppers on the Bridge until one of our Superintendents 'thought it was not a very good idea'. He thought it was a distraction for the bridge team and I had to agree. I didn't really mind but the Singaporean officers were a bit upset because they used to eat the chilli peppers straight off the tree! My Bridge gardening phase was over but my cabin garden flourished and when I retired I removed all the plants to a new home in Yorkshire where I managed to harvest a good crop of chilli peppers for a couple of years.

To my eyes she was a good ship and I thoroughly enjoyed my time there. It had its moments but then I imagine every career in the world must have its ups and downs. Overall, and here I go back to page one, I would do it all again. Might put a bit more thought into a few things along the way but - yes - if we still had a Merchant Navy, I would do it all over again.

The last few years at sea in command of this ship passed quickly and mainly happily. I started off with a Philipino crew but then changed to a Mainland Chinese crew. I have spoken about the Philipino's and briefly about the Chinese but the latter deserve a few words more. Generally they were a good bunch but they lacked the sense of humour of the Philipino's and they were generally not team players. One cook, who's only training was as a welder, caused a stir onboard. Even the Hong Kong and Singaporean officers found his food unpalatable so at the end of the fifty-six days of near starvation he was sent ashore for re-training. I do believe that he turned out to be one of the company's top cooks after this period ashore. Anyway, during his fifty-six day stint the Chief Engineer and I did some serious home cooking. Fortunately we had a small pantry on our shared deck which had a mini oven and a hot plate.   I had a friend who would have been able to prepare a feast on these limited resources   -   we merely sought to survive.   My wife has a good way of preparing roast potatoes and I recall phoning her from somewhere near Suez to get instructions.   She joined for the European coastal voyage and I told her to bring a lot of sandwiches. She didn't and she regretted it.   However, for those few days the Chief Engineer and I had a relief cook!

But apart from Cookie, we did have language difficulties and the 'yes' problem really was a problem.   They were not an inspired bunch and did only what was required of them whereas the Philipino's took some pride in what they were doing.   I realise that it was probably a cultural thing but it could be annoying at times.   It was around about this time that the company decided to get their ships registered with Det Norske Veritas on a scheme that covered shipboard knowledge, safety,   and just about anything else you can think of that has something to do with shipping   - however vague.   Now, trying to instil some urgency into my Mainland Chinese crew took some doing.   Apart from language difficulties, instilling some enthusiasm was virtually hopeless. We were given about four months notice to prepare for the examination or survey to make sure that everything onboard was up and running and correctly labelled and that all members of the crew knew where things were and what they were for and, in the end, what they were supposed to do with them. On the days allotted, the team of DNV surveyors were due to board and survey the ship and also question individuals onboard re anything and everything. The day approached and I for one was suffering from hypertension, sleep loss and a surety that my team was about to fall into the abyss. The day arrived and a severe bunch of DNV surveyors and assistants - they weren't that bad - descended upon the ship. The actual crew examination lasted over two days. The Boat Drills, Fire Drills and Emergency Drills were spread over four days on passage from Hong Kong to Singapore. The blood letting was on the last day after I had been grilled. Having sweated through the last few days I don't feel that I put up a brilliant show but that was it - show over, results to come. Our shortcomings were aired, critisized and suggestions put forward and then we were given the overall result - and 'heavens to murgatroyd' we passed!   I inhaled a few beers after that as did my officers   -   and the DNV surveyors!   Routine then continued and life was back to normal and the voyage continued.

The above I view as a partly cloudy period in my last few years at sea.   However, we got through it and everything settled back into the routine shipboard life that we knew and loved. We took pirate precautions when approaching the Singapore Strait or the Malacca Strait,   we suffered the pilots of the Suez Canal.   The God 'schedule' dictated our lives as we pushed to 'keep up'.   In Northern Europe the weather could intervene but it was mainly ship delays and the consequential backing up of arriving ships that played hell with the schedule.   In the Far East the berthing arrangements were just about spot on but a Typhoon could totally mess up a carefully planned schedule.   The latter could also make life at sea a little difficult but with the up to date weather reporting, typhoon tracking and the ships own instruments we could take evasive action. 'Save the ship and sod the schedule'.   Safety of life, safety of ship and in the eyes of the company, safety of cargo, meant more than schedule at these times.

From day one, I was enchanted by the daily wild life to be see at sea. From the gulls dipping and diving or flying alongside the ship to the size and majesty of the albatross, again as it skimmed the waves over the wash aster. The ever popular dolphins as they flashed across the bows or appeared alongside in huge schools. I was told early on. That if the school was going in the opposite direction to the ship, then this was a bad sign, but I can't remember any adverse happenings related to these incidents. Be it tramp ship, container ship or passenger ship, the sighting of a school of dolphins would always create great surge of interest onboard. The flying fish viewed from the high decks of a passenger ship, were interesting, but viewed from deck level on a small ship, they were fascinating and if the ship was rolling, they sometimes provided an extra food source. This was especially popular with Chinese crews. I found them very nice with a fiery sauce as served in a beautiful club restaurant in Bridgetown, Barbados! But I digress. I had a sad encounter with a whale in the Bay of Bengal on passage from Suez to Singapore. My afternoon was disturbed when after a slight shudder, the engineroom alarms sounded. This followed by a swimsuit attired crewmember who urged me to follow him. With the ever present walkie-talkie strapped to my belt, I ran. We made it to the forecastle head - the forward mooring deck - and I peered over the side. On top of the bulbous bow and stretching approximately twenty-five feet on each side was the body of a whale. Under my instruction to the bridge watch we weaved from starboard to port and back again in an effort to dislodge the huge carcass, but without success. In the end we had to stop the ship and then go 'full astern' to shake it off. The choice was either to carry it on to Singapore and suffer the loss of speed and the higher fuel consumption along with the expense of having it manually removed or to lose time and shake it off as we did. I was told some time later, that the whale must have been dead or dying when we hit it. That was an unfortunate view of one of these mighty creatures, but other sightings, of spout, hump or tail, were much more enjoyable. A swarm of locusts in the Red Sea, was not so enjoyable but I mention it tp point out the variety of wildlife we could observe at sea. The dazzling white of the gannet community off Cape Kidnappers, New Zealand as they crash dive into a shoal of fish. The pelicans off Panama flying slowly and stately past the ship or diving for fish in the calm clear waters of the Gulf of Panama or the Gulf of Darien. The seals and sea otters off the west coast of the USA and Canada or the teeming bird life off the coast of Peru and Chile. The sharks, the rays, the occasional turtle and the hosts of jellyfish of all sizes - if you looked carefully there would usually be something to see. And I haven't mentioned the wildlife in the Unimak Passage and the Bering Sea. Birds, whales, dolphins and seals - magnificent.

One of the gripes held by containership Masters and Chief Engineers was against those 'wise wizards within the office' who planned the schedule. If a ship achieved a speed of say 25 knots during sea trials, said wizards would go ahead and plan the schedule at 24 knots. This meant that the ship was running at maximum throughout and any adverse weather could throw things awry. Push, push, push! I will say it again 'the god Schedule is an angry god'. I went to sea a reluctant Christian and left the sea a token

Pagan.

I went to sea when Britain controlled fifty percent of the world's merchant fleet and had a Navy big enough to protect that fleet. I left the sea, forty years on, when Britain controlled less than one percent and had a Navy which had suffered a similar catastrophic decline. Back to where it all began for me, the fleet employed somewhere around half a million men - British, Chinese, Laskar. I hate to think what the figure is these days. OK, ships have changed and with it the number of men required to safely man them but, hey, it is still a catastrophic decline. I tell people that, if I was to come back I would do it all again, but it appears that I wouldn't get the chance, at least not under the Red Duster. And so, without drum roll or fanfare I climbed down the gangway and climbed into the agents van and away, leaving a lifestyle and a lifetime behind. A van because it was full of my plants. Forty years later it wasn't a grey day in Liverpool but a warm sunny day in Felixstowe. At least this time, forty years later, I didn't have to struggle with my luggage. Willing hands carried it all down for me - garden an all! Forty years on and I called it quits!

CLAYE   'Get abaft the aft mast you half daft barmy bastard'

Edgar Watson   circa 1970

THE END

XXX

Printed in Great Britain
by Amazon

54421324R00241